# How to Do E
# with Onlir

## About the Author

**Andrew Shalat** is a designer, illustrator, instructor, and former actor. This combination of experiences and skills can be taken as either a manifestation of severe adult attention deficit disorder or a deep-seated need to multitask. He has been working as a graphic and commercial designer and a writer for over 20 years. He has an extensive background writing technology columns ("Shalat's Web" on Macweek.com, "Tech Talk" on Start Magazine), feature articles (*Macworld, Macworld UK, Creative Pro, Indesign Magazine*, and more), and reviews and such for both consumer and trade magazines, newsletters, and blogs. He has lectured and given instructional seminars on subjects as diverse as digital imaging, Shakespeare, rhetoric, business writing, advanced web design, architectural criticism, and doing your homework in a timely fashion. He currently teaches Digital Illustration and Design at Sessions.edu online design school and in person at Orange Coast College. Mr. Shalat speaks Italian, Spanish, and French with an odd Tuscan-like accent. Will someone just shut him up? Mr. Shalat lives in Los Angeles, if you can call that living.

# How to Do Everything with Online Video

Andrew Shalat

New York   Chicago   San Francisco   Lisbon
London   Madrid   Mexico City   Milan   New Delhi
San Juan   Seoul   Singapore   Sydney   Toronto

The *McGraw·Hill* Companies

**Cataloging-in-Publication Data is on file with the Library of Congress**

## How to Do Everything with Online Video

1 2 3 4 5 6 7 8 9 0 FGR FGR 0 1 9 8 7

ISBN    978-0-07-149643-8
MHID    0-07-149643-2

**Sponsoring Editor**
Roger Stewart

**Editorial Supervisor**
Janet Walden

**Project Editor**
Agatha Kim

**Acquisitions Coordinator**
Carly Stapleton

**Technical Editor**
Jennifer Ackerman Kettell

**Copy Editor**
Bill McManus

**Proofreader**
Susie Elkind

**Indexer**
Claire Splan

**Production Supervisor**
George Anderson

**Composition**
International Typesetting
and Composition

**Illustration**
International Typesetting
and Composition

**Art Director, Cover**
Jeff Weeks

**Cover Designer**
Pattie Lee

*Dedicated to the Next Thing, and to Dun and Erik who will take it on.*

# Contents at a Glance

# Contents

# Acknowledgments

I would like to thank several people without whose help and support this book would have been extremely difficult to finish. Roger Stewart, my editor, gave me great encouragement throughout the process, as well as helpful ideas and nudges in one direction or another, and Carly Stapleton made sure at every turn that I got this in the proper form. Agatha Kim gets credit for her tolerance and insight. Terry Hart, the second-funniest person I know, also gave me considerable help when it came to explaining how to make a story. I must acknowledge the help of several people from the software and public relations world, including Ryan Luckin, JoAnn Cerutti (nee Peach), Stephna May, and Anne Yeh, who provided me with some Adobe software; the Adobe team, for developing such a comprehensive suite of apps; Chris Breen, for his informative articles on podcasting; and Karina Bessoudo and the rest of the Toon Boom team, for letting me play with their software for this project. Wendy Wilsing deserves mention for her help taking a few still photographs. I also want to acknowledge Scott Sheppard, of Inside Mac Radio, for being, as always, a friend who has my back; Joe Jennings, for inspiration; and David Leishman, for his polemical ideas on all things media. And thank you, Charissa, for all the rest.

# Introduction

You're just in time. The online video revolution is under way. Yeah, yeah, I know. *Another* revolution. It seems like we have a new revolution every 18 months or so. And that's *why* you're just in time. This revolution is gaining momentum, establishing its foundations, and becoming focused. You know something is going on right in front of your eyes. Every week, you hear about new "amateur video" shot at the scene of a crime, of a sports event, of a scandal. You've no doubt recognized that something is going on right now that we're watching unfold. Heck, we should be running as fast we can just to keep pace with the movement of online video. Another train is leaving the station, and we have to figure out how to get on board. That is what this book is going to attempt to do: get you on board.

Every time we see another example of off-the-cuff or, more accurately, out-of-the-pocket newsmaking, we're seeing that train move ahead. Our technology has burdened us all with a new job—perhaps something we may not have wanted or asked for, but something we all are involved in, whether we like it or not. We're all news reporters now. We're all electronic news gatherers. In the broadcast world, that's called ENG, for electronic news gathering. That's the professional terminology. But for us today, it's just being out and about.

We may not be carrying high-end video cameras on our shoulders or have a news van waiting for us at the corner with a satellite uplink, but we have something that makes us on-the-spot professionals. We have video cameras in our pockets and still cameras in our hands. We have our cell phones.

You've heard the hype about smart phones and the like. Well, it's real. And cell phones with cameras constitute more than mere convenience (and who says they're that convenient anyway?). Where the digital revolution of the late 20th century put the power of print publishing into all our hands, the advent of instant handheld video cameras gives us the power to change the world. Let me repeat that for emphasis: each of us now has the *individual power* to coerce, comment upon, and finally *change the world* through our ability to publish video online.

It doesn't stop there. Sure, we can think of ourselves as news gatherers, always equipped with our trusty recoding devices. But we are also just people. And as people, we are sons and daughters, brothers and sisters, mothers and fathers. We're members of a community. And as members of a community, we have this primordial need to share our experiences, to make shapes on the wall, to tell how the hunt went, how the sunset looks, or how the birthday party sounded. As people, we have the innate need to tell a story. Sometimes it's our own story, and sometimes it's a story about someone or something else. We're at a rare moment in our history when we are able to create complex and sophisticated stories and publish them around the world … and we don't even have to change out of our pajamas to do so. We're not just reporters; we're all potential filmmakers. But we need schooling if we want to do that right. This book will help you do that right. This book is just as much about making stories, films, home movies, and slideshows as it is about capturing the news.

If you were to read only Chapters 5 through 8 of this book, you'd have enough film school knowledge to be dangerous. And that's my intent. I want you to be dangerous.

# The 800-Pound Gorilla

YouTube. You know you've heard of it. You've probably even visited YouTube.com, haven't you? You can admit it. Perhaps it was through a friend's e-mail link to a funny snippet from a comedy show last night; or a not-so-funny rant on a comedy show stage; or an unfiltered news event; or the spurious video diaries of a lonely teenager. You may not have even been aware that the content you were watching was an embedded link from YouTube.com. That's how pervasive (and some may say "insidious") this site has become in a very short time.

YouTube.com is not the only so-called "unfiltered" video upload site on the Internet. MySpace.com, Dailymotion.com, and others are also popular. And along with every blog out there, the more traditionally modeled sites also contain video: newspaper sites, magazine sites, and so forth. Pretty much any site you care to design can have video. Of course, YouTube.com and the rest of the online video sharing sites, private and commercial, aren't the only places, or even necessarily the preferred destination, for your work. Video podcasting (or *vodcasting*, as opposed to podcasting, which is audio) is easy to achieve, using the right software. I make a distinction here between online video you'd upload and share to YouTube and vodcasts because vodcasts are a specific genre of online video that has, among other distinctions, the specifics of authorship. Vodcasts are covered in Chapter 3.

Throughput issues still factor into the process but not nearly as much as in previous years partially because broadband service is now widely available and also because compression techniques and streaming data methods are also so much better than previously. Streaming video file formats and protocols continue to be changed, refined, and improved. So it pretty much doesn't matter what format your original footage is in; you can convert it to whatever best suits your publishing needs without too much trouble. That's one of the things you'll learn how to do in this book, but you'll also learn about the choices of file format you have at hand and why one choice might be better than another. A lot of it depends on your intentions as a video movie maker, and the audience you intend to send your video to watch.

Before you get any further into the book, there are a few things we want to put in context. In filmmaking, we call this your establishing shot. We need to describe the environment we find ourselves in, in order to understand what we're about to do, where we're about to go, and what, if any, conflicts we might encounter. We can use the filmmaking analogy because we're about to embark on creating video, the little sibling of filmmaking.

People are saying online video is exploding. Hopefully that doesn't mean your camera is about to be obliterated into flames and detritus (although that can be arranged), but that the move toward uncensored, immediate, worldwide publishing is growing at an astounding rate of speed. That observation shouldn't make your jaw drop. After all, instant video has been around since well before the end of the last century. Remember Rodney King? And even though we don't use the same media to record things, we do use a legacy set of words to describe the act. For example, we still say that we "tape" video when in many cases we're not "taping" anything, but rather registering data bits on memory cards and disks. Of course, in many cases, we will be recording to tape as well, so this term isn't really obsolete. Many camcorders include both memory sticks or flash memory cards as additional storage media to DV tape. Some camcorders have abandoned tape altogether and write directly to DVD media. (Your humble author suggests this is not the best way to go, for various reasons I will discuss later in this book.)

The main concern isn't really what we record our video on so much as how we transfer *from* that medium to our editing tool: the computer and its software. Obviously, we don't deliver our online video on tape. We upload it to a server. Essentially there are three tools we're going to use. I break down the tools into three categories: capture, edit, and delivery. It's similar to the print publishing world, where you have input (human with mouse, scanner, or digital camera), editing (computer, layout software), and output (printer). So after we go through our capture tools (camera, cell phone, and so forth), we have to figure out how to get our footage to our editing tool (computer and software) and then send our edited piece to our publishing tool (the live web site, or online server). There are, of course, variations to this one-two-three formula, and we'll explore those, finding shortcuts and workarounds. But for the most part this is how we're going to approach online video.

# Not Limited to...

Because this book takes on the whole scope of digital video capture from cell phones to camcorders to DV cams, we're going to be working with a lot of radicals and variables. Just as a web page designer can't possibly know which hardware and software every visitor to the web site will be using, I can't know what your specific hardware and software situation is. With that in mind, I've tried to keep the discussion as generic and all-encompassing as possible while still giving you all the information you need to take on any video capture tool and use it to your fullest capability. Some tools are easier than others to learn, and some require workarounds and some spit and glue. We're going to take on video capture with the attitude that whatever limits us only frees us to innovate to find other solutions.

Let's keep things simple. And let's get started. Since you've already picked up this book and are reading these words, I can assume that you don't need any more pep talk on the power and utility of posting video on the Web. You've already figured that out. That's why you're here. What you want from this book is a clear and direct guide to creating your video and putting it online. In the words of the movie industry, you want me to just *cut to the chase*. And in Chapter 1, that's just what I'll do. So check your seatbelt and unhook that cell phone from its holster. The rules have changed. It's time to be dangerous.

*—Andrew Shalat*

# Chapter 1

## Shoot Video

## How to ...

■ Shoot video with your cell phone

■ Transfer your cell phone video to your computer using USB, Bluetooth, e-mail, or microSD

■ Use your webcam for video capture on a PC or a Mac

■ Shoot video for the Web using a camcorder and transfer it to your PC or Mac

In this chapter we're going to shoot video using three capture devices: cell phone, webcam, and camcorder. It sounds easy, and in many ways it is. But in many ways it's not, with all the different and variable ways of shooting video, saving video, and delivering video to your computer.

NOTE   *Don't get confused by the terms shoot, capture, and transfer. When we say "shoot" video, we are referring to the act of aiming your video device (a cell phone, camcorder, digital camera, or webcam) and recording your footage. While we can say "capture" video to mean shoot video, when a software program uses the term capture, it usually means moving the video from the recording device into the software program. I know what you're thinking. This sounds a lot like transferring video. However, we say "transfer" video when we want to bring the footage data from the camcorder tape, the SD Disk, or the micro disk, to the computer hard drive, where it can then be captured into the software.*

# Shoot and Save Video Using Your Cell Phone

We start from the ground up. Actually, let's start a few feet up from there, from what's in your pocket: your cell phone. Now I'm not going to listen to any excuses. You're in the twenty-first century, you've bought this book, so you have a cell phone. Further, that cell phone has a camera. And beyond that, your cell phone will shoot video. So no whining, and no excuses. Take the phone out of your pocket, and put it in front of your face. It's time to get our feet wet. We are going to shoot some short video with our cell phone and then save it.

Here's the first hurdle we must jump. Depending on which cell phone you have, your video-taking experience on your cell phone will vary. And depending which carrier you're shackled to, and sometimes even which service plans you've been paying for, your video-saving experience on your cell phone will vary as well. But I'll try my best to help you through it all.

## Shoot Video with Your Cell Phone

Depending on which cell phone you have, your video-taking experience will vary. The big problem is that there is no single standard operating system for all cell phones. It's the Wild West. Every cell phone manufacturer and every cell phone may have a different user interface from the next (see Figure 1-1 for a few examples). And as we all well know from experience, they're not exactly user friendly either.

No two phones are alike. Each has its own menu system, and rarely do they make much human interface sense.

By default, many cell phones have the camera set to take still images rather than video. Because of the wide variety of cell phone user interfaces, for the purposes of this book, we can't go into the specific button-pushing steps that are necessary to get your particular cell phone to shoot video rather than still images. If you go to your menu, however, you can change the setting without too much trouble. Look under Games and Apps, or Camera Settings, and you'll probably find the video icon to select. Figure 1-2 shows examples. Be aware that finding the video application on your phone probably won't be as obvious or apparent as you would think it should be. It's always a guessing game with cell phones. If you can't find the video setting, refer to the manual that came with your phone.

Don't worry so much about quality of image, lack of resolution, or even frame rate. Resolution (pixels per inch on a screen) and frame rate (how many frames of video per second run across the screen) are important, but at this point they're not critical. Our machines do most of the work for us anyway. At this point, our intention is to go through the process once and

**FIGURE 1-2** Every phone has a different interface and a different way to find the video settings.

create our workflow. Follow these steps, again keeping in mind that which buttons you push to start and stop shooting the video depends on your particular camera:

1. Choose a subject to video: a pet, your spouse, a friend. Make sure it's something that moves. Plants probably won't cut it.

2. Start your video recording at least a second before the action you want to capture begins. This is called a lead-in. When we get to editing footage in Chapter 2, you'll see why the lead-in is important. For now it's more of a habit that you should try to adopt.

3. Film your subject. While filming, count out five seconds to yourself.

**NOTE** *The maximum length of your video directly correlates to the amount of free memory you have on your phone.*

4. Just as it's a good idea to start with a lead-in, give at least one second of lead-out to your footage.

5. Your phone should ask you whether you would like to save the video or discard it. Save the footage.

We now have some real footage. It may not be news-making, but that's not important here. We need to do two things: first, check the video footage to make sure we captured what we thought we were recording, and second, save the footage either directly to the Web or to our editing tool.

## Save the Footage

Cell phones carriers are a funny bunch. While they can obviously communicate with each other, they still can't seem to agree on which wireless standard to communicate over. If you're in Europe or Asia (with the exception of Japan, which uses a different standard), your carrier is most likely on a GSM (Global System for Mobile communications) network. In the United States, you may be on a GSM carrier, or you may be on a CDMA (code division multiple access) or TDMA (time division multiplex access) carrier. You don't need to understand anything about these mobile communications technologies beyond how they affect where you save your video.

If you are using a CDMA carrier (Sprint, for instance), you most likely do not have to worry about in which memory bank to save your video. You really don't get a choice. The phone stores your data and media in the phone itself. If you are using a GSM carrier (T-Mobile or AT&T/ Cingular, for example), your options are more numerous.

GSM carriers utilize SIM card technology. SIM cards have a small amount of free memory that lets you copy your contacts, your pictures, and your video (if it fits). GSM allows you to remove the SIM card without losing any data. If you are using a GSM carrier (T-Mobile or AT&T/Cingular, for example), you can save the video either to your phone's built-in memory or to its SIM card. You GSM-compatible phone should offer you the choice.

**TIP** *If you save your video to the SIM card, you can transfer the SIM card to a SIM card reader, from which you can transfer the video to your computer.*

Be aware of the space limitations. Many phones also have added the convenience of microSD memory slots that act as mini flash drives with the ability to store your images, video, and the like. External portable storage that connects to your cell phone via Bluetooth and Wi-Fi networking is now entering the marketplace as well. microSD, Bluetooth, and Wi-Fi are discussed later in the chapter.

**NOTE** *The next time you are shopping for a new cell phone, consider more than meets the eye. The more you understand about the cellular environment, the better informed your choice will be as to which service, which carrier, and which capture device (phone) you will decide upon.*

Therefore, to save your video, use the following guidelines:

1. Review your footage. You've made your video. Review it to make sure it's what you want, or at least close to what you want.

2. If you have a GSM phone, like ATT, or T-Mobile, for instance, then you can choose where to save your video—to the phone or to the phone's SIM card. If, however, you subscribe to a CDMA or TDMA carrier, like Sprint or Verizon, you may have no choice. It will save to the phone because there is nowhere else to put it.

3. If possible, you may want to rename the video something appropriate to the subject matter. Even something like "video1" will work. But your phone will assign a name if you don't, and that may work just fine as well.

After saving, or renaming, your video, it's a good idea to find where it is located in the labyrinth of your particular cell phone's interface. Knowing how to locate your video is an important issue to our next step, sending the video to the editing tool.

# Transfer Video from Your Cell Phone to a PC or Mac

Before we attempt to get our videos from our phone to the PC or Mac, we have to do some house chores. We can't be sure of what format our phones might record in. It could be any number of formats, from AVI, to 3GP, to MOV. So, to make certain that we will be able to view and edit our videos once we have them on the PC or Mac, we need to have resident on the computer an application that will ensure that we can actually view and edit the footage. At present, the best all-around application to see and perhaps even edit video is QuickTime. So let's go online with our PC and download the free version of QuickTime. (If you're using a Macintosh, you don't need to worry. QuickTime comes built in). I'll walk you through this:

1. Point your browser to www.apple.com/quicktime.

2. Click Download on the left side of the window to open the page from which you can download the QuickTime player, shown in Figure 1-3.

3. Download the reader, and follow the wizard steps to install the program. Figure 1-4 shows the wizard installing QuickTime.

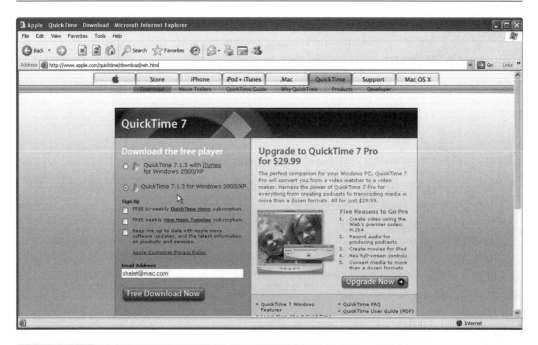

**FIGURE 1-3**    You have the choice of the free reader or the Pro version. For now, choose the free reader. You may want to upgrade at a later date.

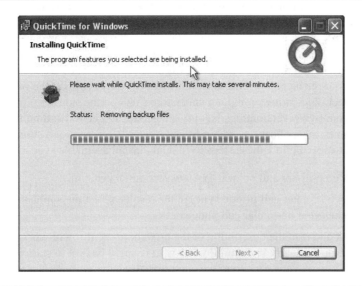

**FIGURE 1-4**   Depending on your processor, the QuickTime installation process can take some time.

Now comes the hard part. There are several ways (surprise!) to get the video from your phone to your PC or Mac, or if you like, even directly to the Web. In this section, we'll deal with the most popular methods:

- Send via USB
- Send via Bluetooth
- Send via e-mail, as an attachment
- Transfer via microSD disk

Each method has its advantages and disadvantages. And once again (you're gonna get sick of me telling you this), the best method depends on a combination of things, including your hardware, your carrier, your present location, and your whim. So let's examine each briefly so that you can make your choice. Whichever method you choose, the end result is that you will have the video file on your PC or Mac, ready to be edited, the subject of Chapter 2.

## Transfer via USB (PC Only)

Wireless schmireless. Sometimes you have to take one step back to go two steps forward, right? One would think this method would be pretty direct, pretty simple. Well, think again. Your phone probably didn't come with a USB cable that connects to your PC. It probably didn't even come with any software to help you sync directly to your PC. Of course, there is a reason for that.

The cell phone carrier doesn't make any money from you when you're sending files via USB. It only makes money when you're using its system, wirelessly.

If your phone didn't come with a synchronization software package, you can easily find one online. In order to correctly connect your cell phone to your computer, you need a special USB cable. In the cell phone world, they are also known as *data cables*. Make sure the cable has the correct adapter for your phone on one end, and a normal PC USB adapter at the other. You can find them at most electronics stores, computer superstores, and online stores.

Versiontracker.com (www.versiontracker.com) is a good resource for finding freeware, shareware, and commercial applications and utilities for your PC. Synchronization software ranges from free up to $30. Follow these steps to find and install a suitable sync application:

1. Open your web browser and point it to www.versiontracker.com.

2. In the Search box, enter **cell phone sync**. In the results, select the application that most closely matches your particular cell phone needs.

3. Click the link and read the description of the product to see if it will work with your phone. You won't actually know until you try, so it might be best to start with the shareware and work your way up to the commercial.

> **NOTE** *The choices shown in the figures in this book are for demonstration purposes. Your particular cell phone may or may not be supported.*

4. If the software's description indicates that the software will work with your phone, click the Download Now link. You'll be greeted with a dialog box, similar to the one shown in Figure 1-5, asking whether you want to run the file or save it to disk.

Work your way through the installation wizard.

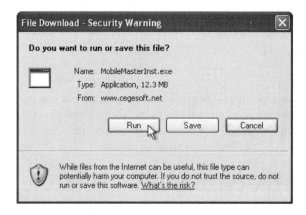

**FIGURE 1-5** Either run the file from the Web or save to disk. You won't know whether it works until you try it.

5. Once you've installed the software through the wizard, run the software. Each application differs as to interface and drivers.

**TIP** *If one application doesn't work, another might. Go back and try again with another. An alternative is to find a newsgroup or message board online for users of your cell phone company or particular cell phone. There's a good chance you'll find someone who has gone through the same travails you find yourself in. Most often, you can find recommendations and cautionary tales that will help.*

6. Establish contact between your PC and your phone. You may have trouble at first. Some software will help you out, as shown in the example in Figure 1-6.

7. Locate the video file in your phone.

8. Transfer the file to your PC. You may be asked to accept or deny the incoming file. Accept it.

9. Place the video file on your Desktop.

10. Double-click the file. If the video doesn't open automatically in Windows Media Player, it will in QuickTime (which you downloaded earlier).

11. Review the video file. If it runs, then you've successfully transferred it from the cell phone world to a place from which you can take it to the world online.

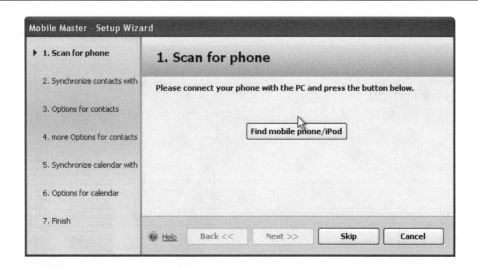

**FIGURE 1-6**    Some software will walk you through establishing contact between your PC and your phone.

## Transfer via Bluetooth

This method is perhaps the easiest way to transfer files to and from your cell phone. Of course, the requirements are as such: you need a Bluetooth-enabled phone, and you need a Bluetooth-enabled PC or Mac. While all Macs for the last few years have come with Bluetooth built in, PCs are a hit or miss situation. The process, however, if you do have Bluetooth, is pretty much the same as it would be for the Mac, so we'll start here with a Macintosh-based transfer. First, we must pair our devices with each other (phone and computer), and then initiate a file transfer. Simple as that. Let's do it.

### Connect Your Phone and Mac via Bluetooth

To connect your cell phone with your Mac via Bluetooth, follow these steps:

1. On your cell phone, go to Settings, or Tools, and select the Bluetooth option. On a Samsung phone, for instance, it may be under Settings | Bluetooth (see Figure 1-7, left image). On Motorola phones, you will find the Bluetooth control by going to Settings | Connection | Bluetooth Link (see Figure 1-7, right image). Again, each phone will differ slightly or tremendously in its user interface.

2. Make sure Bluetooth on your phone is enabled, or turned on. Keep your phone on, with the Bluetooth settings selected.

3. On your Mac, open System Preferences | Hardware | Bluetooth to open the Bluetooth window. As shown in Figure 1-8, click the Devices tab and click Set Up New Device.

4. In the Bluetooth Setup Assistant, follow the onscreen instructions and click Continue.

**FIGURE 1-7**   Each phone will bury its Bluetooth secrets in a different place.

**FIGURE 1-8**   You can have several devices as recognizable favorites for whenever you need to connect via Bluetooth.

5.  Select the type of device you want to set up; in this case, Mobile Phone (see Figure 1-9). Click Continue.

6.  The Assistant will search for your device. Go to your phone and make it discoverable. It may say something like "Find Me." Select the appropriate item. The phone should show up in the Bluetooth Setup Assistant's window. If it doesn't, check your phone for its discoverability.

7.  The computer will now generate a specific passkey (see Figure 1-10). Write that number down, for future reference, and click Continue. Enter that number in your phone (see Figure 1-11).

8.  If your phone allows it, you will be able to sync your contacts, etc. Select the appropriate choice and click Continue.

9.  You can bypass the next screen by clicking Continue. It deals with setting up your cell phone as a wireless modem, which doesn't pertain to what we're trying to do here. The next screen confirms your phone-to-Mac Bluetooth capabilities. Click Quit.

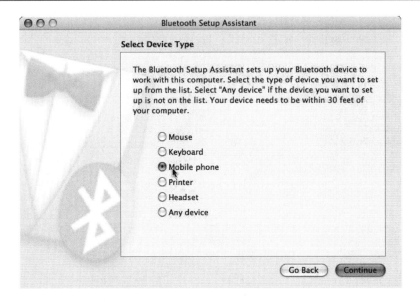

**FIGURE 1-9**    You can set up any type of Bluetooth device. Choose Mobile Phone.

**FIGURE 1-10**    The computer generates a passkey to pair it with your phone.

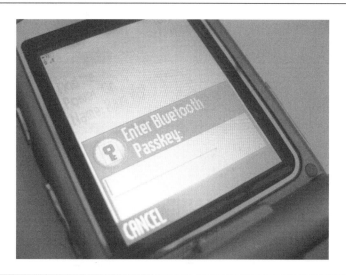

FIGURE 1-11    Enter the passkey into your phone.

## Send Your Video to Your Mac via Bluetooth

Now that you've set up your phone to communicate with your Mac over Bluetooth, it's time to send your video file:

1. Find the Bluetooth icon in your menu bar on the desktop.
2. Select Browse Device, as shown in Figure 1-12.
3. Select your cell phone from the list and click Browse.

FIGURE 1-12    This is where you go to connect your phone to your Mac (from under the Bluetooth icon in the menu).

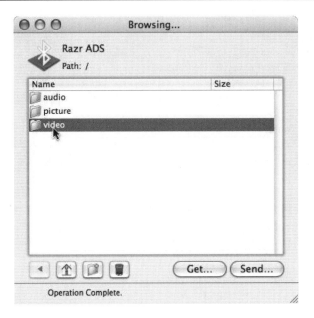

Each directory system will differ depending on the type of phone.

4. You're now communicating with your phone. Scroll through to the video folder and double-click it. See Figure 1-13.

5. Select your video and click Get.

6. Save the file to your desktop.

7. Quit the Bluetooth file exchange program.

You can now open your file from the desktop. It will open in QuickTime.

## Connect Your Phone and PC via Bluetooth

Unfortunately, most PCs (including yours, probably) are not Bluetooth-enabled. While next-generation PCs might include Bluetooth, only a few current PCs do. But that shouldn't stop you from using Bluetooth. There are many USB Bluetooth adapters available for the PC for around $50. If your PC doesn't have built-in Bluetooth, then an adapter is a convenient way of giving your PC connectivity to your phone. The process is somewhat similar to that previously described for the Mac. You have to install a driver for the adapter, however, and run through the install wizard. Once the driver is installed, you run another wizard that searches for and pairs with your cell phone via Bluetooth.

## Transfer via E-mail

This *should* be the easiest method of all. You would think all it requires are a few bars of connection and a valid address for the recipient. But let's not forget, this is the cell phone wireless communications industry here. Despite the commercials, nothing with this technology is as easy as it should be. Don't be disheartened. If you're determined to shoot video with your cell phone, then you're one of those intrepid people who don't let small technological crevasses stop you from reaching your goal.

There are two basic roads we can take on this route. The first necessitates a smartphone with what is commonly called "push e-mail." That means your e-mail notification comes directly to your phone, rather than the second path, where your e-mail comes via your carrier's online server. The second path requires you to check in, to seek out your email online, via your phone's browser.

Since we're trying to get the video to your own computer, it's your e-mail we'll send it to:

1. Locate your video file. In the example in Figure 1-14, you would open the Media folder to locate your video file.

2. Select the file. Don't open it or play it.

3. Select send as e-mail, or e-mail attachment.

4. Send the file. In most cases, the subject line of the e-mail will be filled in with the name of the video file. (So now you see why distinctive naming might be a good thing.)

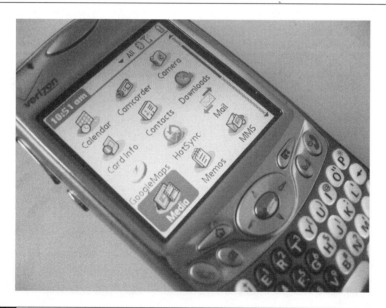

**FIGURE 1-14**    Depending on your phone, the menu item might be up front, or buried in the submenus, under Media.

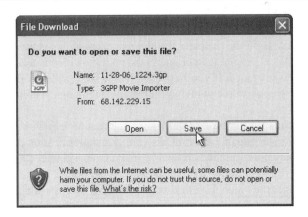

**FIGURE 1-15** Save the video file to the desktop.

5. Go to your computer and check your e-mail to make sure the file has arrived. Open the file.

6. Save the video file attachment to your desktop. See Figure 1-15.

7. Because you downloaded and installed QuickTime earlier in this chapter, you have an application that recognizes the native format of this video file, as shown in Figure 1-16.

8. Open the file into QuickTime. Here you can review it on the bigger screen of your PC, and finally see what you have.

**FIGURE 1-16** Note the icon for the file is that of QuickTime, even though the file format is 3GPP.

# Transfer via microSD (PC Only)

It's important to have as many ways to save files these days as it is ways to capture them. As cell phones have become "smarter" (and I use that term loosely), the designs of the phones have started to come in line with the way people actually work with them, rather than with how the cloistered engineers or product managers might *want us* to work with them. In other words, through enough complaints and competition, cell phone designers are getting it into their heads that accessibility across various types of devices makes more sense than not.

Flash drives, those small, solid-state, key-sized memory storage devices, are now about as common as key fobs. In fact, most of them act as key fobs. We use them for our digital cameras, for our digital camcorders, for transferring files from one computer to the next, and for personal and work-related backup. They also make for great spy-movie devices. Finally, cell phone designers are starting to see their benefits as well. To which we say, in as academic a tone as possible, "duh!" It's a world of adapters, and you may find yourself walking around now with a collection of card readers so that you can transfer files back and forth to all of your digital apparatuses. One of the new options for portable data storage is the MicroSD card, which is the same as what you usually find in a digital camera, only about one fourth the size. These usually come with an SD card adapter, that lets it use standard SD sized media card readers. See Figure 1-17.

The best thing, however, about using the microSD method of transfer is that it's simple. It also works … assuming you have a smartphone with the microSD slot. Once again, due to the absurdly

**FIGURE 1-17**   Clockwise from top, a multicard reader, a flash drive key fob dongle, a microSD card and adapter, and a USB SD card reader adapter. All that, your cell phone, and your laptop, and you're ready to go.

varied phone interfaces, the following directions just show a generic method of getting your video from your phone's memory (where it was originally saved to) and onto your memory card. Even if the following steps don't work exactly for your phone, you should get the basic idea of how to get your video from the phone to the memory card, and then from the card to the PC.

**NOTE**    *If this is the first time you've inserted the microSD card into your phone, you may have to format it to have access to it. If you find you can't save to the drive, then back out to the Settings menu and format the drive for use. Once that's done, follow the next basic steps.*

1.  Locate your saved files on the phone.
2.  Drill down to the Videos folder.
3.  Inside the Videos directory, you have some preloaded material as well as your own homemade work. Find yours. See Figure 1-18.
4.  Select the video that you want to transfer.
5.  Press the Options key and select Move to Memory Card (see Figure 1-19). Every phone may have a different specific command for this. But once you have a memory card inserted in your phone, you should find the way to transfer the file easily enough.
6.  The file is now copied to the memory card. Remove the card from the phone and insert it into its adapter.
7.  Plug the SD/microSD adapter plug into your PC (or Mac) and copy your file across to the Desktop.

Ta-dah. You're done with the transfer. Check the video for clarity and completeness, or at least just to make sure it's the right one. Once again, you'll note that the file will open with QuickTime.

FIGURE 1-18    The Videos directory contains downloaded videos and other sundry items, not just the files you've created.

FIGURE 1-19    Move the file to the memory card.

## Got the File on Your PC or Mac—Now What?

Even though we now have the video file on our PCs or Macs, we haven't touched it other than to make sure it works. Because of the proclivities of each online destination point (YouTube, MySpace, your own web page, etc.), we'll have to deal with the specific format distinctions and requirements as well before we upload the file to the world at large. These issues will be dealt with, discussed, and delineated in Chapter 3.

## How to ... Choose a Smartphone with Video Capabilities

The rigmarole we have to go through just to get our phones to connect with our PC or Mac should act as a cautionary tale when we're looking to buy a new smartphone suitable for video. Let's go over a few of the more important features we should insist upon, or at the very least ask for politely:

- Bluetooth
- An uncomplicated, intuitive user interface; it should make sense to how we want to work
- An extra data card (microSD, for instance) that will let us transfer files directly
- E-mail capabilities

# Capture Video via Webcam

Capturing video to your PC or Mac is much easier when you're using the camera already attached to your computer. You don't have to worry so much about how you're going to get your video from one device to another; it's already there.

A webcam can be defined as a real-time, or video, camera attached to your computer, and whose images can be accessed directly, or indirectly, via the Web. A real-time camera is one of those snap-on cameras sold as webcams. A video camera can be considered a video recorder that works as a stand-alone as well as a webcam when attached to your computer. Pretty much any video capture device that you can hook up to your PC to allow it to feed video in real time to your hard drive can be a webcam. So although you might find yourself longing for the convenience of a small, bug-like widget made of plastic that clicks onto your laptop and plugs into your USB, you can also just use your camcorder sitting on the desk, connected via FireWire (also known as IEEE 1394) or USB. The point is, the webcam is a dumb lens and the PC or Mac is the brains. We control the video from the PC, not the lens.

Webcams work pretty much the same on PCs and Macs, until you get the video on your computer. While the majority of PCs use a USB connection for input, the Mac will either have a built-in iSight camera or connect to an external iSight or other webcam via FireWire. In this section, I've separated the instructions for capture into PC- and Mac-specific sections.

## Capture Video via Webcam on a PC

You don't need to spend a lot of money on a webcam. Webcams can be found for as little as $20, or as much as you're willing to spend. Remember, any digital camcorder with a USB output can be used as a webcam for your PC. Figure 1-20 shows an example of a basic webcam.

FIGURE 1-20    Example of a simple, inexpensive USB webcam for the PC

All we want to accomplish here is a simple video capture onto the PC, so we'll use the software that comes with the PC, in this case Windows Movie Maker, using Windows XP. Vista has some slight differences, but for the sake of the majority of us, we'll stick to XP here. We won't be doing any editing until the next chapter, so don't get all crazy excited when you capture a video clip and that timeline beckons. We'll get to that soon enough. That said, if you're ready, let's capture some more video:

NOTE    *If your version of Windows didn't come with Movie Maker, follow the link listed here to find and download it:*
*www.microsoft.com/windowsxp/downloads/updates/moviemaker2.mspx.*

1. Make sure your webcam is connected to the USB port of your PC.

2. Open Windows Movie Maker (Start | All Programs | Windows Movie Maker).

3. The Movie Maker workspace is broken up into four panes, with three on top and one running along the bottom. From the left, they are the Movie Tasks pane, the Collections pane, the Preview pane, and, below them all, the Timeline. From the Movie Tasks pane, click Capture from Video Device, as shown in Figure 1-21.

4. In the next window, select your webcam. Click Next. If you have more than one video device attached to the PC, they will all show up in the Available Devices pane. Select the one you want to use.

5. Name your captured video. For this example, use **Webcamcapture**. It's important to name things simply and clearly. Click Next. See Figure 1-22.

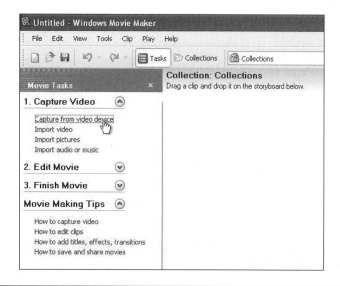

FIGURE 1-21    Choosing to capture from a video device

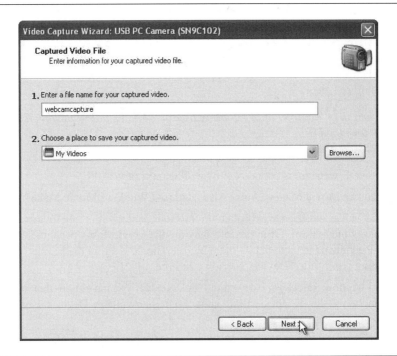

**FIGURE 1-22** Name your captured video something you'll easily recognize and understand.

**6.** In the Video Setting window, choose Best Quality for Playback on My Computer (see Figure 1-23). Note all the settings for the video capture. In this case, it will capture directly to Windows Media Video (WMV) format. This will become important later. Click Next.

**7.** Frame your subject, and click Start Capture. When you're finished (as we did earlier in this chapter, use the five-second count), click Stop Capture.

Your clip will now appear with a thumbnail in the Collections pane. Note the collection has the name you gave it earlier. A thumbnail of your clip appears in the Collections pane and, once selected, will also appear in the Preview pane to the right.

**8.** Drag the clip thumbnail down into the Timeline, as shown in the example in Figure 1-24.

**9.** Once you have a clip in the Timeline, you have ostensibly created a video. Save the video and name it **Webcamcapture**.

**10.** Locate the completed file in your My Videos folder (see Figure 1-25) and double-click it. By default, it will open and play in Windows Media Player.

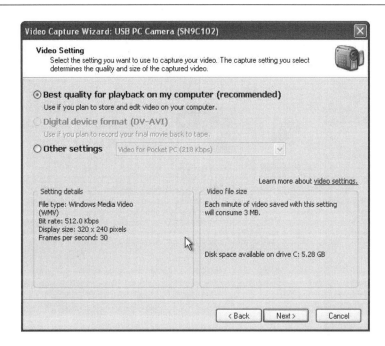

**FIGURE 1-23**   Note the settings for format and size.

We've successfully captured video to our PC via webcam. However, we have created a WMV file, which, according to the best practice guides on YouTube, is not among the formats recommended. We'll deal with this in a bit, but be sure it will include ponying up $30 for a QuickTime Pro upgrade (see "Upgrade to QuickTime Pro" in the next section).

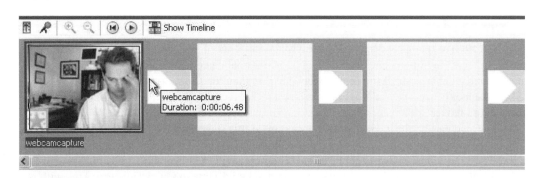

**FIGURE 1-24**   By dragging the thumbnail from the Collections pane to the Timeline, you are creating the video as a video sequence. Note that the clip's duration is visible as you hover your mouse over it.

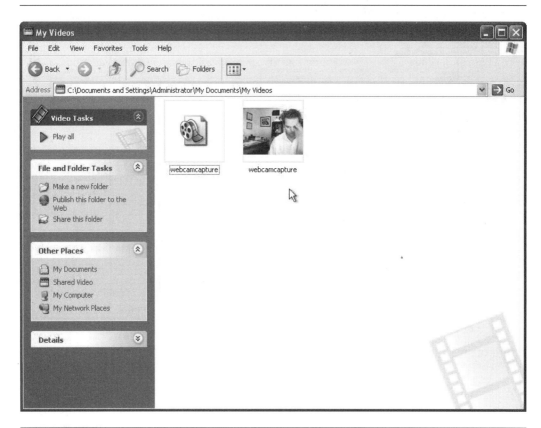

FIGURE 1-25
Both the Collections file and the actual video file are found in your Videos
folder.

## Capture Video via Webcam on a Mac

Since the switch to Intel processors, all laptop Macs and iMacs have come with the iSight camera
built-in, so there's no immediate need to plug in an external camera for video capture. If you
happen to have either a Mac Mini or a Power Mac Pro, then the situation is different, and you'll
need to attach either an external iSight camera or another type of (preferably) FireWire-enabled
video capture device.

As I've said earlier, the device isn't so important at this stage as is the act of capturing video
easily on the computer. In this section, we'll use two methods of capture. By "methods," I mean
we'll use two individual software applications. The first is QuickTime. Although QuickTime
comes already loaded on the Mac, we want to upgrade QuickTime to QuickTime Pro. This will
cost $30, and can be done completely online.

## Upgrade to QuickTime Pro

To upgrade to QuickTime Pro, follow these easy steps:

1. Open QuickTime Player. If you aren't accosted by a small Upgrade Now dialog box, then open your browser and point it to www.apple.com/quicktime.

2. Click the Upgrade Now button and have your credit card ready. It will cost $30.

3. Follow the online steps for purchasing and downloading the upgrade and, voilà, you will be upgraded to QuickTime Pro.

Under the QuickTime Player menus, you will now find access to a number of options that were previously grayed out, like New Movie Recording and New Audio Recording. Now that we're all QuickTime Pro users, we can move on to simple video capture using our iSight camera.

## Capture Video with iSight and QuickTime Pro

This is simple, unedited, straight-from-the-hip (or I should say, more appropriately, straight-from-the-screen) video capture:

1. Open QuickTime Player Pro. When you first open the application, you will be greeted by a QuickTime Content Guide pushing whatever video, concert, top movies, top songs, and products happen to be hot that week. Dismiss this window by clicking the red Close button in the window's upper-left corner.

2. Select File | New Movie Recording. See Figure 1-26.

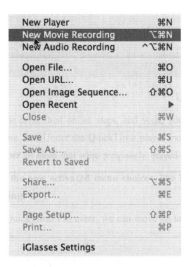

**FIGURE 1-26**    This is one of the reasons we went Pro: the ability to make new movies right from within QuickTime.

FIGURE 1-27    Your face goes here.

3. Notice the single red button at the bottom of the QuickTime window. If you are at your laptop, then you'll also notice your own big mug staring back at you. See Figure 1-27.

4. Click the red button to begin recording. Record for five seconds.

5. As you record, note that the red button has now become a gray square. When you're finished recording, click the gray square to stop.

6. Your recording is automatically saved as Movie.mov on the desktop. If you do it again, the next recording will be Movie 2.mov.

The files saved in MOV format will open in QuickTime Pro. When we're ready to upload them online, we'll convert them to MPEG-4, or another preferred file format, for online viewing.

We've now captured video on the Mac using the iSight camera and QuickTime. Next we're going to capture video using the iSight in conjunction with iMovie HD:

1. Locate iMovie in the Applications folder on your startup hard drive (Macintosh HD | Applications | iMovie HD).

2. In the initial window, click Create a New Project. See Figure 1-28.

FIGURE 1-28 Creating a new project in iMovie HD

**3.** The default project name for iMovie is always "My Great Movie." While we understand that we're proud of our work, let's just tone it down a bit and rename it **iSightCapturetest**, as shown in Figure 1-29. Also note that this project will end up in your Movies folder by default.

**4.** Make sure the Video Format option is set to iSight, as shown in Figure 1-30.

FIGURE 1-29 Name your project so that it makes sense to you.

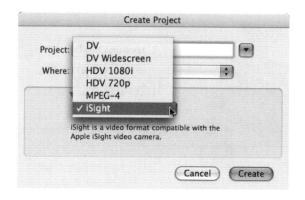

**FIGURE 1-30**    Select iSight for this particular instance.

**5.** Click Create.

**6.** The iMovie workspace has three main panes: the large Preview pane on the upper left, the Media well on the right (which changes with each tabbed button below), and the Timeline below. Just under the blank Preview pane are two icons and a toggle switch. On the left is a video camera icon and on the right is a scissors icon. Slide the toggle over to the Video Camera side.

**7.** Click Record with iSight, and begin recording. Again, use the five-second clip rule. After you click Stop Recording, your clip will appear in the Clips well, to the right.

**8.** Drag the clip from the well to the Timeline below, as shown in Figure 1-31.

**9.** Save the project (File | Save Project).

**FIGURE 1-31**    When you place the clip into the Timeline, you've created a video.

FIGURE 1-32    There are many ways to share your video with iMovie. For this exercise, choose QuickTime.

**10.** iMovie gives you many methods by which to save your video. Since we're just going to save it here as though it were intended for upload to the Web, select Share | QuickTime. See Figure 1-32.

**11.** In the next dialog box, choose Web from the pull-down menu. Each choice has its own advantages. iMovie will give you a brief explanation of each as you go through each choice. Save the file to the Movies folder. Remember to save the file with a name that reflects what you intend to do with the project.

Done. You've now captured and created a five-second (give or take a few) video using iMovie and iSight as the capture device. Editing would be the next step in the process, before the video is ready for viewing online. But again, that will be covered in the next chapter.

# Capture Video with a Camcorder and Transfer It to Your PC or Mac

The big daddy in the world of video capture is the DV cam (digital video camera). DV cams range from the consumer level to the professional level. Each month, improvements are made, features are added, and prices are lowered, but the versatility of the handheld camcorder remains the best way to capture video on the spot, with quality and convenience.

Never mind that the media the DV cameras capture is beginning to vary as much as cell phones do in their own odd little proclivities. The fact that you can capture hours of video on mini-DV tape, writable DVD, or Memory Stick and SD cards is not as important as the fact that you can transfer that footage directly to your computer via USB or FireWire using just the software that comes with that computer. And we've already discussed in this chapter the software that we use to capture that footage. For the PC, it's the Windows Movie Maker, and for the Mac, it's iMovie HD.

**FIGURE 1-33**   This is a standard-issue DV camcorder. It records to mini-DV tape as well as to SD memory cards.

So the final section of this chapter shows how to transfer video from your DV camera directly to your PC. Then it's on to the real making of a video in Chapter 2: editing.

First, take a look at an example of a pretty typical DV camcorder, shown in Figure 1-33.

The most important feature of the camcorder is not the media it records to, but the digital outputs it features. In the case of the camera shown in Figure 1-34, you'll note it has a DV in/out plug for FireWire as well as a USB connection below that.

We won't go into shooting the video content on your camcorder here. Later on in this book we'll show you how to best frame shots, how to lead in, pan, and keep your shots interesting, and we'll give you some tips on how to light them as well. But for now, we're really more concerned with getting your footage, raw though it may be, from the camera to the computer.

## Transfer Your Footage from the Camcorder to the PC

So we're making a few bold assumptions: you've already taken some footage on the camcorder, and you've recorded to tape or DVD media. Now you're ready to transfer it to the PC. Here's how:

1. Put your camcorder into Play mode (sometimes referred to as VCR or VTR mode), rather than Record mode.

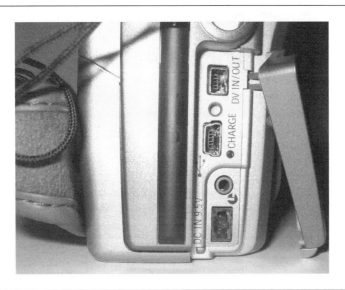

FIGURE 1-34  This camera has pretty much all you'll need as far as input/output possibilities: FireWire and SD memory card. The upper plug is for FireWire.

**2.** Using a USB cable that has on one end a small male plug for the camcorder, and on the other a regular USB male plug for the PC, connect the camcorder to the PC.

**3.** On your PC, open Windows Movie Maker.

**4.** In the Movie Tasks pane, select Capture from Video Device (refer to Figure 1-21).

**5.** In the video capture device dialog window, select the DV camera.

**6.** Give the captured video a name. Click Next.

**7.** On the Video Setting page (refer to Figure 1-23), leave the default settings. Click Next.

**8.** In the wizard, you will have DV camera controls. These control the actual camera as it transfers the video footage to the PC. When you locate the correct in point (where you want your capture to begin) on your footage, click Start Capture.

**9.** When the footage reaches the out point (where you feel your clip should stop), click Stop Capture.

**10.** Click Finish. The footage will now appear in the Collections pane of Movie Maker.

We can save our video by dragging the clip into the Timeline and then saving it as a WMV file (refer to the "Capture Video via Webcam on a PC" section).

## Transfer Your Footage from the Camcorder to the Mac

Earlier we captured video in iMovie using the iSight camera. This process is essentially the same, only instead of using the iSight, we're using a DV camcorder, where the video footage has already been recorded and resides on a mini-DV tape:

1. Connect the DV camcorder to the Mac via a FireWire cable with a small male plug on one end for the camera, and a standard FireWire 400 plug for the Mac.

2. Turn the DV camcorder to Play mode (sometimes labeled as VTR or VCR mode).

3. Open iMovie HD. Select Create a New Project.

4. In the Create Project dialog box (refer to Figure 1-29), name the new project **DVcamTransfer**. In other words, name the project something that makes sense for its purpose or content, something that will make sense to you later.

5. Select MPEG-4 for the video format. This makes the most sense for sending a video to a web service like YouTube. Click Create.

6. Make sure the camera is on, and connected to the Mac. In the iMovie workspace, toggle the mode to the Camera setting.

7. Use the Forward, Back, and Play buttons to find your In point for the footage.

8. When you're ready, click Import.

9. Click the Stop button in the controls when you've imported your clip.

Again, we're not so interested right now in making a video (although we did complete a video clip in the section on importing from iSight in iMovie), so we won't bother to drag our clips into the Timeline and then Share to QuickTime (although you can if you want). We've done what we wanted to do, which was go through the process of transferring video footage from the DV camcorder to the Mac via FireWire.

The next chapter will deal with what we need to do to make that captured video watchable. In other words, we'll be editing our footage. It should be pretty easy to understand, since in this chapter you've just played around with some of the tools you'll be using for editing.

# Chapter 2

# Edit Video for Posting Online

## How to...

■ Plan a scene using different shots

■ Edit video using Movie Maker (PC)

■ Edit video using QuickTime Pro (Mac/PC)

■ Edit video using iMovie HD (Mac)

In this chapter we're going to edit video footage with the specific intention of taking it online. That means we will have to work with an eye toward several key factors, including, but not limited to, duration of the footage, transitions between clips, sound quality, dimensions of the video, and file format. That's a lot of stuff to think about. Alternatively, we could just slap some clips together, butt them end to end, and upload them to the Web. There are no real rules; just guidelines, choices, and whatever fits best. As the video producer, in the final analysis, it's up to you.

In the preceding chapter, we went over the various methods of uploading video to your computer. The content of the video was unimportant, so we just shot footage randomly for around five seconds—long enough to have a file to transfer. In filmmaking they call that decoy element a *McGuffin* (also spelled MacGuffin or Maguffin). It's a plot device that motivates characters in a film, moves the story forward, but has little intrinsic value in and of itself. I throw that in since this is moviemaking we're flirting with, and I'd hope Alfred Hitchcock, the purported coiner of the term, would appreciate it. But I digress.

Where the video footage was the *Maguffin* of the last chapter, it becomes the main character of this one. The whole point of editing is to sharpen, focus, and articulate. You can't do that with something that's inconsequential. So, in order to edit, we need to have something substantial to edit. Therefore, our first task will be to use whatever capture device we have on hand, and capture some usable video footage. After that, we'll explore how to edit our video using a basic PC tool "MovieMaker." Mac users, don't fret, we'll next show how to edit video using QuickTime Pro 9 which works for both Mac and PC. We'll also look at iMovie HD.

NOTE *iMovie HD has a new sibling called iMovie '08, which uses a completely new approach to making video and uploading them to the web. So we've added a chapter; see chapter 11.*

# Plan a Scene Using Different Shots

To make things manageable and interesting, let's capture four separate video clips. All that means is we want to stop our recording between *shots*. Now just because we're shooting four shots, and plan on editing them together, on the computer, that doesn't mean we shouldn't try *while shooting* to make the shots as clean and to the point as possible. We may not be cinematographers, but we can try to act as though we are. And what is the difference between a cinematographer and a director?

The cinematographer wants to get the shot as correct as he can, while making the shot. He doesn't want to edit the shot. He wants each shot to be able to stand on its own, complete and integral. The director, on the other hand, sees the shot as footage; fodder for the editing machine.

The digital age has done more than just make digital imaging and editing easier—it has blurred the distinction between cinematographer and director somewhat, but the distinction still stands. It's all a matter of perspective. The particulars of each job have overrun each other now that the tools are so much more capable. You can be either or both, it seems. Just don't tell that to a professional director. He might hit you with his riding crop.

What, then, do these related professionals have in common? They plan their shots. Photographers, designers, cinematographers, and directors all have a map that they use, sometimes to a great degree of accuracy, and at other times loosely. Our starting point, therefore, will be to plan out our four shots.

I'm planning the following four shots of a ball rolling down a ramp:

- A side shot of the ball rolling down the ramp
- A shot from behind as the ball rolls down the ramp
- A shot from the bottom of the ramp looking up as the ball rolls toward the camera
- A shot taken from above as the ball rolls down the ramp

Of course, this isn't as compelling a video as I'm sure you'd come up with on your own, but for the purposes of editing a short video, it will work just fine. Think of it as a simple sentence, "The ball rolls down the ramp." We're working with basic elements so as not to distract ourselves from the real point, which is learning how to edit for online video. Sort of like reading a *Sally, Dick, and Jane* book, we're worried more about subject, predicate, and verb, not so much what dramatic conflict Sally has with Dick, while Jane looks for Spot. A simple sentence: if we look at our planned shots, that's pretty much what we have. The subject of the shots is the ball, the predicate is the ramp, and the rolling is the verb.

Sometimes before shooting video, we make a storyboard. We'll talk about this later on in the book, in Chapter 7, but for now I've supplied you with a set of illustrations. Take a look at Figure 2-1 for a guide. The illustration gives you an idea of how to set up these simple shots. Take the first, or establishing, shot from the side. This shows the complete action of the ball rolling down the ramp. Shot 2 starts from just behind the ball's point of view. It's another view of the same action we see in Shot 1. Shot 3 is from the point of view of the bottom of the platform. The ball rushes toward us. Shot 4 is from above.

Remember that when you take your video, you should give yourself a second or two before and after the actual action as lead-in and lead-out footage handles. We've all heard the classic director line, "Lights, camera, action!" Those three commands signify the setup:

- **Lights**    Make sure everything is lit correctly.
- **Camera**    Film is rolling before the action begins.
- **Action**    The action of the shot takes place.

Just remember to give a second or two before you shout "Cut!"

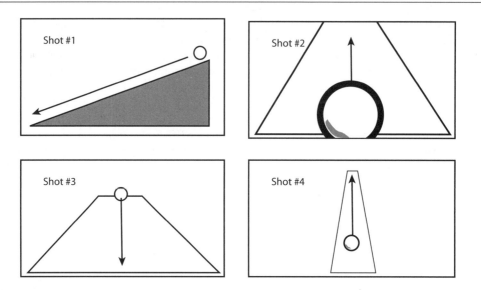

**FIGURE 2-1**    Drawing out the shots before you take them is always a good idea.

Now please set up your four shots, take the footage, and transfer it to your computer. If you need help transferring your footage from whatever capture device you're using (and it doesn't really matter which you use as long as you get the footage in an acceptable digital video format, preferably MP4, MOV, or WMV), refer to Chapter 1 and find the most applicable method of completing that transfer.

With our footage on the computer, we can begin editing. Note that we took four separate shots, or clips. If they transferred over as one continuous shot, we'll rectify that in the editing software. Otherwise, we should have four separate clips ready to be edited. The first major section covers editing on the PC using Movie Maker, the second covers editing on either the PC or Mac using QuickTime Pro, and the third covers editing on the Mac using iMovie HD.

# Edit Video Using Movie Maker

This section covers how to perform the following editing techniques in Movie Maker:

1. Order video clips
2. Trim and split video clips
3. Apply video effects, including transitions
4. Add audio, such as narration or music
5. Add titles
6. Save your file

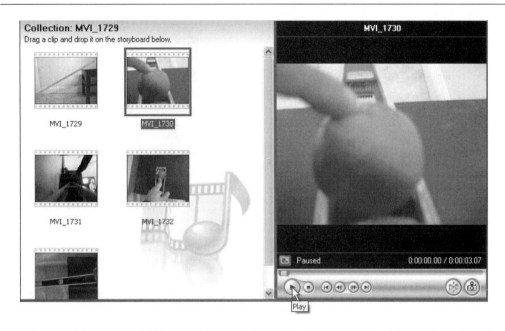

**FIGURE 2-2**    Be sure to review each clip in the Preview pane.

## Make a Rough Order of Clips

Working on the PC, have your clips ready as files on your Desktop and then follow these steps:

1. Review each of your clips. Load your clips in Movie Maker; you should see your clips in the Collections pane. Click a thumbnail in the Collections pane, and watch the preview in the Preview pane to the right. See Figure 2-2.

2. Drag each clip, in the order of shots (refer to Figure 2-1), into the Timeline pane. Once you've done that, you now have yourself a storyboard, as shown in Figure 2-3.

3. With the clips in order, select the first clip in the Storyboard and click the Play icon. The Storyboard lets you watch each clip in order in the Preview pane.

4. Click Show Timeline (located just above the active Storyboard and shown in Figure 2-4) to switch to the Timeline.

5. Expand the Timeline pane so that it shows not just the Video track, but the Audio track as well, as shown in Figure 2-5. Do this by positioning your cursor over the divider between the upper panes and the Timeline pane and clicking and dragging up to expand the Timeline pane.

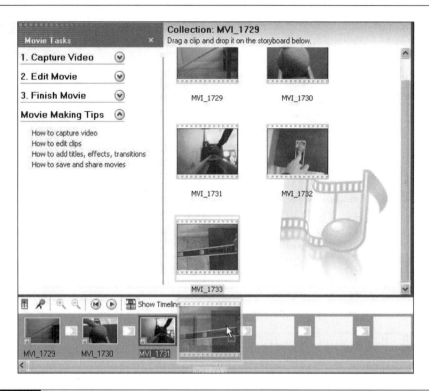

**FIGURE 2-3**    Movie Maker calls this the Storyboard, but it toggles to become a Timeline as well.

Before we deal with the Audio track, we need to do some basic editing on each clip. Our first task is to look at each clip to see whether it needs to be edited. Most likely, we'll want to cut out some of the beginning and some of the end. That is why when we recorded the footage, we began rolling before we started the action. Now we have to select an *In* marker.

**FIGURE 2-4**    The Timeline is used for editing clips.

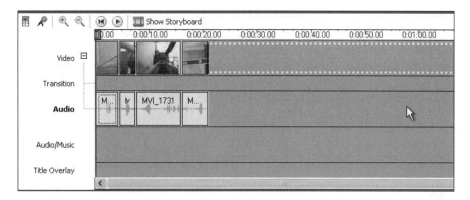

**FIGURE 2-5**    The Timeline lets you see both Video and Audio tracks.

## Split and Trim Clips

Don't worry that splitting and clipping footage is going to damage it. In this application, it's a nondestructive process. In other words, the program automatically keeps an original of your footage. Any edits you do to the Timeline won't affect the original, just the clip in the sequence you're working on in the Timeline.

In the Timeline, select the first clip and preview it. Note where you want to first see the action. For editing, our goal is to come in late, get out early. (See the sidebar of the same title.)

# Come In Late, Get Out Early

In screenwriting scenes for the movies, there is a basic rule of thumb: come in late, get out early. What that means is that there is little need for excess when telling a story. If a scene involves a man having a conversation with another person in a hotel room, there is no need, other than artistic, to show the man enter the room, walk across the room, and take a seat before the conversation begins. At the other end of the scene, there is no real reason to show the man get up, push his chair in, walk back across the room to the door, open it, and finally close it behind him. Rather, the story makes just as much sense if it shows the man knock on the door, cuts to the conversation at the table, and then moves on to the next scene at the end of the conversation. *Come in late, get out early*. Remember, though, when you're shooting your video, you want to do the opposite. You want excess footage on either end of the video you capture.

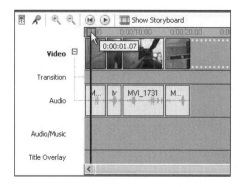

Depending on how long your clip is, this method might be less accurate than sliding the playback preview as shown in Figure 2-7.

Undoubtedly, when viewing the clip, we'll notice that we have extra film at either end of the action that we want to show in the video. We have a choice to make. We can either *split* the clip or we can *trim* it. Let's examine each choice.

Splitting the clip cuts it into two. There is an advantage to splitting a clip. It gives you two clips instead of one, letting you use either part in other places, without having to go through the trimming process. To split a clip, do the following:

**1.** Either position your cursor in the Timeline ruler above the clip, at the point where you want to split it (see Figure 2-6), or slide the playback in the Preview pane to the position you want to designate as the split point (see Figure 2-7).

It's better to actually watch your video in the Preview pane and see where you'd like to split it. Always take note of the exact time in the Timeline. In this case, it's 01:60.

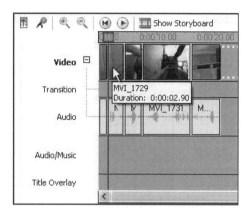

FIGURE 2-8    The clips are split cleanly, making them more versatile. The Audio tracks are split as well.

TIP    *Always remember to save incrementally. It's at points like this, where you've done a bit of detailed work, that you might want to do a Save command.*

**2.** With the video clip at the correct frame, choose Clip | Split (or press CTRL-L).

**3.** The Timeline now has two clips where only one was before, as shown in Figure 2-8.

Since we don't really need the first part of the clip we split, it makes more sense to just trim the clip to the point where we want the clip to start. Here's how to trim a clip:

**1.** Find the point in the video where you want to insert your In marker by jogging the play slider in the Preview pane (refer to Figure 2-7). Make note of the time code on the bottom right.

**2.** Go back to the Timeline. Click the magnifying glass icon so that your trim will be accurate.

**3.** Position your cursor over the left edge of the clip in the Timeline. The greater the magnification you use, the better the chance that you'll get an accurate in point.

**4.** With one eye on the Preview pane, put the cursor on the Timeline, and drag the edge of the clip to the right until it reaches the point you want your clip to start. See Figure 2-9.

**5.** Release the mouse. Your clip is now that much shorter. It will begin at the point to which you dragged the edge of the clip. Check the Preview to make sure it's correct. You'll also notice that the time code in the Preview now starts at 00:00, as shown in Figure 2-10.

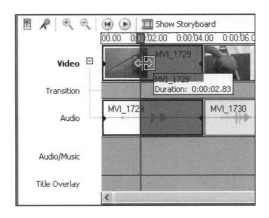

Drag the edge to the exact point of your In marker.

**6.** Your clip probably runs a second or so beyond where you'd like it to stop. If that's so, then simply repeat the previous steps, but instead of dragging the trim edge from the left, use the right side of the clip and drag to the left, thereby shortening the clip, and creating an Out point, as shown in Figure 2-11.

When you get the hang of trimming your clips, a whole world of possibilities opens up. Note that even though you're trimming or splitting your clips in the Timeline, the clips that live in your Collection, in the Collections pane, remain in their original form, so this is nondestructive editing. You're changing an instance of the clip, but not the clip itself.

The time code now says 00:00 because the trim made your In marker the new starting point of the video.

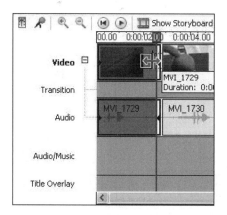

**FIGURE 2-11**    Drag from the right end of the clip back to the left to move the clip's Out point.

And since this is digital editing, you can copy and paste clips along the Timeline as you see fit. But first, follow these steps:

1.  Preview each clip separately.

2.  Trim or split each clip according to what you want to show in the video. In the case of our four shots, you should trim each beginning and end so that they *come in late and go out early.*

3.  Review each clip individually after you've trimmed them.

4.  Review the whole sequence of trimmed clips, with an eye toward continuity.

This is a raw edit. Next we want to refine it somewhat. Let's split Shot 1 and shuffle the order a bit. We should have Shot 1 trimmed so that it shows the ball beginning its roll down the ramp and ending just before it hits the bottom. Admittedly, it's a short clip. But let's make it shorter:

1.  Using the Preview pane to guide you, split the clip at the point where the ball is midway down the ramp. Use the Next Frame button in Preview, as shown in Figure 2-12.

2.  Choose Clip | Split.

3.  With Shot 1 now trimmed and split into two, select the second half of the split in the Timeline. See Figure 2-13.

4.  Click and drag that clip over the top of the following clip, and place it after it in the Timeline.

NOTE    *Step 4 shows you how to easily play with the clip order of your movie. Don't feel obligated to keep the adjustment you've just made.*

**FIGURE 2-12** Using the Next Frame button, you can move the video clip forward one frame at a time for a precise split point.

**5.** Review the complete clip sequence from beginning to end.

**6.** Trim Shot 2 so that it shows the ball midway through its trip down the ramp. When you review the sequence in Preview, you'll now see how the shots are starting to make a new, contrived sense.

We can repeat and adjust this type of editing for each of the clips in our sequence. We want to make the simple event of a ball rolling down a ramp more interesting. So we cut into each clip, trim and split, making each an element of the whole sequence. Do not be afraid to copy and paste your clips along the Timeline.

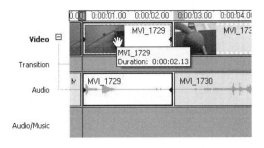

**FIGURE 2-13** Place your cursor over the body of the clip and it becomes a hand, for grabbing.

# Apply Video Effects

After we have our clips in sequence, we can start to look at the transitions between them. Movie Maker keeps rudimentary transitions, effects, and speed controls under Video Effects. To apply video effects, follow these steps:

1. To access the Video Effects pane, click the Edit Movie drop-down arrow in the Movie Tasks pane and choose View Video Effects. The Collections pane changes to become the Video Effects pane.

2. You can apply any of the effects by dragging the Video Effects thumbnail from the Video Effects pane directly on top of the clip you want to effect in the Timeline.

3. Alternatively, you can choose your effects and apply them from the menu. That is, choose Clip | Video | Video Effects. When the Add or Remove Video Effects dialog box appears (see Figure 2-14), choose the effect or effects from the Available Effects column and click Add to add them to the Displayed Effects column.

4. Click OK, and the effects are immediately applied to the clip. If you don't like the effects once they're applied, you can remove them through the same dialog box (Clip | Video | Video Effects).

Remember that these effects aren't permanent, so you always have the ability to remove or adjust them. Since our four-shot sequence is very short, and probably very fast, there is one effect we may want to apply to all the clips: Slow Down, Half. But how do we apply this effect to all of our clips at once? You'd think that all you'd have to do is hold down the SHIFT key on your keyboard and move your cursor across the Timeline to the last clip and click again to select

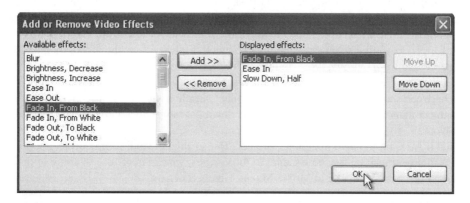

**FIGURE 2-14**    This method lets you apply more than one video effect directly to a clip.

all the clips at once. Unfortunately, you can't apply the video effect to all of the clips that easily. Try it, you'll see. Nope, doesn't work. We have to take the more tedious route:

1. In the Timeline, select the first clip.
2. Drag the Slow Down, Half effect from the Video Effects pane onto the clip. Notice that the clip in the Timeline now has a small star icon. That signifies that it has some sort of effect applied to it.
3. Review the clip in the Preview pane.
4. Make it slower by half again by repeating Step 2. Note that the clip has a different star icon, showing multiple effects. The clip will now run at one-quarter speed of the original.

NOTE     *Multiple stars means multiple effects, even if it's the same effect applied twice.*

Repeat Steps 1–4 on each individual clip you want to slow down. It's up to you as videographer to decide which clips need the particular effect.

You've no doubt noticed that we haven't spent much time on the specifics of making this short video make perfect visual sense. We're working in a skeletal manner here. Depending on your footage, you'll have to make specific decisions about where to trim, where to split, and how to shuffle your clips.

In the case of our four-shot sequence, we have pretty limited choices. But we can experiment a little further without verging on the ridiculous. Many of the video effects you'll find in Movie Maker are gratuitous in most cases, and inappropriate for the majority of simple projects. Sepia tones, aged film, and the like are great effects for very specific and particular situations. But if they don't add to the original intention of the video, then leave them alone. Simplicity is a good thing, although it's surprisingly more difficult to achieve than you might expect.

When you decide to add effects, you have to ask yourself whether they're essential to your video (they add to whatever message or story you're trying to tell) or draw attention away from the video. In most cases, we want to keep the attention of the viewer *inside* the video. If we add effects just for pizzazz, effects that draw the viewer's attention *outside* of the video, then odds are we're detracting from our own work and its own *effectiveness*.

With all that in mind, let's revisit our four-shot sequence. As it stands, we have no real transitions between shots. Of course, for this particular "simple sentence" of a sequence, that's fine. The subject matter is always the ball as it rolls down the ramp. So a hard cut from one angle to another works.

But what if we want to move to another subject? Rather than the ball rolling down the ramp, say we want to now transition to a new scene. In those cases, we can make use of some of the built-in video transitions available in Movie Maker. Here's how:

1. In the Movie Tasks pane, click View Video Transitions.
2. You'll notice that the former Video Effects pane is now the Video Transitions pane. Scroll through the various transitions. They do get a bit crazy.

The best way to choose a transition is to experiment with them. Again, remember that simpler is usually better. When you decide on a transition, drag the thumbnail icon from the Video Transitions pane to the point *between* your clips. When you drag the transition into the Timeline, the transition has its own track in the Timeline. The translucent area in the Timeline is where we've laid in our transition. It shows the video clips that are affected by it.

NOTE *Video Transitions work in much the same way as Video Effects, but you drag and drop them between your clips.*

**3.** Review your sequence with your transitions, and make sure they fit not just the pace of your video but its intention as well. Unless you want viewers to say "wow, what a cool transition" instead of "wow, what a cool video," use your transitions with delicacy.

**4.** If the duration of each transition is not what you want, you can adjust it. There are two basic approaches. The first, as shown in Figure 2-15, is directly in the Timeline. You can drag along the edge of the transition to adjust it. The other way is to choose Tools | Options to open the Options windows, shown in Figure 2-16, and then adjust the default Transition Duration setting.

## Add Audio

So far we've dealt with editing video clips, including splitting and trimming them, slowing them down, and adding effects and transitions to them, but we haven't approached the audio aspect yet. If we break down movie making into its simplest components, we might say that it consists of image, movement, and sound. In Movie Maker we have some limited audio capabilities, but if we use them right, they can be very effective.

If your video footage includes an audio track, then it was imported along with the video. You can see the audio track in the Timeline. When we shot the ball rolling down the ramp, we weren't concerned with the audio, so we probably have nonessential, nonuseful audio attached

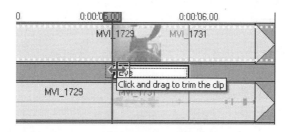

FIGURE 2-15    Adjust the duration of the transition by dragging on it in the Timeline.

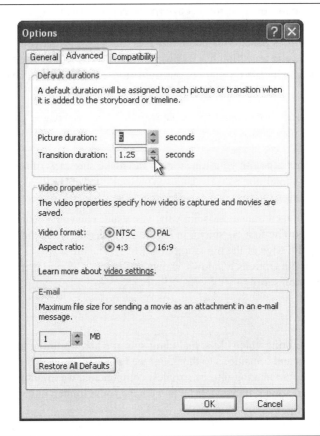

FIGURE 2-16    From the Options window, you can adjust the default settings of clips, stills, and transitions.

to each clip. We don't want that particular audio in our video. We want to get rid of that audio. Unfortunately, Movie Maker doesn't allow us to strip our imported clips of their embedded audio tracks. However, it lets us mute the audio, so that is what we will do:

1.  In the Timeline, select a clip with audio.
2.  Press CTRL-U to open the Audio Clip Volume window, shown in Figure 2-17.
3.  Check the Mute Clip box in the lower-left corner.
4.  Repeat this process for each clip.

NOTE    *As for most CTRL commands, you can also execute them through either the Timeline or the menu bar. To mute audio through the menu bar, for example, choose Clip | Audio | Mute.*

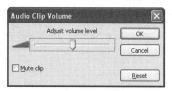

**FIGURE 2-17**    Adjust the audio levels for the clip from the Audio Clip Volume window.

Now that we've silenced our video by muting the embedded audio track, we can consider what kind of audio we'd like to add to this sequence. We can add narration or music. First let's add narration.

## Add Narration

To add narration, you can attach a microphone to your PC or use the built-in microphone if your PC has one. Whatever your sound input is, you must first adjust your levels, or at the very least make sure that you have a reliable input source. To access the narration controls, follow these steps:

1. Choose Tools | Tools | Narrate Timeline. Your Movie Tasks pane and whatever happened to be in the central pane will combine to show the Narrate Timeline pane.

2. Click Show More Options. The pane will open to reveal several more controls, as shown in Figure 2-18.

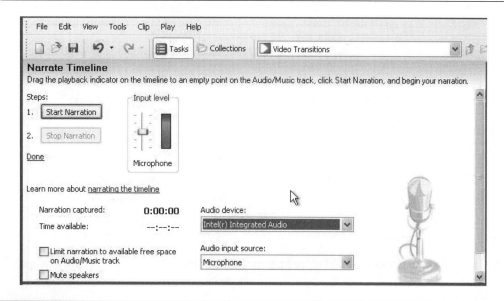

**FIGURE 2-18**    Controls for input levels and an Audio Input Source drop-down menu

3. Check your vocal levels before you begin. You'll be able to monitor your levels on the Input Level gauge.

4. Place your cursor at the point on the Timeline where you would like your narration to begin. Click to make sure that the playhead sits at that point.

5. When you're ready, click Start Narration.

> **TIP** *While you may think you're an expert at extemporaneous oration already, it's always a good idea to have, if not a complete script of what you are going to say, at the very least a few bullet or talking points. Read them a few times aloud before you click Start Narration, and get used to speaking into a computer. You may want to keep these notes in front of you while you do your narration as well. Narration might seem easy, but the reality is that it takes practice.*

6. If you want to limit your narration to the length of the existing video sequence, check the Limit Narration to Free Space on Audio/Music Track check box in the lower-left corner. If, however, you're feeling verbose today, you can leave that box unchecked and narrate beyond the length of the video. If you do this, you may have to go back to your clip editing to make it make sense, unless you want narration over a black screen. That is an artistic decision.

7. When you are done recording your narration, click Stop Narration.

8. After a moment, a Save File dialog box appears. By default, the audio file you've just created will take the name of the file, with the added word Narration. In this case, since the project name is ballonramp, the narration will appear as ballonramp Narration. If you decide to save it and do a second or third try, Movie Maker will automatically add a number to the end of the filename. Save the file with a name that's recognizable.

If you look at your Timeline now, you'll see that the Audio/Music track is now populated. The name of the file that populates it is the very same that you just created as the narration, as shown in Figure 2-19. One great feature about this track is that you can slide it back and forth along the Timeline to make finer adjustments of synchronization with your video.

## Add Music

Adding music rather than narration is a breeze:

1. Choose File | Import into Collections (or press CTRL-I).

2. Locate your music files.

> **TIP** *Locating your music files is easier if you keep them in the obvious place, like My Music.*

3. Inside your music folder, choose any MP3 (or similar format) file to import. In this example, I'm importing a prepackaged sample. You'll find MP3, AAC, and other compatible formats

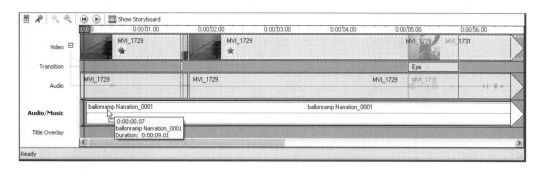

**FIGURE 2-19** With your narration file in place on the Audio/Music track, you can slide it to the best position in correlation with your Video track.

ready and available. Click Import. You've now imported the music file into your Collections pane. It resides next to your original video clips. See Figure 2-20.

**4.** Drag the music clip onto your Timeline. It automatically takes up residence in the Audio/Music track. If you had narration there before, it will be replaced by the music clip. That is one of the limitations of this software package.

**5.** Review your video, with its audio, transitions, and effects.

Is there something missing? Well, maybe just one small thing. Which leads us to our next step: adding titles and credits.

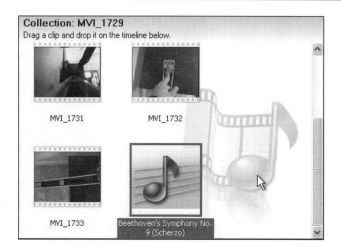

**FIGURE 2-20** Beethoven's Symphony No. 9 (Scherzo) is a pre-packaged sample.

## Add Titles and Credits

Including titles in a video is not required; it is a choice for you, the videographer. You can use them to introduce your video, to comment upon the action or some characters in the video, or for any other suitable purpose. This is all up to you. Credits are sometimes good to have as well, not only to let viewers know such things as who helped to make this project, but also to indicate to viewers that your video has come to an end. We can apply titles and credits to our video with the built-in tools in Movie Maker.

Movie Maker takes a wizard approach to adding titles and credits. To access this wizard, revert your workspace to its original layout: the Movie Tasks, Collections, and Preview panes on top, and the Timeline on the bottom. The easiest way to do this is to click the Tasks button in the menu until you get to the configuration just described. In the Movie Tasks pane, click Make Titles and Credits. The pane now becomes our wizard.

### Add Titles

The steps for adding a simple title shot are straightforward:

1. Click Add Title at Beginning of Movie.

2. In the ensuing pane, type the text for the title. As you do, you'll see it appear on the right in the Preview pane, as shown in Figure 2-21.

The title also appears automatically at the start of your video clip sequence in the Timeline. In this instance, it shifts the rest of your video down the track, but note that it doesn't shift the Audio/Music track.

Since we're adding this as a clip, at the front end of our sequence, the title shifts all the other video clips in the track down for the span of its duration. Drag and shift on the Audio track to match the sequence, or have some overlap.

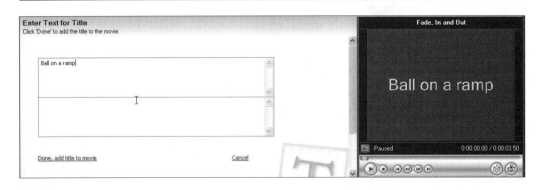

FIGURE 2-21    You type on the left, and it appears in the Preview pane.

Preview your video sequence with the title. It should have a nice effect now; a more mature aspect. It has a title, after all.

Let's now revisit our wizard. Even though some aspects here are somewhat self-evident at this point, we can look at the overlay title. Click the Tasks button and then follow through to the Add titles and credits wizard.

1. In the Timeline, select a clip in the middle of the sequence.

2. In the Titling pane, click Add Title on the Selected Clip in the Timeline.

3. Type in something innocuous, like "ball rolls down."

4. Click Done, Add Title to Movie.

5. Play the movie in the Preview pane. Your overlay title should be in place. See Figure 2-22.

You should also note that your overlay title lives not in the top Video track of the Timeline, but in its own Title Overlay track at the bottom. Let's do something clever here. Let's convert our original title that opens the sequence to an overlay title.

In the Timeline, place your cursor over the opening title clip and drag it from the top track down to the Title Overlay track. Note that the video clips shifted back to the left. Click Play in the Preview pane. Instead of appearing in its own frame, the title now overlays nicely on your opening clip. You don't have to shift any of your narration or music at all!

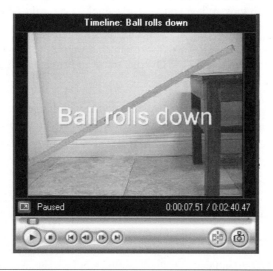

**FIGURE 2-22**    Overlay text adds sophistication and information to your video.

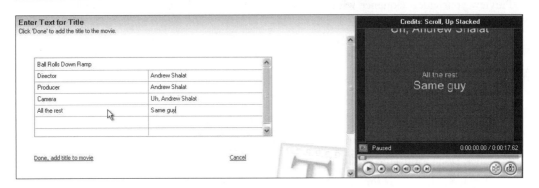

The credits text form is a little different from the standard title text form.

## Add Credits

To add your credits, return once again to the titling wizard, by clicking the Tasks button, and
follow these steps:

1.  Click Add Credits at End of Movie. Note that the text layout for the credits text form is
    slightly different from the title text form, as shown in Figure 2-23.

2.  Fill in the particulars. As you do, note the Preview pane on the right gives you an idea of
    how your credits will look. When you're ready, click Done, Add Title to Movie.

3.  Since we chose to add the credits at the end of the movie, Movie Maker adds them as a
    video clip to the Video track. But we now know that we don't have to be satisfied with
    that. We can drag the clip to the Title Overlay track and have our credits crawl over
    existing video. See Figure 2-24.

Well, there you have it. You've completed an edited video, with music or narration, and titles
that overlay and credits that roll. One last step and then we're ready to upload, which we'll learn
how to do in Chapter 3.

## Save Your Movie

When we save our movie, we want to save it for our intended purpose of putting it online. So we
will have to save it in a format that best fits that need:

1.  Select File | Save Movie File.

2.  The Save Movie Wizard appears. From the choices, select The Web. Click Next.

NOTE    *Each time we save a video, we'll want to know where we intend to use it. In this case,
and in the case of all projects in this book, we want to go online. So save for The Web.*

**FIGURE 2-24**   It adds a touch of sophistication to have titles overlay video rather than just a blank background.

**3.** Choose an appropriate name. You may want to add "web" after the main name so that you can tell at a glance what your intentions for the file are. Click Next.

**4.** Select DSL, Cable Modem, or Higher (384 Kbps), as shown in Figure 2-25. Click Next. The wizard saves your file.

**5.** In a bit of heavy-handedness, Movie Maker now asks you to provide a web host for your video. Since we're not going to just take Microsoft's options as our options, click Cancel. See Figure 2-26.

**6.** Don't panic when the next warning window comes up. Just click Yes, you want to cancel.

Your file has already been saved. Your editing job is done. You can close out of Movie Maker and take a break. Get a cup of tea or coffee. If you do not intend to use QuickTime Pro or iMovie HD to edit your videos, you can go straight to Chapter 3. If you are considering using one or both of these other editing programs, then read the corresponding section or sections.

# Edit Video Using QuickTime Pro

Using the four shots of video with the ball rolling down the ramp, we can use QuickTime Pro (on either a PC or a Mac) to do basic editing of our video sequence. We can trim and split our video clips and reorder them, and we can add music or narration. But we'll be doing these things very roughly. It won't be as polished or sophisticated as what we're able to do with Movie Maker, or iMovie HD, let alone Adobe Premiere or Final Cut Express or Pro. But this book is about

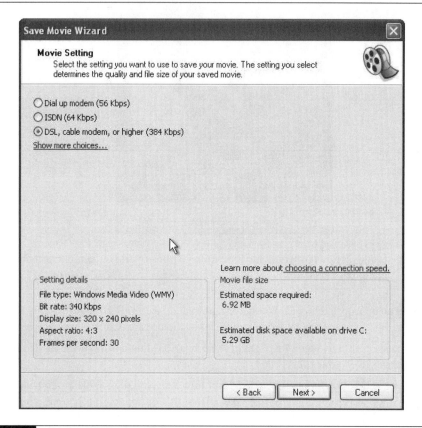

FIGURE 2-25    Dial-up? Who has dial-up anymore? How 20th century.

how to do *everything* with online video. So short of making a hearty spaghetti sauce with online video, or a nice soufflé, we can certainly rough out a quick edit in QuickTime Pro and make it a reasonable candidate for putting online.

To begin, gather your four shots depicting the ball rolling down the ramp. By hook or by crook, get the video onto your computer (see Chapter 1). In any case, we want to have the four video shots as separate files in our computer for this short exercise. Open the four clips in QuickTime. Here's what we're going to do in this section:

- Copy and paste the first shot, so that we have five QuickTime windows open instead of four.

- Use that fifth QuickTime window as the Timeline/workspace for our video sequence.

- Cut and paste portions of each of the original four shots into the fifth window to make our edited piece.

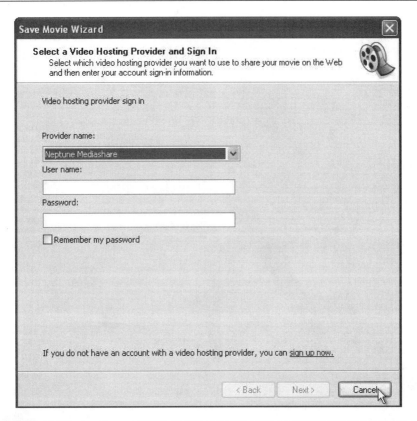

**FIGURE 2-26**   Unless you have an account at one of the two options that Movie Maker is giving you, click Cancel. Don't be pushed around by your software.

- Edit out the embedded sound and add a new audio track.
- Make some finer adjustments to the audio.
- Save the video in an appropriate format for online viewing.

We start by copying and pasting the first shot so that we have five player windows open:

**1.** Situate your four video shots on your desktop so that you can see each, as shown in Figure 2-27. You may have to reduce them in size.

**NOTE**   *QuickTime Pro works the same no matter whether you're working on a PC or a Mac. If you find that the screen shots in this section aren't* exactly *what you see on your screen, you likely are using the other platform. Don't fret; the mechanics of the program are the same. Really, they are.*

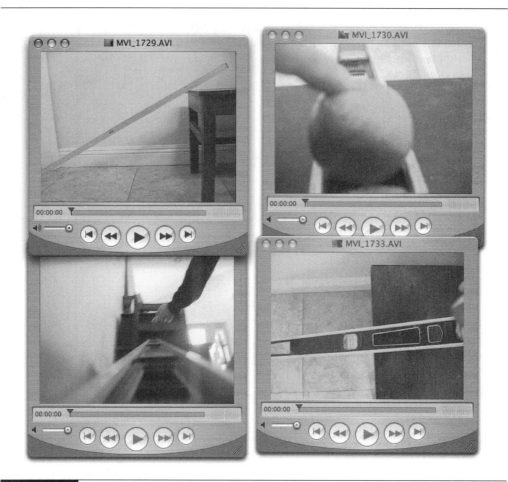

FIGURE 2-27    To start, it's a good idea to see all four shots at once.

2. Select the first shot.

3. Click inside the video window.

4. Execute the Select All command (PC: CTRL-A; Mac: ⌘-A). Notice the progress bar in QuickTime completely darkens. Also, notice that there are now two markers in the progress bar: one at the beginning (In marker) and one at the end (Out marker).

5. Copy the selection (PC: CTRL-C; Mac: ⌘-C).

6. Select File | New Player.

7. In the new Untitled player, paste the video copied from shot 1 (PC: CTRL-V; Mac: ⌘-V).

Let's edit our footage now.

# Trim Your Shots

As you remember, when you made the first shot, you gave yourself a little lead-in and lead-out at the beginning and end of the shot. Let's trim those parts out, first the lead-in and then the lead-out:

1. Click and drag the rightmost (Out) marker along the progress bar to the point at which you want your video to begin. See Figure 2-28.

2. Choose Edit | Cut or press DELETE. When you delete, the playhead triangle resumes its position at the zero point in the video. You have successfully trimmed the opening of shot 1.

3. Save the new player. Name it something like BallonrampSequence. Save it as a self-contained movie.

4. Trim the end of the clip. Drag the Out marker all the way to the end of the video, at the right. Make sure to drag the marker, not the playhead.

FIGURE 2-28    Select the Out marker. Note that the space between the markers is dark, which means it's selected.

5. Click and drag the In marker to the point at which you want the video to end.

6. Press DELETE.

7. Save the player.

We just trimmed our video footage. Now that we understand how to trim the video, we'll want to do a variation on it *before* we bring in more video.

So let's start our trim on shot 2 and then bring it into our sequence. This time, however, we're not going to delete anything. We're just going to copy the selection from the footage and paste it into our sequence.

1. Select the player depicting shot 2.

2. Because of the nature of the QuickTime Pro Player, we have to choose our Out point first. So click and drag the right Out marker to the point where you want the clip to *end*. See Figure 2-29.

3. Release the Out marker, and select the In marker on the left. Drag it to your preferred In point. See Figure 2-30.

4. Copy your selection.

5. Select BallonrampSequence player.1

6. Drag the playhead to the end of the video.

7. Paste the selection. The result will be that your footage from shot 2 is at the end of this sequence. Save your file.

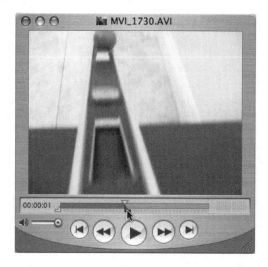

FIGURE 2-29    Select the Out point first.

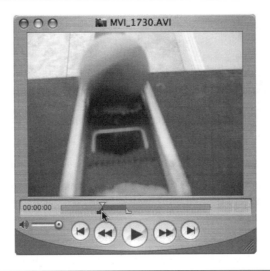

FIGURE 2-30    Select the In point next.

Continue this process of trimming, copying, and pasting from your original shots into your master video sequence. Don't be afraid to take small pieces of footage and copy and repeat them in the sequence. When you have a reasonably finished product (remember, this is a rough way of editing), save the player.

## Edit Out Embedded Sound and Add a New Audio Track

We still have to replace the audio with either a narration or a music soundtrack. So let's do that right now.

First, let's record a narration:

**1.** Select File I New Audio Recording to open the Audio Recording window, shown in Figure 2-31.

FIGURE 2-31    Audio Recording window

The same trim process we used for video works for audio as well.

2. Click the red Record button, record your audio, and then click Stop.

3. Play back your recording to make sure it's up to snuff. When you're satisfied, trim out any parts you do not want (see Figure 2-32) and copy the rest. You may want to save the narration just in case.

4. In the audio player, choose Window | Show Movie Properties.

5. In the Properties window, we can see all sorts of information. For now, our concern is the audio track, so select the soundtrack, as shown in Figure 2-33.

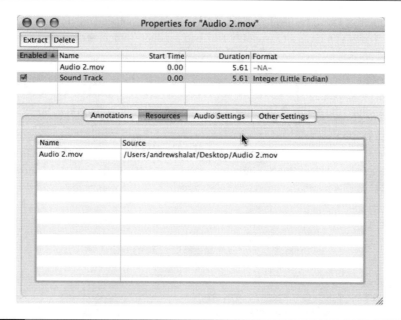

Select the soundtrack.

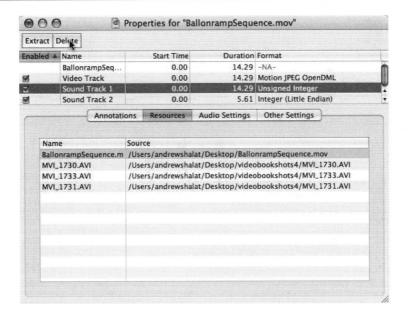

**FIGURE 2-34**    You can add soundtracks to your video and they won't cancel each other out.

6. Click Extract. A new untitled audio recording will appear.

7. Go back to BallonrampSequence. Place the In marker at the point where you want your narration audio to begin.

8. Choose Edit | Add to Movie.

9. You've now added your narrative to the video. Open the Properties window in the video player (Window | Show Movie Properties). You'll see an extra Sound Track (see Figure 2-34). You can remove the old one. But wait! Think of the possibilities. You could add another, such as a music track, using the same simple process you've just learned.

Now that you have learned how to add a sound track to an existing video sequence, the possibilities open up. You can add music too. Any audio you can open in QuickTime Pro can be used (we're not talking about copyrighted material, of course—don't break the law). You can also decide which channel you want your audio to occupy: right or left.

Select an audio track in the Properties window and click the Audio Settings tab. Look at the Channel/Assignment section. Click the Assignment pull-down menu and you'll see the options, as shown in Figure 2-35.

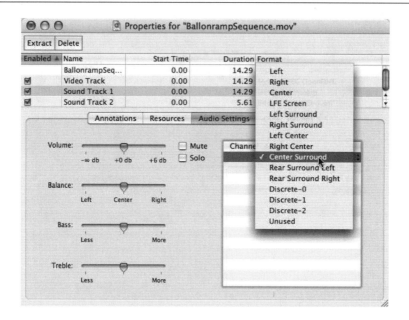

**FIGURE 2-35** You can mix your audio to a pretty fine degree with this simple $30 program.

There are other A/V controls available in QuickTime Pro, which I encourage you to experiment with. You'll find them in the Window menu under Show A/V controls.

## Save Your Video for Online Viewing

Finally, we must ready our sequence for delivery to the Web. This is the easiest thing you'll have to do all day:

1. Choose File | Export.

2. Choose either Movie to iPod or Movie to MPEG-4. See Figure 2-36.

If you choose MPEG-4, you'll also have access to the Options button on the right. Click Options. You may just want to keep the settings as is. The defaults are a good place for us right now.

With your file saved as MPEG-4, you're ready to upload it, as described in Chapter 3. However, if you are interested in editing using iMovie HD (Mac only), read the following section before you jump ahead to Chapter 3.

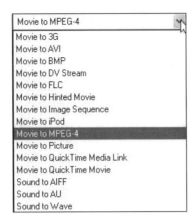

**FIGURE 2-36**    Many choices for output.

# Edit Video Using iMovie HD

iMovie HD is not something to be taken lightly. It's not just a plaything to be frivolously dabbled in. Well, actually it is that too. But it's also a very powerful and integrated video editing program that will give you results that are as professional as you have the skill or patience to manufacture. It's also a lot of fun.

We won't worry too much about how we're going to capture our footage here. iMovie makes it very easy to acquire video footage, as well as stills, from diverse sources. You can drag your files directly into the clip well, or import them directly via FireWire from a digital camcorder. You can even drag them in from iPhoto. With so many methods of acquiring our footage, I'll let you choose how to get those four video shots of the ball rolling down the ramp into iMovie. See Chapter 1 if you need assistance.

iMovie's interface is rather simple. Although it doesn't provide many instructions, it's not that difficult to figure out how to do the basics. The following exercises will give you a few more insights and tricks, though, so follow along.

When you first open iMovie, you're asked what type of project to create. Choose Create a New Project for this exercise to open the Create Project dialog box, shown in Figure 2-37. You'll have to name your project before you start actually editing. iMovie also asks you to define the format for the video. A short explanation of each format accompanies each choice. In this case, just keep it at the default setting of DV.

> **TIP**   *You can also determine where the file is going to be sent on your hard drive. In this case, it will live in the Movies folder in your account. Also note that each format in the Video Format drop-down menu has an explanatory note.*

When we finally get to the iMovie workspace, we see that it's broken down into three main areas, as shown in Figure 2-38: the large Preview pane, the Clips well to the right, and the Timeline below.

**FIGURE 2-37** Before you start, you must assign a name to your project.

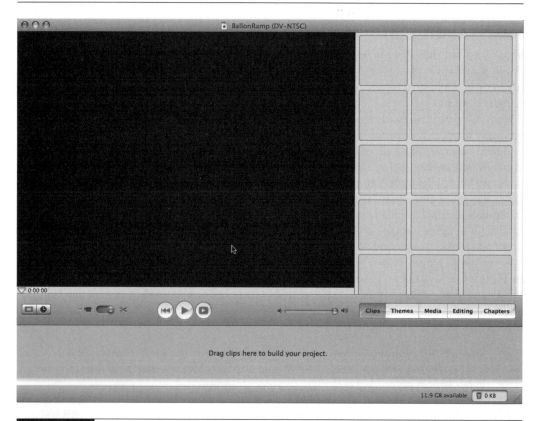

**FIGURE 2-38** The basic iMovie layout

You'll also see that the Clips button is just one choice of five in the lower-right corner. With each of those choices, the area above the buttons changes to reflect what area you're working in. So, when you click Editing, for instance, the controls above change to show all the editing controls for titles, transitions, video effects, and audio effects. But we're getting a little ahead of ourselves. More about that in a minute.

Since we already have our four shots on our computer, we can simply choose File | Import, locate the files, and bring them into iMovie.

Once the files have been imported, as clips, they take up residence in the Clips well, as shown in Figure 2-39. If you care to explore, hold down the camera icon, and you will see a choice of capture modes, form normal to time lapse. See Figure 2-40.

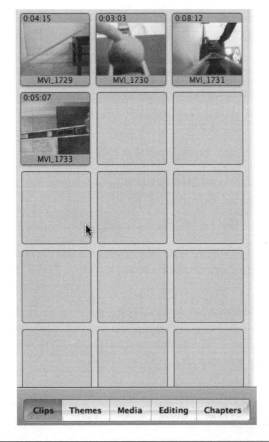

FIGURE 2-39    Clips fill the Clips well.

**FIGURE 2-40** There's more than meets the eye with the capture mode.

## Trim, Split, and Order Clips

It is time to put our four clips to work. The first thing we'll do is trim our clips:

1. Select the first clip from the Clips well. You'll see it in the large Preview pane to the left. Take note of the In and Out markers in the progress bar. There are three components to be aware of in the Preview pane: the playhead, which is the inverted triangle that rides along the top part of the progress bar, and the two markers, one on the left (In marker) and one on the right (Out marker), that ride along the bottom edge of the progress bar. See Figure 2-41.

2. Drag the Out marker to the point at which you want the video clip to end.

3. Drag the In marker to the point at which you want the video clip to begin. The space in between those markers is the footage we want for our video. So let's crop (trim) the clip to those points. Select Edit | Crop.

> **NOTE** *Cropping your clips is destructive. You are actually affecting the data on the clip. Sometimes it's a good idea to use Edit | Split Video Clip at Playhead instead of cropping your clip. This splits the clip into two, which gives you a few more clips to work with, but also saves the footage.*

4. Drag the cropped clip from the Clips well to the Timeline below.

> **NOTE** *When you drag your clips to the Timeline, you are essentially ordering them. You can pick them up and drag them, shuffle them and such by selecting the clip mode for the Timeline.*

5. Repeat the process with the second clip, only this time, let's split the clip rather than crop it. Choose Edit | Split Video Clip at Playhead. You never know when you might want that bit of outtake. See Figure 2-42. Also take note that in the Clips well, there are now two clips where there once was one.

**FIGURE 2-41** Note the three components of the Preview pane's progress bar.

| | |
|---|---|
| **Undo Move** | ⌘Z |
| Can't Redo | ⇧⌘Z |
| **Cut** | ⌘X |
| **Copy** | ⌘C |
| Paste | ⌘V |
| **Clear** | |
| **Select All** | ⌘A |
| **Select Similar Clips** | ⌥⌘A |
| **Select None** | ⇧⌘A |
| **Crop** | ⌘K |
| **Split Video Clip at Playhead** | **⌘T** |
| **Create Still Frame** | ⇧⌘S |
| **Special Characters…** | ⌥⌘T |

**FIGURE 2-42**   Split Video Clip at the Playhead makes two clips out of one.

**6.** Since we only split the front part of the clip, we now have to take the back end and do the same. Position the Out marker where you want the clip to end. Make sure the playhead is also at the same point.

**7.** Choose Edit | Split Video Clip at Playhead (or press ⌘-T).

**8.** Drag the resulting clip with the footage you want from the Clips well to the Timeline.

**9.** Repeat this process with the remaining two original clips.

**10.** When you have all four clips, trimmed and ready, in the Timeline, click from the Film Frame icon to the Clock icon. For reference, see Figure 2-43.

Once you're in Timeline mode, shown in Figure 2-44, peruse for a moment the different aspects of the Timeline and how it depicts your clips. You'll no doubt see that the ruler at the top shows the passage of time in a very accurate way. Also, the clips have a volume control line running through them. We'll deal with that adjustment when we work with audio a few steps down the line here.

**FIGURE 2-43**   The two modes for the Timeline. Use Film Frame mode to order your clips. Use Clock, or Timeline, mode to actually work with the clips.

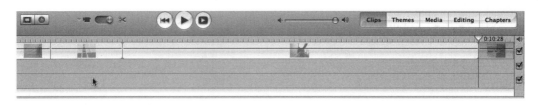

**FIGURE 2-44**    The Timeline is a more accurate method of editing.

# Work with Effects and Transitions

Now that our clips are in order in the Timeline, let's look at some possible effects and transitions that we can apply. But first, review your video by clicking the Play button at the foot of the Preview pane. Now, follow the steps below to see how to apply effects to your footage.

1. Click the Editing button.

2. Click the Video FX tab at the top.

3. In the Timeline, select the first clip.

4. Just for the sake of experimentation, select Aged Film in the Editing pane. Look at the effect in the Preview pane.

Okay, enough of that. You get the idea. You like an effect, you click Apply, and there you have it. But we aren't interested so much in effects right now. I just wanted you to be aware of the Effects tab, and its ease of use. We do want to see transitions, however. So click the Transitions tab at the top of the Editing pane.

Transitions are perhaps the easiest things to misuse, and yet they carry with them the most subtle aspects of a good video. If we use transitions correctly, no one will even notice them. And that's a good thing. We don't want to draw attention to the transitions … we want to draw attention to our video.

In many cases, no transition at all is fine, leaving a hard cut from one angle to another. In fact, with the four basic shots we have here, that may be the best bet. But we're not seriously going to worry about the content of our short video. We're using it only as an example on which you can learn new editing techniques, a laboratory rat, if you will. So let's apply a transition and see what happens:

1. On the Transitions tab of the Editing pane, select Cross Dissolve.

2. Drag the Cross Dissolve *between* two of your clips in the Timeline, as shown in Figure 2-45.

3. If the clips on either side of the transition are too short, you'll get a warning, as shown in Figure 2-46.

FIGURE 2-45    Transitions sit between your clips.

4.  Return to the Transitions tab of the Editing pane and select Cross Dissolve again. At the bottom of the pane, you'll see a control that says Speed, with a slider and a number.

5.  Slide the slider to the left until the corresponding number on the right becomes 2:00, as shown in Figure 2-47. The Preview pane will display what your final transition will look like.

6.  Apply the Cross Dissolve transition by dragging it between the clips in the Timeline. See Figure 2-48.

Preview your video sequence, with the transition in place. Better? If not, merely delete the transition before you go any further. It's a good rule of thumb to use transitions sparingly and with great attention to the clips they are working with. Again, the best transitions are those that no one notices.

## Add Narration

In our clips, we still have the residual audio that was embedded when we made the shots. It's doubtful that it's very good, or that it fits our edited piece. So we want to extract it, remove it, and then add a narration track.

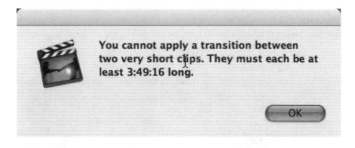

You cannot apply a transition between two very short clips. They must each be at least 3:49:16 long.

OK

FIGURE 2-46    Oops. Uh oh. Time to go back to the Transitions controls.

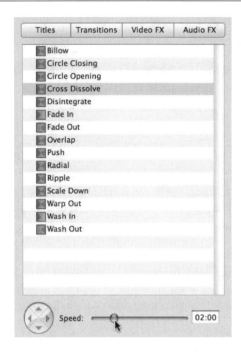

FIGURE 2-47 Making the transition faster will help it fit between shorter clips.

## Extract Residual Audio

To extract the existing audio, follow these steps:

1. Select the first clip in the Timeline.

2. Select Advanced | Extract Audio, which separates the video from the audio. When we extract the audio from a video clip, it doesn't disappear. It merely finds its place on a separate Audio track directly below it, as shown in Figure 2-49.

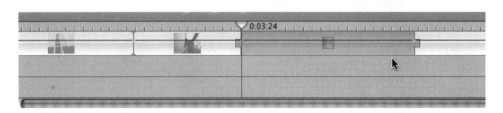

FIGURE 2-48 Transitions look different than normal video clips in the Timeline.

**FIGURE 2-49**    Extracted audio finds its place on the track just below it.

**3.** Repeat Steps 1 and 2 for each clip in the sequence.

NOTE    *If you find yourself doing this in a project with many clips, do this as soon as you drop the clips onto the Timeline. To accomplish this wholesale, simply use the Select All command (⌘-A) and then choose Advanced | Extract Audio. All your clips with embedded audio will immediately separate.*

With all of your audio extracted to the first Audio track, notice that there is a small thumbtack icon on both the video and the corresponding audio below it, as shown in Figure 2-50. This thumbtack icon means that the audio is still locked with its corresponding video. Let's *unlock* the audio and video. Select and slide one audio clip to the right. Note that it moves alone, without the video above it. You've essentially moved it off its synchronization. Even though you've moved the audio, the thumbtack icon means that if you move the video clip, that (now off-sync) audio clip will move with it.

## Remove Residual Audio

There are two ways to remove the audio. The first, nondestructive method is to uncheck the check box at the far right of the Audio track. That check box is a sort of mute button, that turns off or on its respective Audio track. The second method is to delete the audio completely.

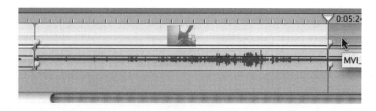

**FIGURE 2-50**    The thumbtack icon means the audio is still locked to the corresponding video clip.

Removing the audio altogether is easy:

**1.** Select the audio clip and press DELETE.

**2.** Do the same now for all the audio tracks.

## Add a Narration Track

After you've removed all audio, you'll want to do a narration track. In iMovie, it's called a Voiceover.

**1.** Click the Media button.

**2.** Make sure you have either a built-in microphone or an external microphone, possibly through your iSight camera. If you aren't sure, go to the System Preferences, select Sound, and check your Sound Input settings.

**3.** In the Media pane, note the Microphone levels and the red Record button, as shown in Figure 2-51.

**4.** Talk into your microphone, and watch your levels. If they seem good, by which I mean they don't live completely in the red, but just tickle it every so often, then click the red Record button and start speaking.

> **TIP** *While you may think you're an expert at extemporaneous oration already, it's always a good idea to have, if not a complete script of what you are going to say, at the very least a few bullet or talking points. Read them a few times aloud before you click Record, and get used to speaking into a computer. You may want to keep these notes in front of you while you do your narration as well. Narration might seem easy, but the reality is that it takes practice.*

**5.** As you record, watch the Audio track in the Timeline (see Figure 2-52). It will show your recording in real time in direct relation to your video. When you're finished, click Stop.

If your voiceover didn't make the grade, you can always do it again. Just select the audio clip and press DELETE. Then start over.

**FIGURE 2-51** Microphone, levels, red button. I wonder what that means.

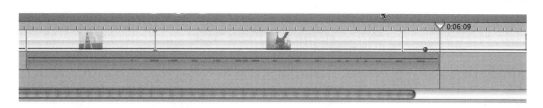

**FIGURE 2-52**   Real-time visual feedback for your voiceover

Narration is fine, but sometimes it can sound hollow if it's not backed up with some music. Odds are, since you're on a Mac, you've got a good music collection in iTunes as well. Which is a good thing, since iMovie is directly integrated with iTunes through the Media pane.

## Add Music

Adding music is easy. Choosing the music is not. So we're going to concentrate on adding music, and leave the choosing to you. In order to do that, let's look at the Media pane again.

**NOTE**   *iMovie lets you sample all your music before you commit to placing it in the Timeline. Of course, there are built-in samples of music, but we all know you have your own ideas about what music you're going to use as a soundtrack for your video. Still, I wouldn't be doing my job if I didn't point out to you all the choices open to you.*

But how do we know if the music we choose is appropriate? We test it, of course.

1.  In the Media pane, click the Audio button.

2.  Scroll through the listing, to your iTunes collection.

3.  If you have playlists in iTunes, they will be available to you via this list. Select iTunes. You may have to click the triangle to its left to expand the full listing of songs and playlists.

4.  Select Library. To see all the songs available, you may want to adjust the songlist pane by clicking and dragging it up or down. See Figure 2-53.

5.  You can also sort your song list by duration, rather than by title or artist, by clicking the Time column heading. This may be handy if you want the song to begin and end at the same time as the video itself. So, for instance, if your video is 1:02, you may want to search out a song that is near to that length of time.

6.  If you have a particular song in mind, you can also use the built-in search function to locate it.

FIGURE 2-53   View your song titles in the songlist pane.

7. Once you have a song selected, sample it with the Play button.

8. Satisfied? In the Timeline, place the playhead where you want the song to begin. See Figure 2-54.

9. Back in the Media pane, now that you have chosen your song and played it in the sampler, click Place at Playhead, as shown in Figure 2-55.

10. The song is now in place on your Timeline. You can shift it right or left to match your video better, if need be. Or you can select it and delete it if it isn't what you want, and then you can start over.

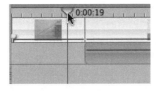

FIGURE 2-54   Place the playhead where you want the music to begin.

**FIGURE 2-55**   Place the song at the playhead by clicking the button.

**NOTE**   *The audio controls we use here are pretty simple. We might want to be "ducking" our music under narration, which means lowering the levels on the music enough so that our narration is not drowned out. We can adjust these levels using points in the Timeline, by clicking a point and dragging it up or down to suit our needs.*

# Apply Titles

The final step before we send our video off in proper format is to apply titles. Once again, the process is similar to applying effects and transitions. Here's how to apply titles:

1. Return to the Editing pane.

2. Click the Titles tab.

3. Choose a title style from the list. In the text input area just below the list, type in your information, as shown in the example in Figure 2-56.

4. The preview pane shows how your titles look, before you commit to them. If they appear over a black background, but you want them to overlay on your video, deselect the Over Black check box in the lower-left corner of the Editing pane. You can also adjust the speed of the titles, as well as whether they pause or not, as they run. And don't forget to format the size, style, color, and family of the type. See Figure 2-56.

5. Move the playhead in the Timeline to your preferred In point for the titles. Then click Add.

Preview your video. If you aren't satisfied with your titles (or your transitions, for that matter), even after applying them, you can delete them and start over. Here's how to remove titles (or transitions):

1. Select the clip or clips that contain the title or effect you want to remove in the Timeline.

2. Switch the Timeline to Clip Viewer mode.

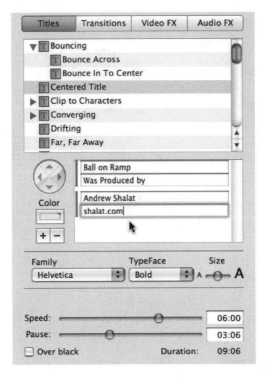

FIGURE 2-56 Your titles can be long or short.

**3.** Select the title's icon in the Clip Viewer, as shown in Figure 2-57.

**4.** Press the DELETE key.

**NOTE** *If you want to select all of your transitions at once, select a transition and choose Edit | Select Similar Clips.*

FIGURE 2-57 In Clip Viewer mode, select the effect, transition, or title from the clip's icon.

Review your video, titles, transitions, and effects. If everything is ready for delivery, Save Project (File | Save Project).

# Prepare for Online Delivery

We've finally arrived at the point where we want to put the video in a suitable format for upload. All we really have to do here, then, is make the right choice of format. But don't worry if you make the wrong choice. There are no *wrong* choices. Just more appropriate ones.

1. Choose Share | Share.

2. In the ensuing dialog box, we need to make a selection. Since we're not exactly sure whether we're going to send this to iTunes, to a web page of our own making, or to a free online service like YouTube.com, iFilm.com (Spike), or even MySpace.com, let's hedge our bets a little and select QuickTime, as shown in Figure 2-58.

3. In the QuickTime selection, we have some further choices, for compression, as shown in Figure 2-58. We can scroll through the various presets and read each description to better understand what we're about to do. For this exercise, choose Web.

4. Click Share.

5. In the Save As dialog box window, shown in Figure 2-59, name the file and navigate to where you'd like to save it.

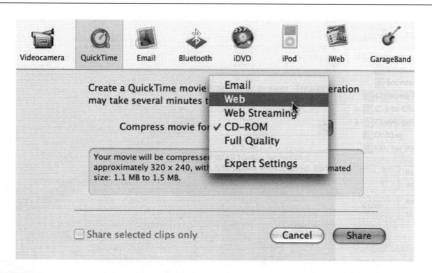

---

**FIGURE 2-58**    Select QuickTime, and then choose to compress for the Web. The final output will be perfect for YouTube, MySpace, or even iPod.

FIGURE 2-59 Save your file where you know you can find it later.

After you've saved your file, you're done here. You've edited your video to a point of viewability. You're ready to share it with the world. You're ready to upload it. Forge on, seeker. The next chapter will show you how.

# Chapter 3

# Upload Your Video

## How to...

- Set up a YouTube account
- Upload video files to your YouTube account
- Set up a MySpace account
- Upload video files to your MySpace account
- Create a simple web page and embed QuickTime and Flash video files
- Encode QuickTime video files as Flash Video files
- Embed video files from outside sources
- Launch a vodcast with iTunes

There are almost as many places to deliver your video online as there are ideas of what to shoot a video about. The online video community (for lack of a better term) continues to grow and adapt to both newer, previously unforeseen applications and better technology. You can upload your videos to one of the readily available, and free, prepackaged video sites, such as YouTube, iFilm, and MySpace; you can embed videos on your own web site; you can upload your videos to a blog, or you can create a video podcast and list it on iTunes or FeedBurner. You can achieve a mix of all of these as well, linking, embedding, and pointing to videos from one source to the next. Each YouTube video has information accompanying it that allows you to send just a URL link to it, or embed the actual video, interface and all, on a web page you're designing, or just a line of text that points to the video where it lives on YouTube.

In this chapter, you'll learn the fastest and best ways to get your video online using popular video hosting sites such as YouTube, MySpace, iFilm, and others, and learn how to make vodcasts.

# Deliver Your Video on YouTube

This section leads you through the steps of signing up for a YouTube account, uploading your video to your account, and editing your video information after uploading your video to your account.

## Sign Up for a YouTube Account

To sign up for your own YouTube account, follow these steps:

1. Point your browser to http://youtube.com.
2. Click the Sign Up link.
3. In the Join YouTube window, note that several levels of account type are available in the Account Type drop-down list (see Figure 3-1): Standard, Director, Musician, Comedian, and Guru. For informational purposes, check out the description for each account type (other than Standard) by selecting it in the drop-down list. A description appears immediately above the Account Type field.

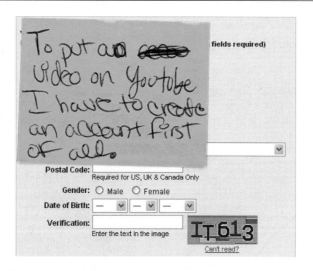

*(handwritten note: To put a ~~video~~ video on Youtube I have to create an account first of all.)*

**FIGURE 3-1**    Each level of account type has different requirements and protocols. Check out each one, but to start, just choose Standard.

**4.** Choose Standard.

**5.** Fill in the rest of the form. You must fill in all the fields to create an account

> **NOTE**    *The Sign Me Up for the Broadcast Yourself Email check box lets you send e-mails directly from your YouTube page to a large number of recipients. You can check or uncheck the box, but by default, it is checked.*

**6.** Click the Sign Up button.

**7.** Check your e-mail for a message from YouTube. You will be required to respond to the automatic e-mail from YouTube service.

**8.** Follow the instructions in the e-mail. Click the link, or copy and paste the individual URL supplied in the e-mail into your browser, to complete your signup process.

You now have a YouTube account. In the following section, we'll figure out what to do with it. Of course, you know that means *upload your video*.

# Upload Your Video to YouTube

Login to your YouTube account and locate the Upload Videos link. See Figure 3-2.

Uploading video on YouTube is a two-step process. First, you fill in general information about your video, including the Title, Description, Tags (keywords, essentially), and Video Category fields (refer to Figure 3-3). Be sure to write a clear and succinct description of your video. Also, think of about 12 keywords that you think would be applicable as search words for your video.

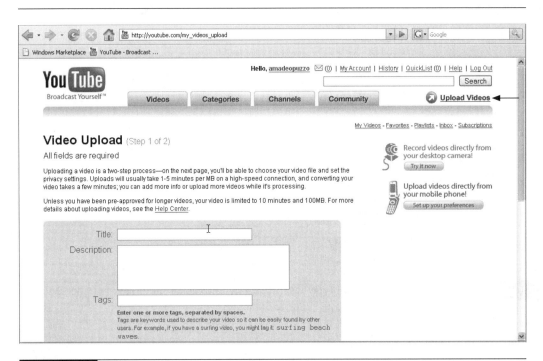

**FIGURE 3-2** The gateway to the future.

> **TIP** *You may consider having a description and a set of 12 keywords ready to go before you've even logged in.*

When you finish filling in the basic information for your video, the second step of the two-step process is to identify your file and choose to whom you want to broadcast it, as follows:

1. Click Browse (see Figure 3-3) to locate your video file. It cannot be larger than 100MB. If you've followed the instructions from Chapter 2, your video should be in an acceptable format (YouTube accepts video files in WMV, AVI, MOV, and MPG file formats). Select your file, as shown in Figure 3-4, and click Open.

2. Make sure you have the correct file chosen in the File field.

3. For the Broadcast option, choose Public to set the video to be available to the Internet world at large, or choose Private to designate a list of specific people with viewing privileges.

> **NOTE** *You can also populate your Friends and Family lists in the account settings. Nothing is etched in stone, though, so if your cousins diss you at Thanksgiving, you can always go into your settings and remove them. Exile them until Memorial Day, if you like.*

4. Click Upload Video. You will see a status bar of the upload progress.

**FIGURE 3-3**   Browse for your file.

After the video has been uploaded, and it's safely somewhere on the YouTube servers, you can take some time to go over some of the details and privileges pertaining to it.

## Edit Your Video Information after Upload

Since this is *your* account on YouTube, you can add or retract privileges and change settings on your uploaded video, even after you've uploaded it. Let's examine the YouTube web page that you arrive at after you upload your video. The following figures and descriptions are all part of the same web page. The page is presented one section at a time so that you can better understand and decide which settings are important and which are not essential.

**FIGURE 3-4**   Find your file and prepare to upload.

You can change the settings on your video even after you've uploaded it.

## Video Details

In Figure 3-5, note the Tags and Video Category settings. If, after uploading your video, you decide that your original tags or categories are not as accurate as you'd like, you can change them here.

## Date & Location Details

Figure 3-6 shows the Date & Location Details section. In many cases, the time, date, and place of the video may be very important, not just to you, but also to your viewers. Sometimes, the context of a video makes it more relevant than not. If that is true for your video, then fill in this information.

Date, time, and place can be important features for the context of a video.

## Sharing

Sharing or access privileges for viewing the video are very important. Which options you should choose in the Sharing section, shown in Figure 3-7, depends on how thick your skin is. Of course, one of the main reasons for uploading a video to YouTube is to share it with the world. However, occasionally, you may want to restrict video viewing privileges to a few specific individuals but for now let's parse out the basic options of the Sharing section, listed next.

NOTE  *When available, you should opt for the Yes, with Approval option. This gives you control over what follows your video.*

- **Broadcast**    Unless you really want to keep your video private, choose the recommended choice and select Public.

- **Allow Comments**    Selecting Yes, with Approval helps mitigate unwanted or rude commentary. If you're feeling more democratic, select Yes, Automatic, which leaves your video open to all sorts of criticism, good, bad, and mostly ugly.

- **Allow Video Responses**    Choosing Yes, with Approval is recommended. Again, you can let the comments fly, or you can have some editing control over them.

- **Allow Ratings**    If you're sincere, and open, you should want to allow these.

- **Allow External Sites to Embed This Video**    This is probably the best and easiest way to market and popularize your video. Enable this option. I'll talk further about methods of marketing your video in the next chapter, but in the case of YouTube, this is the place to start.

**Sharing**

| | |
|---|---|
| **Public URL:** (Non-Editable) | http://www.youtube.com/watch?v=GmAiLw6cbwY |
| | Email this video to others using YouTube's share feature. |

**Broadcast:**
- ⦿ **Public:** Share your video with the world! (Recommended)
- ○ **Private: Only viewable by you and those you choose.**
  **Email this video and enable access now to the contact lists below.**
  - ☐ Family
  - ☐ Friends

**Allow Comments:**
- ⦿ **Yes, with Approval:** Allow comments to be added to this video after you have approved them.
- ○ **Yes, Automatic:** Allow comments to be added to this video immediately.
- ○ **No:** Don't allow comments to be added to this video.

**Allow Video Responses:**
- ⦿ **Yes, with Approval:** Allow video responses to be added to this video after you have approved them
- ○ **Yes, Automatic:** Allow video responses to be added to this video immediately.
- ○ **No:** Don't allow video responses to be added to this video.

**Allow Ratings:**
- ⦿ **Yes:** Allow people to rate your video.
- ○ **No:** Don't allow people to rate your video.

If you disable ratings, this video will no longer be eligible to appear on the list of "Top Rated" videos.

**Allow External Sites to Embed This Video:**
- ⦿ **Enabled:** External sites may embed and play this video.
- ○ **Disabled:** External sites may NOT embed and play this video.

**FIGURE 3-7**    Take your time going through these options. You won't always want to use the same settings for every video you make.

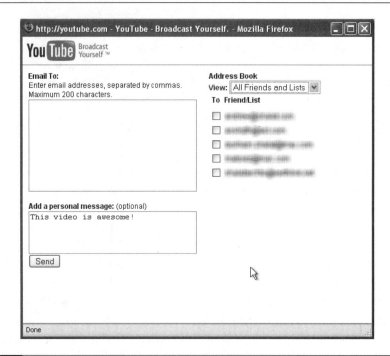

FIGURE 3-8 This is a simple but powerful feature that lets you directly e-mail your video to specific recipients, along with a short message.

Under the Public URL option at the start of the Sharing options, you'll see a link to YouTube's Share Feature. Click the link. A new window opens, as shown in Figure 3-8.

This feature allows you to enter specific e-mail addresses and add a short message to accompany your video. This is an excellent option to get your video out and seen. Remember that you can always use this option, and then go back to the normal Public broadcasting option. This *ensures* that certain designated people will see your video.

## Embed HTML

Finally, you have the embedded video options. The generated code at the bottom of the page (see Figure 3-9) lets you embed the video itself on any web page you have the ability to edit. See the section "Embed Video from Outside Sources," later in the chapter, for more information on how to do this.

Just below the Embed HTML code is the Update Video Info button. If you have uploaded your video but want to change the settings for access, sharing, tags, or category, you can easily update the video's information by clicking this button.

**FIGURE 3-9**    The code is generated by YouTube automatically. Use it to embed the video directly on your web site.

# Update Your Video Information in the Future

Any time you login to your YouTube account, you can edit and update your video information. Just click My Account, click My Videos, and, in the cell containing the respective video that you want to edit, click Edit Video Info, as shown in Figure 3-10.

This will return you to the video information page.

**NOTE**    *You will find that most video and photo uploading sites like YouTube, such as PhotoBucket and iFilm, use pretty much the same step-by-step method of uploading and categorizing. Once you are familiar with one, you should be able to drop into any of the other sites and not have any trouble adjusting.*

**FIGURE 3-10**    You can change your settings on any of your videos at any time.

# Deliver Your Video on MySpace

If you're under 40 years old, you probably have a MySpace account. If you're a celebrity, you have a MySpace account. If you're a musician trying to get a gig, or a musician who already has a gig, you probably have a MySpace account. If you're a celebrity publicist or assistant or just the person in the celebrity's entourage designated to keep things up to date, you either have or, at the very least, have experience with a MySpace account.

If you're none of those people mentioned, you still might have a MySpace account. You may just be a politician. And that's okay. It shows that you are hip to one of the easiest and most cost-effective methods of getting a message out to the world, and have point of contact to filter that world right back in.

NOTE
*There's been a lot of rumor surrounding having a MySpace account lately. MySpace gets a lot of notoriety for its singles-oriented aspects. There's no accounting for what people do with their time, or their energy. But if you don't have a MySpace account because you've heard that it's some virtual den of iniquity, some digital Hieronymus Bosch realm, then you're probably not going to be comfortable having an account there. But do some research, check out other MySpace pages and then make a decision. Or, find another place, such as Flickr or Yahoo, to post your videos. MySpace is nothing more than a platform, so whatever you bring to it is what you'll make of it.*

## Sign Up for a MySpace Account

The sign-up process for MySpace is not all that different from YouTube (refer to the "Sign Up for a You Tube Account" section). Go to www.myspace.com, click the SignUp link in the upper-right corner, and answer the questions.

## Upload Your Video to MySpace

MySpace accepts a wider variety of video formats than most upload sites accept, including those listed in Figure 3-11.

Now that you have an account, this section shows you how to put video on MySpace:

1. Login to your MySpace account.

2. In your greeting area, click Add/Change Videos.

3. Select the Upload tab, shown in Figure 3-12.

4. Fill in the information. Remember, tags are search keywords. Also, make sure to check the Public/Private options. See Figure 3-13. Check back to the previous section about YouTube, so you don't mistake these actions for déjà vu.

---

File Size Limit per upload: 100MB.
Acceptable formats: .asf, .wmv, .mov, .qt, .3g2, .3gp, .3gp2, .3gpp, .gsm, .mpg, .mpeg, .mp4, .m4v, .mp4v, .cmp, .divx, .xvid, .264, .rm, .rmvb, .flv.

---

**FIGURE 3-11** Upload alphabet soup.

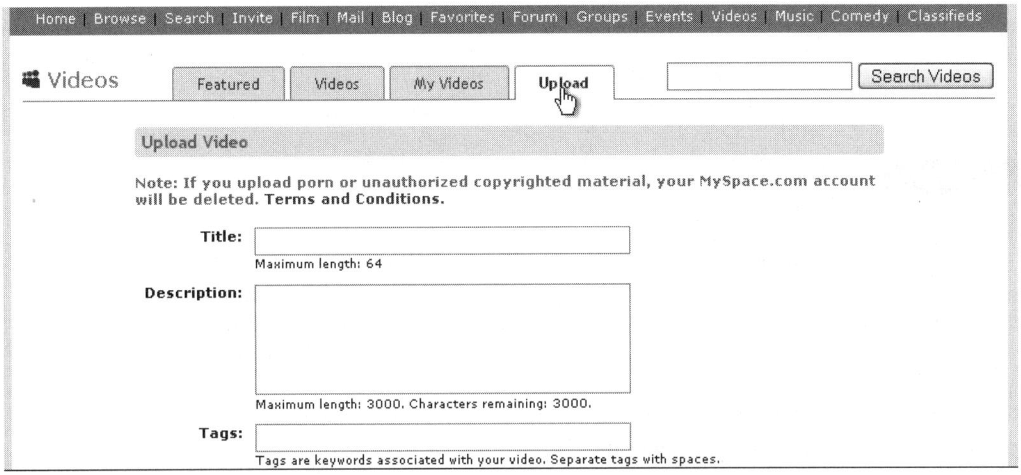

Home | Browse | Search | Invite | Film | Mail | Blog | Favorites | Forum | Groups | Events | Videos | Music | Comedy | Classifieds

**Videos**    Featured    Videos    My Videos    **Upload**    [          ]  Search Videos

**Upload Video**

Note: If you upload porn or unauthorized copyrighted material, your MySpace.com account will be deleted. **Terms and Conditions.**

**Title:** [                              ]
Maximum length: 64

**Description:** [                              ]

Maximum length: 3000. Characters remaining: 3000.

**Tags:** [                              ]
Tags are keywords associated with your video. Separate tags with spaces.

**FIGURE 3-12**   This tab should be familiar to anyone who's used YouTube.

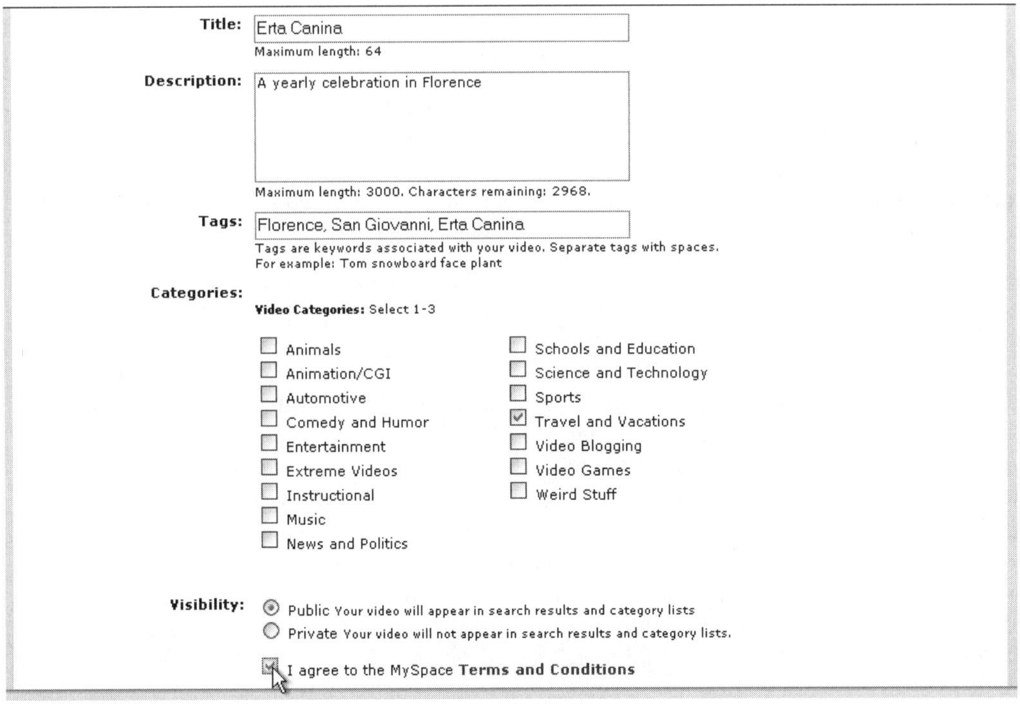

**Title:** Erta Canina
Maximum length: 64

**Description:** A yearly celebration in Florence

Maximum length: 3000. Characters remaining: 2968.

**Tags:** Florence, San Giovanni, Erta Canina
Tags are keywords associated with your video. Separate tags with spaces.
For example: Tom snowboard face plant

**Categories:**
**Video Categories:** Select 1-3

☐ Animals                    ☐ Schools and Education
☐ Animation/CGI              ☐ Science and Technology
☐ Automotive                 ☐ Sports
☐ Comedy and Humor           ☑ Travel and Vacations
☐ Entertainment              ☐ Video Blogging
☐ Extreme Videos             ☐ Video Games
☐ Instructional              ☐ Weird Stuff
☐ Music
☐ News and Politics

**Visibility:**   ⦿ Public Your video will appear in search results and category lists
○ Private Your video will not appear in search results and category lists.

☑ I agree to the MySpace **Terms and Conditions**

**FIGURE 3-13**   Keywords and categories are important. Also be sure to assign access privileges, either Public or Private.

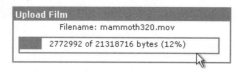

FIGURE 3-14    Uploads can take some time.

**5.** After you assign tags and privileges, click Upload. While your video uploads, you can probably make yourself a cup of tea, shine your shoes, or dust around the house, depending on how large the file is (the maximum size is 100MB). Figure 3-14 shows a typical progress bar during upload.

Once the video is processed, it appears on your MySpace page under Videos. You can send the link to friends and colleagues, via e-mail or via the MySpace network.

**NOTE** *You will find that most networking sites like MySpace use pretty much the same step-by-step method of uploading and categorizing. Once you are familiar with one, you should be able to drop into any of the others and not have any trouble adjusting.*

# Embed Video into Your Own Web Page

Using one of the uploading and sharing sites we looked at earlier in this chapter is probably the easiest, fastest, and most efficient way of getting videos on the Web, viewed by thousands, and distributed around the world. But there are also times when you need to make a more boutique experience for viewers. That's where setting up and using your own web site (your domain, your site, your hosting service of choice) to display video comes into play.

**NOTE** *If you have a blog on Blogger, Google's free blogging service, you can also embed your video in an article, using a simple link (<href> </a>) or an embed link. Check with your specific blogging service to find out what its specific tag is.*

There are as many ways to create a web page as there are, uh, software applications to help you do it. And then there are a few more after that. But most designers and web developers use one of the more familiar programs: Adobe Dreamweaver. If you have experience building a web site, you might have your own favorite program, such as FrontPage (or its replacement, Expression Web), Freeway, BBEdit, iWeb, or Sitebuilder. However, the purpose here is not to show you how to build a whole web site using various programs, but rather to show you how to embed video into a web page. Because of its popularity, I'll use Dreamweaver for the example. From this discussion, you should be able to figure out how to embed video using your own favorite program.

In the following sections, you'll learn how to create a basic HTML page and embed video into it. We're not worrying about page design so much as clean, simple, table-based layout. The rest of the design is up to you, of course. You will learn how to embed two types of video files. The first is a QuickTime (MOV or MP4) file, and the second is a Flash Video (FLV) file. Finally, you'll learn how to embed into your page a video from YouTube.

## Create a Simple Web Page

We will be using Dreamweaver here. But since Dreamweaver lets you work in Code view as well as Design view, I'll also give you the HTML code so that you can use a text editor if you are so inclined. We'll just be making a simple web page, not an elaborate CSS (Cascading Style Sheets) based conglomeration. Since this is not a design book, I won't bore you with aesthetics.

1. Open Dreamweaver.

2. In the opening Welcome Screen window, also called the Start Window, select HTML under Create New, as shown in Figure 3-15 (CTRL-N, or ⌘-N on a Mac).

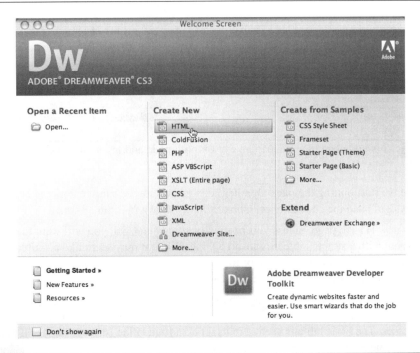

FIGURE 3-15    This is always an easy place to start a new page.

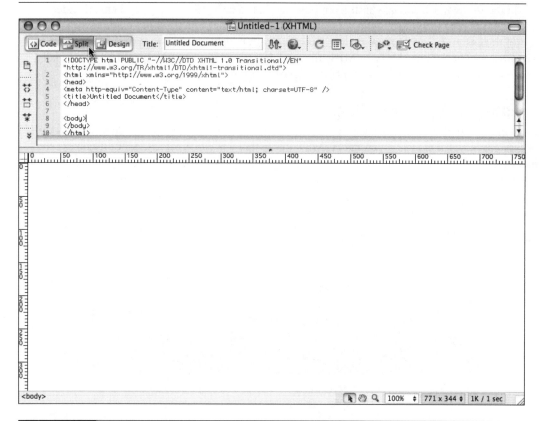

**FIGURE 3-16**    It's not a bad idea to keep an eye on both code and layout at once.

**3.** Before we start putting the page together, let's make sure we can see both the layout (or "design") and the code at once. Click Split, as shown in Figure 3-16.

**4.** In any new HTML page, unless you're specifically using CSS, you will want to control the layout with a simple table. So, insert a table. While it may seem like a simple thing, take a look at the upper Code pane of the window after you do it. Refer to Figure 3-17. If you prefer the code-only view, take a look at Figure 3-18.

**5.** For the sake of symmetry, set up the table with three columns and three rows, as shown in Figure 3-19. You can always combine or split rows and columns as your design progresses. The basic table is used here to set up a foundation for your page and to keep all the elements of your layout in a controllable place.

**6.** Set the alignment for the cells of the table. Place your cursor in the cell you want to work with. In the floating Properties palette, select Center Align, as shown in Figure 3-20.

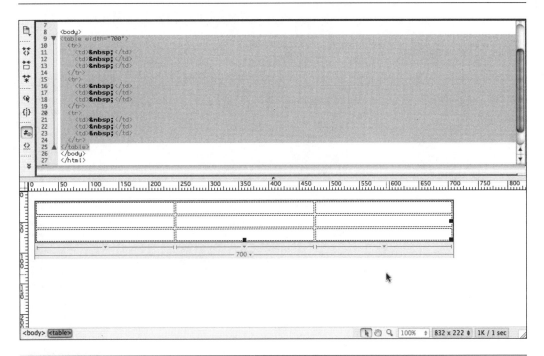

**FIGURE 3-17**    You can see that even a simple table takes some code.

With the table in place on the page, we can insert our video. Unlike inserting simple images, be they GIF or JPG, inserting videos on a web page requires some extra *tlc* (tender loving care). That's not a technical term, but the procedure we use is.

## Embed a QuickTime File

This section makes one basic assumption concerning the video file: that you've saved it in any of the QuickTime-readable formats. Let's begin by embedding a QuickTime MOV file into a web page:

1. Choose Insert | Media | Plugin. There is no specific menu item for QuickTime, but selecting Plugin will fashion the embed code correctly for the file type you are about to insert.

2. In the Select File dialog box, shown in Figure 3-21, navigate to the file you want to embed. If you have a site set up on Dreamweaver, you may already have that file inside the site folder. If not, then Dreamweaver will ask you to copy it to your root folder on its own. If that's the case, click Yes. See Figure 3-22. When you locate the correct QuickTime video file, select it and click Choose.

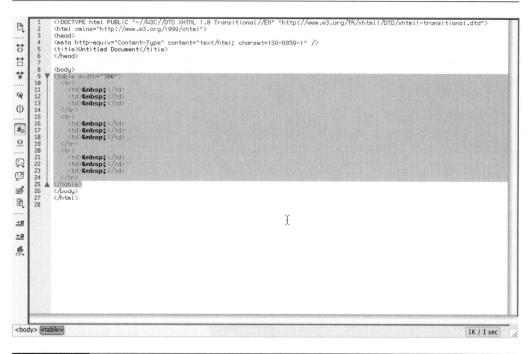

```
1    <!DOCTYPE html PUBLIC "-//W3C//DTD XHTML 1.0 Transitional//EN" "http://www.w3.org/TR/xhtml1/DTD/xhtml1-transitional.dtd">
2    <html xmlns="http://www.w3.org/1999/xhtml">
3    <head>
4    <meta http-equiv="Content-Type" content="text/html; charset=ISO-8859-1" />
5    <title>Untitled Document</title>
6    </head>
7
8    <body>
9    <table width="700">
10     <tr>
11       <td> </td>
12       <td> </td>
13       <td> </td>
14     </tr>
15     <tr>
16       <td> </td>
17       <td> </td>
18       <td> </td>
19     </tr>
20     <tr>
21       <td> </td>
22       <td> </td>
23       <td> </td>
24     </tr>
25   </table>
26   </body>
27   </html>
28
```

`<body> <table>`                                                    `1K / 1 sec`

**FIGURE 3-18**    Just viewing the code alone, you can see that sometimes it's more efficient to work by design and layout rather than writing code. But that may be a personal preference.

**3.** When the file is set in the center of your table, it shows up only as a plug-in icon, similar to the example shown in Figure 3-23. You have to refer to the floating Properties palette to make sure it's the correct file.

**4.** Note that the plug-in icon takes up only a 32 × 32 pixel space, as the W and H settings indicate in Figure 3-24. Because your video has much larger dimensions than that, you need to make a specific adjustment. Your QuickTime video from Chapter 2 (of the ball rolling down the ramp) was set at 320 × 240 pixels, so use those dimensions for this example. Go to the Properties palette and change the H and W settings to 320 and 280, respectively, as shown in Figure 3-25.

**5.** Once set, the correct dimensions of your video are reflected in the layout in Dreamweaver, as shown in Figure 3-26. Check to make sure.

**6.** Save your document. You can give it any name you like. For instance, I called mine movie.html.

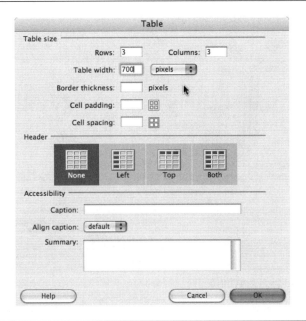

**FIGURE 3-19**   Inserting a table in your web page is just to keep your basic elements in place.

7.  Since the browser feature of Dreamweaver doesn't necessarily have plug-ins, you have to preview your video in a browser, by choosing File | Preview in Browser | *Browser*, as shown in Figure 3-27. In any case, previewing in a browser is the way to go, because your viewers are going to be seeing the online video through a browser. See Figure 3-28. This is also the beauty of web design. Unlike print design, there are no proofs that are other than a final rendition, seen the way they actually go online.

## Embed a Flash Video File

You may be asking yourself, "Well, since I already know how to put a QuickTime video file on my page, why do I need to use a Flash Video file?" This is a valid question. There are several

**FIGURE 3-20**   Set the table cell for center alignment.

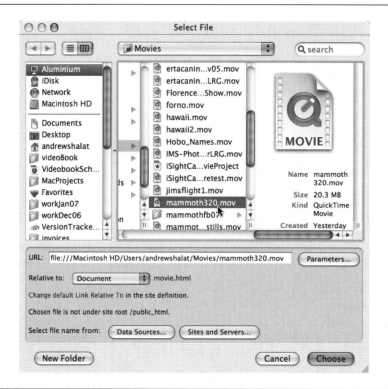

FIGURE 3-21    Select your video file.

FIGURE 3-22    You should choose to copy the file to a place within your root folder.

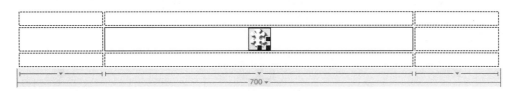

FIGURE 3-23    Even though you know it's a QuickTime video, you'll only see it represented as a plug-in icon in your layout.

FIGURE 3-24    The default size for an inserted media plug-in file is 32 × 32 pixels.

FIGURE 3-25    Adjust the video dimensions to the correct size. You can always check the properties of the specific video file to make sure of the numbers.

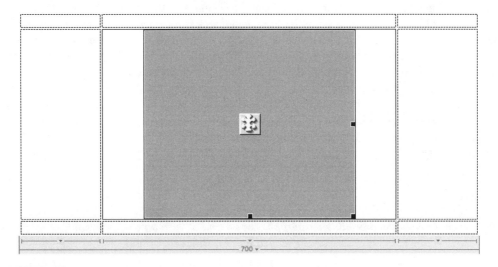

FIGURE 3-26    The dimensions shown here are the dimensions you'll get on the Web.

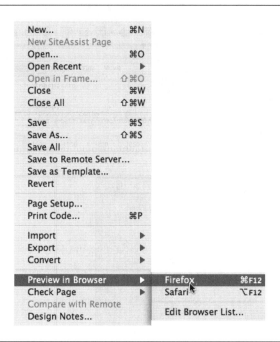

| New... | ⌘N |
| New SiteAssist Page | |
| Open... | ⌘O |
| Open Recent | ▶ |
| Open in Frame... | ⇧⌘O |
| Close | ⌘W |
| Close All | ⇧⌘W |
| Save | ⌘S |
| Save As... | ⇧⌘S |
| Save All | |
| Save to Remote Server... | |
| Save as Template... | |
| Revert | |
| Page Setup... | |
| Print Code... | ⌘P |
| Import | ▶ |
| Export | ▶ |
| Convert | ▶ |
| Preview in Browser | ▶ |
| Check Page | ▶ |
| Compare with Remote | |
| Design Notes... | |

| Firefox | ⌘F12 |
| Safari | ⌥F12 |
| Edit Browser List... | |

**FIGURE 3-27**    In Dreamweaver, you have a choice of previewing your video in your primary or secondary browser.

answers as well. For one, the quality of a QuickTime video and the quality of a Flash video can differ, depending on the codec (compression/decompression protocol) you use for each. Many people find that Flash videos have a glossier look than QuickTime videos. This may or may not be so. But beyond the look, which is adjustable, Flash Video has a distinct ease of locking. That is, whereas you can set up a QuickTime video to be difficult to copy, the default setting of Flash Video makes it uncopyable. That means that your video is relatively safe from piracy.

Flash Video is a format in itself, so before we can embed our video as a Flash Video file on our web page, we have to convert it to Flash Video. The easiest way to convert to Flash Video is to use the Adobe Flash Video Encoder. There are other applications that do the same thing, like GeoVid Flash To Video Encoder, Sothink Video Encoder for Adobe Flash, VX Flash Video Encoder, and others. We're going to use the Adobe Flash Video Encoder.

NOTE    *Flash CS3 Professional, which is part of the Creative Suite 3 from Adobe, is not inexpensive. The Flash Video Encoder is included with Flash, as an added utility application. But this might be an expensive add-on for most of us. The other encoders mentioned in the preceding paragraph cost around $50, so they're reasonable. The main thing is to get your videos encoded into Flash Video format.*

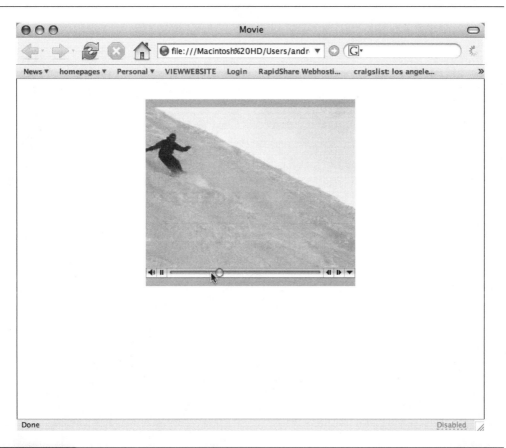

**FIGURE 3-28**   Voilà! Your video on your page.

## Convert a Video to Flash Video

To convert your video to Flash Video format, follow these steps:

1.  Open the Flash Video Encoder. The workspace is very simple, as shown in Figure 3-29. The major pane will contain your selected videos. You can batch encode a number of videos into Flash Video format. Notice the Start Queue button on the lower right.

2.  Click Add. In the subsequent dialog boxes, select your QuickTime file.

3.  The Flash Video Encoding Settings dialog box, shown in Figure 3-30, lets you configure some control settings. By default, the quality control is set at Medium Quality (400kbps). The corresponding settings are listed in the box in the middle of the screen. You can explore the other possible quality settings by clicking the drop-down arrow.

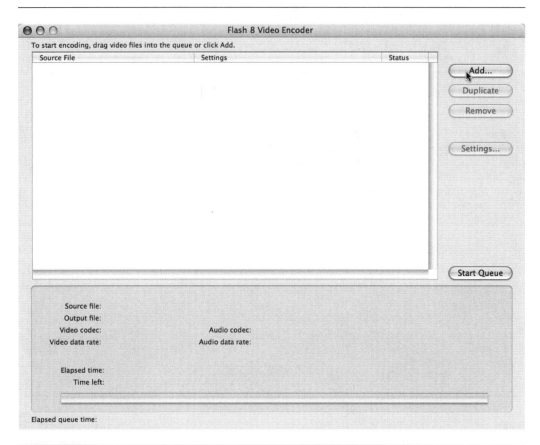

The Flash Video Encoder lets you encode multiple video files at once.

**4.** Click the Show Advanced Settings button to view the additional settings shown in Figure 3-31.

**5.** The advanced settings let you adjust not just the video quality, but also the audio and the in and out points. You can also crop your video to other dimensions. Try adjusting the in and out points. See Figure 3-32. It may be easier to use the preview pane, because editing with a visual cue is always easier. These controls should be familiar to you if you read the "Edit Video in QuickTime Pro" section in Chapter 2.

**6.** One of the more interesting settings is the Crop feature, shown in Figure 3-33. If you shot your video in 4:3 aspect ratio, but would like a more cinema-like screen, you can change your video to a 16:9 aspect ratio. Click the Crop and Trim tab. Make your adjustments in the numerical input areas, but keep an eye on the preview pane as well.

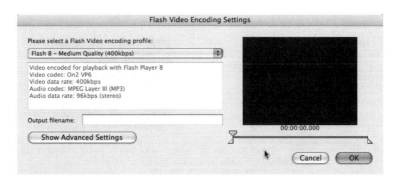

The default setting of Medium Quality is usually good enough for most circumstances.

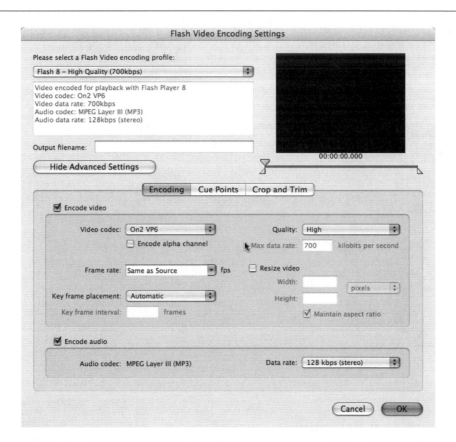

Here you have more settings for audio, video quality, and start and end points for the video.

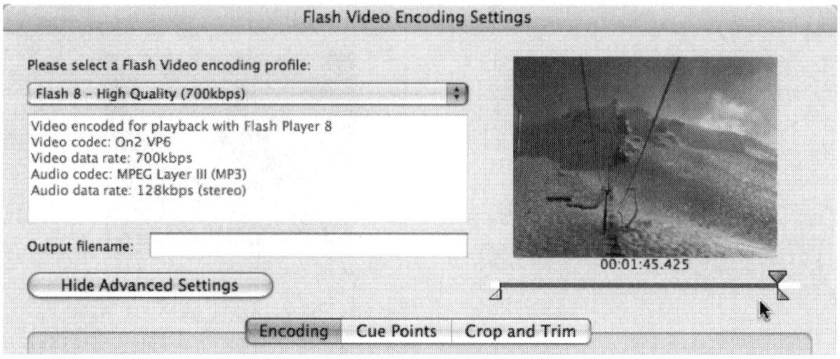

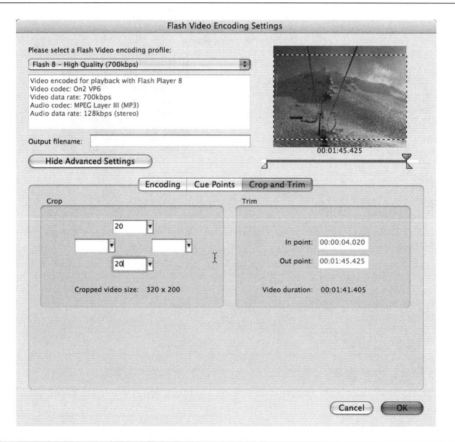

**FIGURE 3-32** The in and out points of your video are completely open to your adjustment.

**FIGURE 3-33** You can change the aspect ratio of your video on the Crop and Trim tab of the Advance Settings window.

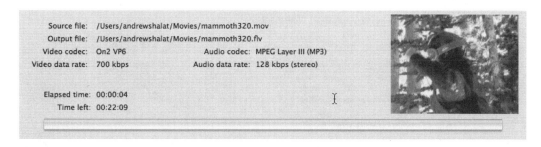

Source file: /Users/andrewshalat/Movies/mammoth320.mov
Output file: /Users/andrewshalat/Movies/mammoth320.flv
Video codec: On2 VP6          Audio codec: MPEG Layer III (MP3)
Video data rate: 700 kbps     Audio data rate: 128 kbps (stereo)

Elapsed time: 00:00:04
Time left: 00:22:09

**FIGURE 3-34**    The progress bar shows both elapsed time and time left. The preview pane
shows the video as it encodes, frame by frame.

7. Click OK.

8. Back in the main encoding window (see Figure 3-29), click Start Queue. You can watch
   frame-by-frame progress as your video encodes, in the window shown in Figure 3-34.

## Embed the Flash Video File

You should now have an encoded video in Flash Video format, signified by the .flv extension.
Let's get back to Dreamweaver and embed this file into our page:

1. Choose Insert | Media | Flash Video.

2. In the Insert Flash Video dialog box, shown in Figure 3-35, use the Browse button to
   navigate to your file and select it so that its path appears in the URL field.

3. In the Skin menu, select a skin, which determines how your video controls appear
   over your video when a mouse rolls over it. The skins come in various lengths and
   complexity. When you select a skin in the list, the box below the selection shows what
   the controls for that skin look like, so you can view different skins before you make your
   selection.

4. Enter the aspect ratio of your video in the Width and Height fields. The easiest way to do
   this is to simply click Detect Size, which fills in the fields.

5. Click OK. If your file is not already in the root folder of your site, Dreamweaver prompts
   you to copy it to the correct folder. This is very important, since the Insert Flash Video
   (Insert | Media | Flash Video) will not let you embed the file if it is not within the site's
   root folder. So when you see the window, don't panic. (Refer to Figure 3-22.)

6. Your Flash Video file is now embedded into your page. Note the Flash Video icon, as
   shown in Figure 3-36. Save your page.

7. Choose File | Preview in Browser | *Browser*. When the browser opens, roll your mouse
   over the video to see the skin you chose, as shown in Figure 3-37.

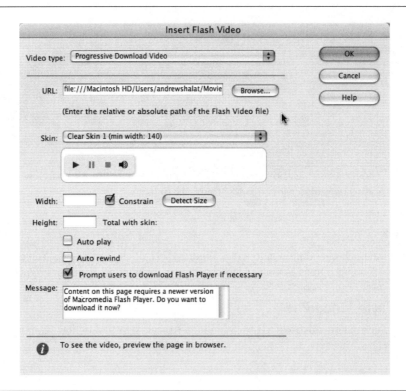

FIGURE 3-35    Select your Flash Video file (FLV) and choose the skin for its play controls.

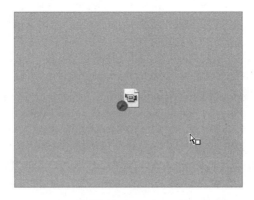

FIGURE 3-36    Flash Video file on your web page

**FIGURE 3-37**    When you roll your mouse over the video, the skin with video and audio controls appears.

If you try to drag the file off your page, or save the Flash Video file off the page from the browser, you won't be able to. That's the antipiracy aspect of FLV files mentioned earlier. But note the clarity and quality of the video. Compare it with the QuickTime video and see which you think is better, or better suits your needs.

## Did you know?

## Your Recommended Daily Code Requirement

Here's the actual code for the simple web page containing the Flash Video file. The emphasis in bold type is mine. It signifies where the Flash either is controlled or resides.

```
<!DOCTYPE html PUBLIC "-//W3C//DTD XHTML 1.0 Transitional//EN"
"http://www.w3.org/TR/xhtml1/DTD/xhtml1-transitional.dtd">
<html xmlns="http://www.w3.org/1999/xhtml">
<head>
<meta http-equiv="Content-Type" content="text/html; charset=ISO-8859-1" />
<title>Movie</title>
<script type="text/javascript">
function MM_CheckFlashVersion(reqVerStr,msg){
  with(navigator){
    var isIE  = (appVersion.indexOf("MSIE") != -1 && userAgent.indexOf("Opera")
== -1);
```

```
      var isWin = (appVersion.toLowerCase().indexOf("win") != -1);
      if (!isIE || !isWin){
        var flashVer = -1;
        if (plugins && plugins.length > 0){
          var desc = plugins["Shockwave Flash"] ? plugins["Shockwave
Flash"].description : "";
          desc = plugins["Shockwave Flash 2.0"] ? plugins["Shockwave
Flash 2.0"].description : desc;
          if (desc == "") flashVer = -1;
          else{
            var descArr = desc.split(" ");
            var tempArrMajor = descArr[2].split(".");
            var verMajor = tempArrMajor[0];
            var tempArrMinor = (descArr[3] != "") ? descArr[3].split("r") :
descArr[4].split("r");
            var verMinor = (tempArrMinor[1] > 0) ? tempArrMinor[1] : 0;
            flashVer =  parseFloat(verMajor + "." + verMinor);
          }
        }
        // WebTV has Flash Player 4 or lower -- too low for video
        else if (userAgent.toLowerCase().indexOf("webtv") != -1)
flashVer = 4.0;

        var verArr = reqVerStr.split(",");
        var reqVer = parseFloat(verArr[0] + "." + verArr[2]);

        if (flashVer < reqVer){
          if (confirm(msg))
            window.location = "http://www.macromedia.com/shockwave/download/
download.cgi?P1_Prod_Version=ShockwaveFlash";
        }
      }
    }
}
</script>
</head>

<body onload="MM_CheckFlashVersion('8,0,0,0','Content on this page requires a
newer version of Macromedia Flash Player. Do you want to download it now?');">
<table width="700">
  <tr>
    <td width="221"> </td>
    <td width="320"> </td>
    <td width="143"> </td>
  </tr>
```

```
    <tr>
     <td> </td>
     <td><div align="center">
       <object classid="clsid:D27CDB6E-AE6D-11cf-96B8-444553540000"
codebase="http://download.macromedia.com/pub/shockwave/cabs/flash/
swflash.cab#version=8,0,0,0" width="320" height="240" id="FLVPlayer">
         <param name="movie" value="FLVPlayer_Progressive.swf" />
         <param name="salign" value="lt" />
         <param name="quality" value="high" />
         <param name="scale" value="noscale" />
         <param name="FlashVars"
value="&MM_ComponentVersion=1&skinName=Clear_Skin_1&streamName=
mammoth320&autoPlay=true&autoRewind=true" />
         <embed src="FLVPlayer_Progressive.swf"
flashvars="&MM_ComponentVersion=1&skinName=Clear_Skin_1&streamName=
mammoth320&autoPlay=true&autoRewind=true" quality="high" scale="noscale"
width="320" height="240" name="FLVPlayer" salign="LT" type="application/
x-shockwave-flash" pluginspage="http://www.macromedia.com/go/getflashplayer"
/>
</object>
     </div></td>
     <td> </td>
    </tr>
    <tr>
     <td> </td>
     <td> </td>
     <td> </td>
    </tr>
</table>
</body>
</html>
```

# Embed Video from Outside Sources

If you have a blog or just a simple web site, as long as you have access to edit the page, you can embed video from an outside source like YouTube.

When you visit YouTube and play a video, to the right of the video, you see a small box that lists its category, its tags, its URL, and a box that says Embed, as shown in Figure 3-38.

The Embed code is the important stuff for us right now. One of the beautiful things about YouTube is the ability to take any video you see on that site and embed it into your own web page.

The process is easy. Follow these basic steps and you'll have any YouTube-like video on your page:

**1.** In Dreamweaver (or whichever HTML editor you happen to be using), either open a new page or use the page you generated in the "Create a Simple Web Page" section.

**FIGURE 3-38**    This information can be found next to each video on YouTube.

2.  If you're using the same page as earlier, then you should have a table with three rows and three columns. Make sure you have access not only to the Design pane but also to the Code pane of the page (in other words, use Split view).

3.  Open your Internet browser and navigate to YouTube. Find a video that you would like to embed into your own page. When you locate the video you want to embed, note the Embed field to the right of the video itself. Place your cursor in that field, select all the text, right-click, and choose Copy.

4.  Return to Dreamweaver (or whichever HTML editor you happen to be using). Place your cursor in the Design pane area, in the table cell where you want to put the video.

5.  In the upper Code pane, you will now see a corresponding insertion point, as shown in the example in Figure 3-39. Click inside that pane, at that insertion point.

6.  Right-click and choose Paste to embed the code from the YouTube page. Your code should now look something like Figure 3-40. Confirm the edit by clicking the Refresh Code button.

```
45        <td width="221"> </td>
46        <td width="320"> </td>
47        <td width="143"> </td>
48      </tr>
49      <tr>
50        <td> </td>
51        <td><div align="center">X</div></td>
52        <td> </td>
53      </tr>
54      <tr>
55        <td> </td>
56        <td> </td>
57        <td> </td>
58      </tr>
59    </table>
60  </body>
```

**FIGURE 3-39**    Be sure you are working in the Code pane, where your insertion point is blinking.

```
45        <td width="221"> </td>
46        <td width="320"> </td>
47        <td width="143"> </td>
48     </tr>
49     <tr>
50        <td> </td>
51        <td><div align="center"><object width="425" height="350"> <param name="movie" value="http://www.youtube.com/v/58_OE7dVa9c"> </
       param> <embed src="http://www.youtube.com/v/58_OE7dVa9c" type="application/x-shockwave-flash" width="425" height="350"> </embed>
       </object></div></td>
52        <td> </td>
53     </tr>
54     <tr>
55        <td> </td>
56        <td> </td>
57        <td> </td>
58     </tr>
```

**FIGURE 3-40**    The Embed code from YouTube is now part of your page.

**7.** If you look at your Design pane now, you will see the icon for the embedded video, as shown in Figure 3-41. Save your page, and then choose File | Preview in Browser | *Browser*. In the browser, your page will look something like Figure 3-42.

If you have a blog, the process is basically the same. Make sure to put the embed tags specific to your blog interface and paste the code.

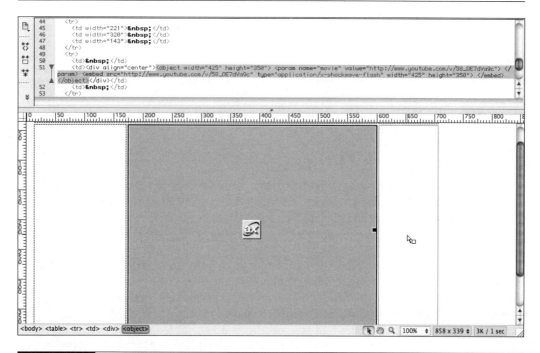

**FIGURE 3-41**    The embed code sets the size for the plug-in for you.

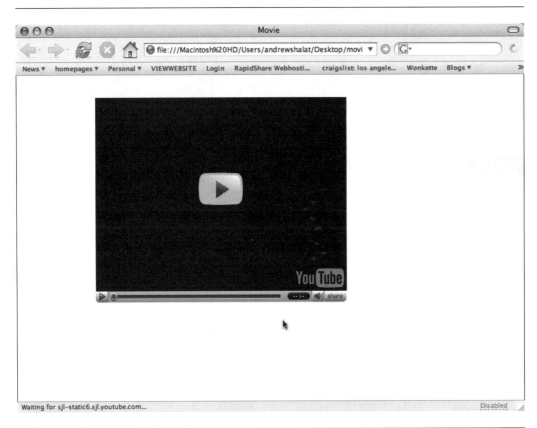

**FIGURE 3-42**    You've embedded an external video on your page.

# Launch a Vodcast with iTunes

If you've read this book from Chapter 1 right up to this point, then you have all the basic tools to create a video podcast (also called a vodcast). A vodcast differs somewhat from a regular video uploaded on YouTube or embedded into your web page. Vodcasts can be listed on the iTunes site, and can be downloaded to a video-enabled iPod. In a sense, it's a combination online/offline video.

The underlying premise of a vodcast is that it is not just a once in a lifetime event, but rather is part of a series, an episode. In a way, it has more in common with a blog than a simple video upload. If you list your vodcast on iTunes, you can choose to have a subscription service notify subscribers when you have uploaded a new episode or show.

Of course, you can call any video that you make a "vodcast," as long as you keep it in a specific output format and size. A vodcast also has a technical side to it, which involves wrapping the file upload in an RSS feed. Now I know that sounds like true geek speak, and it is. But it's one of the necessary evils of the form. It's something you have to learn to deal with if you want to create and publish a video podcast.

*RSS stands for Really Simple Syndication. And that's what it does. Using XML and other tech weenie things, RSS sends out feeds, like headlines, to those browsers and applications open to receiving them.*

Fortunately, there are services online and even on your computer desktop that help you out with RSS. If you're on a Mac, you can use the iWeb software to publish your vodcast. It takes care of the RSS feed information automatically. But many of us aren't using Macs, so we have to figure out other methods of wrapping our vodcasts in RSS. One service in particular works very well. It's called FeedBurner, and is located at www.feedburner.com. We'll get back to FeedBurner a bit later in the chapter.

Right now, let's see what we need to do to make a vodcast. First, we'll want to use QuickTime Pro. If you recall from Chapter 1, it's a $30 purchase, but its versatility and facility makes it worth every penny and then some.

## Create a Vodcast

Of course, the first thing you need to do is create a video. We don't have to go over that procedure here, since you already know how to do that. Later in this book (Chapters 5 through 8), we will go over the finer points of making short movies, with planning, lighting, and sound. But for now we're going to be happy with a basic video that we can make using a webcam, iSight, camcorder, or even cell phone.

*If you've already converted your video to Flash, it won't be importable into QuickTime. Luckily, even if you have converted your video to Flash, you still have the original. For the following steps, use the original.*

The following steps are provided to help you see the how to use QuickTime Pro (remember, the QuickTime Player is the same thing, only in the Pro version it has no grayed out commands) to Compress and Encode your video. QuickTime Pro is a great utility as a conduit to most forms of encoding and compression.

1. Bring your movie into QuickTime Pro.
2. Once opened in QuickTime Pro, you can export it from the File menu. In the Save As dialog box, select Movie to MPEG-4. See Figure 3-43.
3. Click the Options button.
4. In the MPEG-4 Export Settings dialog box, on the Video tab, choose H.264 in the Video Format pop-up menu, as shown in Figure 3-44.

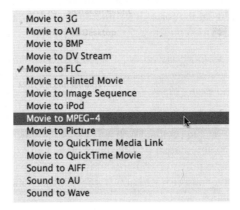

**FIGURE 3-43**   MPEG-4 is the preferred format for a vodcast.

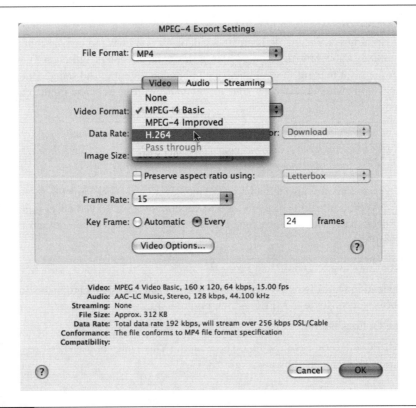

**FIGURE 3-44**   H.264 is a standard for high compression on video files.

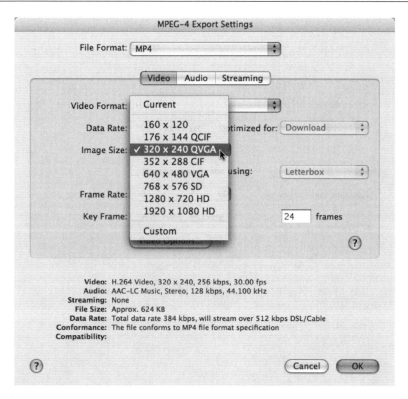

MPEG-4 Export Settings

File Format: MP4

Video  Audio  Streaming

Video Format: Current

Data Rate:
160 x 120
176 x 144 QCIF          timized for: Download
✓ 320 x 240 QVGA
Image Size:
352 x 288 CIF
640 x 480 VGA           using:      Letterbox
768 x 576 SD
Frame Rate:
1280 x 720 HD
1920 x 1080 HD
Key Frame:                          24    frames

Custom

?

Video: H.264 Video, 320 x 240, 256 kbps, 30.00 fps
Audio: AAC-LC Music, Stereo, 128 kbps, 44.100 kHz
Streaming: None
File Size: Approx. 624 KB
Data Rate: Total data rate 384 kbps, will stream over 512 kbps DSL/Cable
Conformance: The file conforms to MP4 file format specification
Compatibility:

?                                          Cancel    OK

**FIGURE 3-45**    Size matters. Keep in mind that the larger the size of your video, the more
space it takes up on your server.

5.  Still in the Video tab, select the size of the video. You can always opt for larger or
    smaller, but since you're going to want to send it to iTunes eventually, 320 × 240 is a
    good size. See Figure 3-45.

6.  To ensure that the file size of the vodcast isn't too bloated, we can trim away unnecessary
    information from the Audio portion. Click the Audio tab in the MPEG-4 Export Settings
    dialog box, shown in Figure 3-46. On this tab, you may want to keep the Data Rate
    at something like 48 kbps (which isn't too much bloating, but it won't lose too much
    either). For the Channels option, you may want to opt for Mono rather than Stereo, and
    then set the Output Sample Rate at a moderate 32.000 kHz. Of course, if you want a
    faster Data Rate, you can keep audio as Stereo and 48.000 kHz.

7.  Click the Streaming tab, shown in Figure 3-47. Check the Enable Streaming check box,
    and click OK.

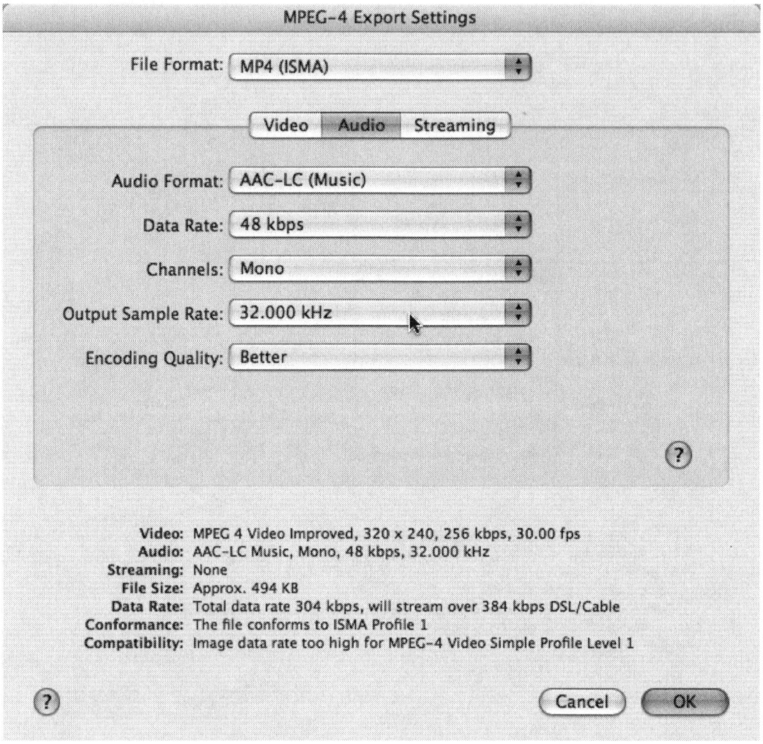

FIGURE 3-46    The settings shown here are moderate. They help to keep your vodcast from becoming bloated.

That should take care of your compression settings. Now, depending on your video, the compression itself might take a little time. In the meantime, we can start working on the more geek-enabling aspects of creating the vodcast.

# Upload and List Your Vodcast

Compressing and encoding the video is only half the battle. Now we have to do a little bit of housekeeping. We have to be sure that we have several things in place.

## Upload Your Vodcast

You need to have a web site where your vodcast will live. Make sure you know the exact path for where your vodcast will be. Here is where it can get a little bit confusing. You can have a remote server that services the web site that in turn delivers your podcast. Or you can keep it on your

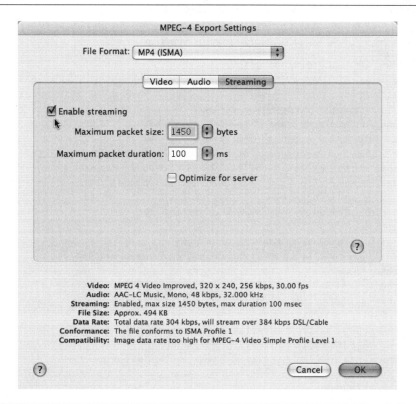

**FIGURE 3-47**   Enable streaming for you vodcast.

own site. The simplest method, of course, would be to keep it on your own site. For instance, the URL for your vodcast might be *yoursite*.com/vodcasts/*yourvodcast*. This path would require that you create a directory called vodcasts on your site.

1. Upload your video file (MP4) to the designated directory. You can use Dreamweaver, or you can use any FTP client that you might normally use to send your files to your site. What matters is that you get the video on your server.

2. Now comes the heavy lifting. Create the corresponding XML file that your vodcast needs in order for iTunes to gain access to your file. Now don't panic. Copy the following XML code in a simple text editor. Microsoft Word may or may not work for this, so if you're on Windows, try using Notepad and saving the file as an XML file (.xml extension). If you're on a Mac, use TextEdit, and save in XML format as well. If possible, use UTF-8 for encoding your feed.

TIP  *The following XML document can also be downloaded, copied, and pasted by visiting http://playlistmag.com/features/2005/07/howtovodcast/index.php (the article is by Christopher Breen, editor in chief of* Playlist Magazine*).*

```xml
<?xml version="1.0" encoding="UTF-8"?>
<rss xmlns:itunes="http://www.itunes.com/DTDs/Podcast-1.0.dtd" version="2.0">
    <channel>
        <title>Vodcast's Title Here</title>
        <itunes:author>Your Name Here</itunes:author>
        <link>http://www.sitename.com</link>
        <description>A description of your vodcast's channel</description>
        <itunes:subtitle>A subtitle for your vodcast's channel</itunes:subtitle>
        <itunes:summary>A summary of your vodcast channel</itunes:summary>
        <language>EN</language>
        <copyright>(c) 2007 Your Name</copyright>
        <itunes:owner>
            <itunes:name>Your Name</itunes:name>
            <itunes:email>youremail@example.com</itunes:email>
        </itunes:owner>
        <category>Vodcasts</category>
        <itunes:category text="Vodcasting"></itunes:category>
    <item>
        <title>Your Movie Title</title>
        <itunes:author>Your Name</itunes:author>
        <description>A description of this movie</description>
        <itunes:subtitle>A subtitle about this movie</itunes:subtitle>
        <itunes:summary>A summary of your movie</itunes:summary>
        <enclosure url="http://www.yoursitename.com/moviename.mp4"
length="1024" type="video/mov" />
        <guid>http://www.yoursitename.com/moviename.mp4</guid>
        <pubDate>Thurs, 25 July 2007 10:00:00 GMT</pubDate>
        <itunes:explicit>no</itunes:explicit>
        <itunes:duration>00:01:35</itunes:duration>
        <itunes:keywords>keyword1, keyword2, keyword3</itunes:keywords>
    </item>
    </channel>
</rss>
```

NOTE  *Apple's web site has a section that ought to help round out your understanding of how to create and upload a vodcast. Visit www.apple.com/itunes/store/podcaststechspecs .html and check out all the links, including the following:*
*Submission and Feedback Processes*
*An Example Feed*
*iTunes RSS Tags*
*Common Mistakes*
*Additional Resources*
*iTunes Categories for Podcasting*

**3.** After you save the preceding code as an XML file, replace the pertinent information between the tags (I put it in italics for you) with your own appropriate information. To fill in the total duration of your video, open the video in QuickTime Pro, drag the playhead all the way to the right, and make note of the timecode.

**4.** After resaving the XML document, place it in the same directory on your server as the directory in which your video MP4 file is located.

**5.** Once uploaded, you can test it in your browser. If, for instance, you uploaded the documents to the http://*yourwebsite*.com/vodcast directory, then type this into your browser: **http://*yourwebsite*.com/vodcast/*yourvodcast*.xml**.

Note that the URL in the Address field of your browser changes to begin with *feed* rather than *http*. In other words, instead of http://*yourwebsite*.com/vodcast/*yourvodcast*.xml, it now says feed://*yourwebsite*.com/vodcast/*yourvodcast*. See Figure 3-48.

**FIGURE 3-48**    The XML document will have given you a feed document. This is an important step in listing and accessing your vodcast via iTunes.

Type the URL of your XML document.

## List Your Vodcast on iTunes

Where do you find your new vodcast? Where does it live? How can people find it? How can you find it?

1. Open iTunes (for Windows users, it's a free download from www.apple.com/itunes/download/).

2. In iTunes, choose Advanced | Subscribe to Podcast.

3. In the Subscribe to Podcast dialog box, type the URL for your XML document. For example, http://*yourwebsite*.com/vodcast/*yourvodcast*.xml. Figure 3-49 shows an example.

4. Click OK. You'll now see your vodcast playing in the bottom left of the iTunes window, similar to the example shown in Figure 3-50, and you'll see your vodcast listed in the main pane of the iTunes window, as shown in Figure 3-51.

Your vodcast should play in the bottom left of the iTunes window. To see it at a larger size, click the live thumbnail.

| Podcast | | Time | Release Date ▼ | Description | |
|---|---|---|---|---|---|
| ● ▶ Inside Mac Radio | | 1:19:22 | 2/17/07 | Nationally Syndicated Broadcast Macintosh Radio Programming | ❶ |
| ▶ MyMac.com | SUBSCRIBE | 56:16 | 2/25/07 | | ❶ |
| ❶ ▶ NPR: Satire from The Unger Report | | 3:56 | 1/22/07 | Commentary. More NPR podcasts at NPR.org/podcasts. | ❶ |
| ❶ ▶ NYT: David Pogue | | 10:02 | 12/21/06 | David Pogue's weekly column on technology. | ❶ |
| ● ▶ Sex With Emily | | 0:46 | 2/11/07 | Hosted by Emily Morse, a talk show about sex and relationships | ❶ |
| ▼ Sierra Cement | | | 2/26/07 | Sierra Cement | ❶ |
| ▷ Sierra Cement | 🖵 | 0:13 | 2/26/07 | When the snow is too heavy and the day is too long | ❶ |
| ❶ ▶ The Onion Radio News | | 0:57 | 11/23/06 | The Onion Radio News is a daily podcast featuring a short new... | ❶ |
| ● ▶ Tiki Bar TV (video) | | 6:28 | 11/30/06 | Forbidden cocktails in a swank pad. | ❶ |
| ❶ ▶ Vintage ToonCast | EXPLICIT | 4:15 | 12/7/06 | Playing public domain vintage cartoons and high quality short f... | ❶ |

**FIGURE 3-51**    Your vodcast now has a listing, with all the information you put in the XML document describing it.

You've now successfully created a vodcast, uploaded it, and listed it on iTunes. There are several other ways of putting your vodcast online for everyone to view. One method is to list it with FeedBurner, which will generate a feed URL for you. The steps are pretty straightforward. Upload your video to your web site. Log into www.feedburner.com, submit the vodcast location to FeedBurner, and let it generate an XML feed for you. Once you have a FeedBurner feed URL, you can list that with iTunes.

Now that you have your video files on YouTube, MySpace, or your own web site, and listed in iTunes too, what more is there to do? Well, you have to let everyone know that your filmmaking ventures are available on the Internet. You have to tell the world. You have to market your work. The next chapter will discuss various methods of how to get the word out, how to link to your video, and how to disseminate your message. So don't just sit on your digital laurels. Read on, voyager, read on.

# Chapter 4

## Let the World Know How to Find Your Video

## How to . . .

- Market your video
- Use tags
- Use reverse engineer marketing
- Use online forums to popularize your video

What's another word for marketing? Advertising. Promotion. Selling. Exposure. Depending on how you made your video, what you intend your video to act as, and what you want your video to do, you could define marketing as any of those words, or all of them. Unfortunately, there is no better way to market something than to do it yourself, on a *degree of separation* basis—you know someone who knows someone who knows three other people who tell their friends, and so on. This is the idea behind the networking sites we're already using. Nowadays, however, "knowing" someone may just mean you have a link to their web site or have their e-mail address.

How do we get our video before the eyes of as many people as possible? Or how do we get our video in front of the specific eyes we want to see our video? These are two related questions that have different answers. Each path we take refers back to the original question of this chapter: what's another word for marketing?

When you uploaded your video to YouTube and MySpace in Chapter 3, you saw the Share options. You can send e-mails directly to people whose e-mail addresses you know or have on hand. You can put your video on a categorized list. You can add tags, or keywords. All those things are essentially marketing tools. In this chapter we're going to look at various tools, methods, and strategies for letting the world know where to find your video.

I like to break down the marketing and exposure process into two basic types of methods:

- **Internal Methods**   The technical methods of wrapping keywords, finder items, and hooks into or pointing to your video file itself. Further, internal markers work within the technical site you upload to, and also to the search engines on the Internet that people use to find items, or surf the Web.

- **External Methods**   The traditional, physical-world processes of marketing, such as snail mail, e-mail, and advertising. Some of these external methods can cost a lot of money, and this isn't a guide to tell you how to spend your money. You can figure that out for yourself. To keep spending to a minimum, we'll look at what we have available for free right in front of us, which means using internal methods of exposure and marketing and an inexpensive external method: e-mailing through networking sites.

# Use Simple Tags

We'll start at the upload point. Point your browser to www.youtube.com and log in (if you want to use MySpace, the steps are very similar—refer to Chapter 3). Click the Upload Videos button. We went over the two-step Video Upload process in Chapter 3, but here we are going to explore in more detail how to refine the Tags choices to help market your video effectively.

As you should be familiar with from Chapter 3, in the Video Upload window, we have Title, Description, Tags, and Video Category fields and options to complete. Entering information on this page is the first, most rudimentary step in getting your video exposure. The most important part of this step is the Tags input.

**TIP** *It's a good idea to write down these classifications and categories and work on them before you begin uploading your video to YouTube. That way, you can consider them carefully and make sure they're not simply random thoughts that you had about your video that could have been influenced by what you had for dinner last night.*

The trick to tags is to make them *likely*. That is, you should think not only about what the video's subject matter is, but also what keywords people are most likely to use when searching for it, or a video of similar content or subject matter (see the example shown in Figure 4-1).

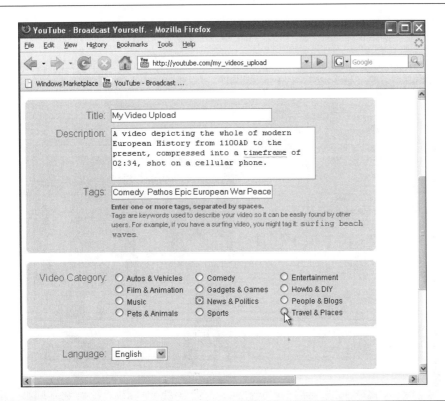

**FIGURE 4-1**   Make sure your tags are appropriate, and that they are *likely*.

## Understand Tags

Let's take a short side trip to the world of the basic HTML web sites. Tags are very closely related to the search engine keywords that we use when building web sites. In web development, we call these keywords *metatags*. They're *meta* because they don't actually *appear* on the web page as you see it in the browser. Rather, they're written in the header of the HTML code. So if you were to look at most web sites—not in the main browser format, but in their *source code*— you could read the various embedded tags that help to make the sites discoverable by search engines. For instance, point your browser to a run-of-the-mill web site. When you have the home page open, select View | Page Source (Mozilla Firefox) from the menu, as shown in Figure 4-2. I liken the source view to having a pair of x-ray glasses—you get to see what's underneath the clothing of the page.

A separate window opens showing you the basic HTML code that makes up the web page and instructs the browser on how to make it appear, as shown in the example in Figure 4-3. All this is actually easy to understand with a little practice. Although you can't change anything in a web page's source code, viewing it helps you to see how the pages were constructed. In particular, note the keywords.

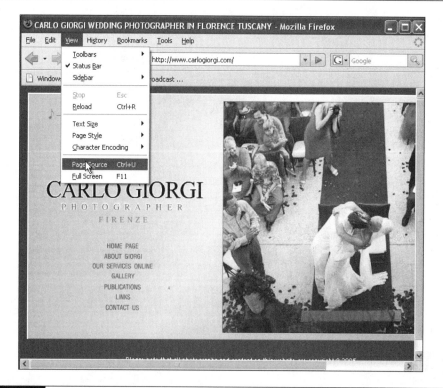

**FIGURE 4-2**    This is an easy way to see how a web page has been constructed.

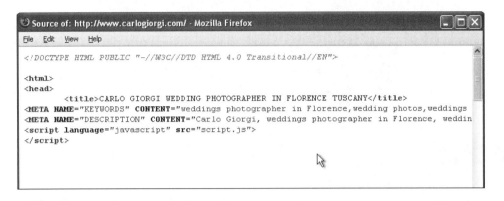

**FIGURE 4-3**   Viewing the source code of a web page

*Including good keywords is the simplest way to help readers locate your web site from a search engine. Tags with which you supplement your video upload act in much the same way.*

## Test Your Tags

Now let's bring that knowledge of keywords and tags back to the video site realm. Dealing with the internal search engine of a video site like You Tube is slightly different from dealing with search engines on the Web. These internal search engines are geared more toward users who are already on YouTube (or whatever site you happen to be using). But they are efficient. Here's a test you can try out to see just how efficient the tags you assign to your video can actually be:

1. Locate the video you uploaded in the previous chapter.

2. Note the tags you used to describe the video.

3. In the internal Search area on the home page of YouTube, enter one of the more unique tags you used for your video upload (see Figure 4-4). It's a good idea to include some unique tag words for your video, along with more common ones. This will help you out in the long run.

**FIGURE 4-4**   Finding unique tag words

**Video results for 'erta canina'**

**Erta Canina 05**
09:42
A celebration of Florence's saint's day: San Giovanni.
Tags: San  Giovanni  Firenze  erta  canina  tuscany
Added: 2 weeks ago  in Category: Travel & Places
From: amadeopuzzo
Views: 0

**FIGURE 4-5**    Note the tags listed in the search results.

**4.** When the search results come up (see Figure 4-5), hopefully your unique tag brought your video to the top of the list. If it didn't, you may want to edit your tags from within your YouTube account, and update them for that particular video.

When your video comes up in the search results, the tag words are listed right there in front. Simple stuff.

Using tags is like using a wide net with lots of large holes in it. We want a wide net with small holes, one that catches minnows as well as whales (it's very impolitic to speak of catching whales, but you get the idea).

To carry the metaphor further, it's not enough to have a big net; we have to know where to throw it. Starting at YouTube and MySpace is a good idea. Within the network of either of those sites, you'll be sure to get some viewers just by selecting the right, and most likely (there's that word again), tags.

## Google Your Tags to Discover Markets

Chapter 3 showed you how to make your video into a vodcast. If this is the route you took, then you've already positioned your video so that it can be accessed by any number of viewers on Apple's iTunes site. But once you have your vodcast listed on iTunes, you still have to notify others about how to find it. Hence, I'll introduce you to my own method of reverse-engineered marketing, which you can use to market your vodcasts and any other videos.

Reverse engineering is a scientific method of taking apart something that works, piece by piece or process by process, to figure out the steps that were used to create it originally. If you do it right, you'll be able to put those pieces back together in the reverse order that you took them apart, and the thing that once worked will work again.

We're going to employ this methodology with a twist. We'll take the tags that we've assigned to our video and use them as *search agents* to root out and discover our niche markets online. So let's go back to our YouTube video and look at our tags.

Let's say we made a video that shows people skiing. Our tags might be *skiing*, *snow sports*, *extreme*, and *Mammoth*. Let's take those tags, as a group now, and put them into a Google search, as shown in Figure 4-6.

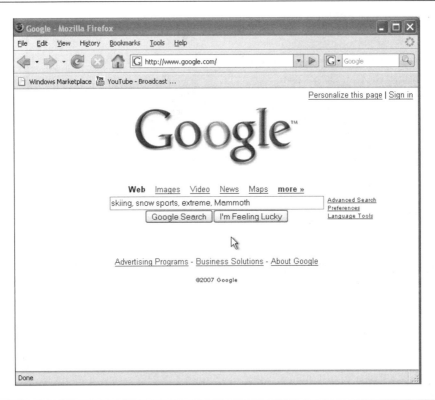

**FIGURE 4-6**   Conducting a reverse search

Of course, the first set of results will give you a listing of related web sites (see Figure 4-7). You can choose to inspect these, but these are mainly for viewing, not interacting. We want to *interact* with the Web, not *react* to it. So in the links above the Search field, choose More to find the other result categories, as shown in Figure 4-8.

If you choose Groups, your results will list any number of interested forums. Here's your field of topsoil waiting to be seeded. Since these groups are in some way or another tied to your subject matter, you have a receptive audience waiting to view your video. You'll find the discussion group link to the right of the main link, as shown in the example in Figure 4-9.

Following the group links will take you to the discussion groups. You may have to subscribe to be allowed to post comments, but that's a simple process, as shown in Figure 4-10. For Google Groups, if you have a Google Account, you simply enter your e-mail address and password, as shown in Figure 4-11.

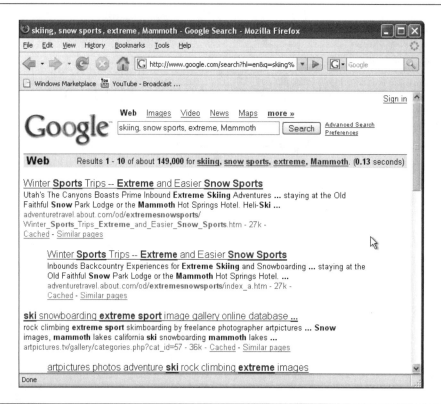

**FIGURE 4-7**   The initial results are web site listings. This is a good starting point, but you'll
want to go a little further.

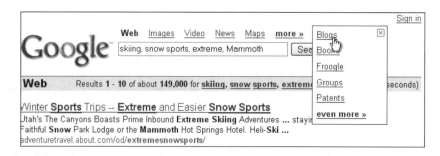

**FIGURE 4-8**   Blogs and Groups lead to online forums and contact points for others in our
niche market.

Inline speed record?     Group: rec.sport.skating.inline
... however, **snow** skis also do this at higher speed, so i'm somewhat used to it. ... 40 mph
or so, motorcycle leathers or kevlars) this is a wonderful **sport** for those ... it seems
to attract people who are also aficionados of steep and/or fast **skiing**. ...
Jun 10 1998 by George Merkert - 19 messages - 11 authors

***The Colorado Skier-"Lost" **Ski** Areas #15, 25 May***     Group: rec.skiing.alpine
... The ghost town of Bodie received 18 inches of **snow** on 17 May. ... Jeff wants to use it
in his **ski** shop: "Summit **Ski** & **Sports** Wear" - Pagosa Springs, CO ... b. Besides our normal
post to rec.**skiing**.alpine/announce, we are also sending direct E-Mails ...
May 29 1994 by Mark Wallace - 1 message - 1 author

**FIGURE 4-9**    Discussion groups are very topic-focused forums.

**Discussions**
+ new post

About this group
Subscribe to this group

This is a Usenet group - learn more
Find or start a Google Group about
**alpine**.

**FIGURE 4-10**    Subscribe to a group so that you can post comments.

Sign in to Google Groups with your
Google **Account**

Email:
Password:
☑ Remember me on this computer.
Sign in

**FIGURE 4-11**    In the case of Google Groups, you only have to enter a login name and
password.

The point of this exercise it to use the tags you added to your own video as leads to find interested audiences who will in turn link back to your video, and hopefully spread the word on their own as well. One of the purposes of posting messages to the newsgroups is also to drum up interest for your video. As you become a regular on these forums and newsgroup sites, your credibility increases with other users as well. Humans are funny that way. We get to know each other through habit and habitat, and as colleagues of both, we start to help each other out. We invest some of our credibility for a little credibility in return.

You can take any results you get from your own tags and drill through their links, amassing a niche market, if you will, always pointing them back to your video.

# E-mail Your Video Through Networking Sites

On the Web, we're best served using the web tools available right at our fingertips. We've talked about keywords and tags. But just attaching unique and likely tags isn't enough. If you recall from the last chapter, you can also point this information directly at a list of e-mail recipients you may have on hand. This isn't something to be pooh-poohed. Word of mouth is one of the best ways to get the message out. Then you're relying on the quality of your content to push your video around the Web. Once your videos are in the works on the networking sites, it's pretty much your job to reach out to as many friends, colleagues, and acquaintances as you can. With every contact, you should include a link to your video. But make sure that the links you use are truly connected to you in some way. We don't want to add to or become spammers.

TIP     *Getting exposure via e-mail doesn't have to be a hard-sell, "spammish" method. You can be more passive-aggressive in your method of getting your video exposure. That is, why not put a live link to your video at the bottom of every e-mail you send? You don't have to make an aggressive marketing effort in each e-mail, but rather have the link in your e-mail signature. Every e-mail you send will passively give your video more exposure.*

Well, you've already taken the first step in marketing your video. You've uploaded it onto the Web. The next step is up to you. Of course, it's not a linear process. Marketing your video online is as nonlinear a process as the Web itself. It's not just what you know, it's who you know. It's who they know. It's where you put it. It's who you tell. And in some ways how you tell it. The most important thing to remember is to equip your video with all the best advantages you can before you send out signals. Like a sailor about to go to sea, make sure it has both its heavy weather gear and its fair weather gear. Make the tags as *likely* as you can, and reverse market them to search out and identify your market. The rest should be smooth sailing.

# Chapter 5

# Film School in a Book

## How to...

- Understand basic filmmaking terminology
- Use different types of shots
- Maintain continuity between shots
- Choose the best audio options
- Get the best lighting with your equipment

Digital filmmaking is actually very simple. You point a camera at the action, record or register on digital tape, or some other memory medium such as a DVD or flash drive, and then transfer the video to your computer. Big deal, right? You already know how to do that from previous chapters. Of course, sometimes your videos aren't the easiest things to watch. Maybe the camera was shaking, or you missed some action, or you can't hear what the people are saying because you didn't use a *boom*, or even a *lavalier*. Maybe the light is too bright and you *backlit* your subjects, or your *key light* was not bright enough, or even too bright. Perhaps your audience has trouble following the action because there's no *continuity* to a shot, or you didn't follow the *180 degree rule*, your camera angle is wrong, your *bookends* don't box in the video *sequence*, and your *coverage* is incomplete. Perhaps your *decoupage* is not ordered, and your *eyeline* doesn't match because you started with a *POV dolly shot* and cross-faded to a *Dutch tilt* instead of using a *head-on shot*. And all of this could have been avoided if you had made a more complete *storyboard*, reviewed your *mise en scène*, used a *static shot* to start, *blocked out* some shots, and, before you called a *wrap*, made sure you checked the *gates*. Simple stuff. Point, shoot, and upload, right?

Okay, don't panic. If you had trouble understanding some of the terminology I used in the previous paragraph, don't worry. I used that terminology (all of which makes sense, by the way) to make a point: When filming, sometimes you *do* need to know some technical aspects of what you're doing. It's not that difficult to translate. Sure, it's easy to just point, click, and record, and for most purposes you'll probably do just fine. But there are times when you'll want to make something more of your video than just a home movie. And when you do, it's not a bad idea to have some understanding of basic filmmaking techniques and terms. This chapter gives you enough knowledge to be dangerous. If you practice, you may even be able hold up your end of a Hollywood cocktail party conversation enough to drop a "log line" of a film idea you have, have the other guy ask you for a "treatment" of the project, turn the project into a "property," and get the ball rolling toward having some meetings. In Hollywood, you can't get anywhere without meetings.

By the end of this chapter, you'll understand all the terminology used in the opening paragraph. The core of the chapter explains the terminology that you probably need to know to actually make your video. First, I'll discuss moving shots, in which the camera is in some sort of motion, and then I'll discuss framing shots, which describe the composition of the shot but not necessarily the action of the camera. I'll then cover audio and lighting options. To wrap up the chapter, I'll define some other terms that probably aren't essential to know but might be useful to you if get more involved in filmmaking.

# Start with Basic Moving Shots

When you're making your video, you are employing a variety of shots. You may not even be aware of it at the time, which is a shame, because the more you know about what you're doing, the more choices you will have to adapt, adjust, and improve.

Camera movement is a big part of making your video. Many times, home movies are almost unwatchable because of the camera movement. The proud father zooms in too close to the subject, follows their every movement the way our eyes do, up and down and across at a speed that makes the viewer feel queasy, and then pulls back and the subject is lost in a jumbled composition of trees, people, and whatnot. To help you avoid such mistakes, this section describes the following basic camera shots that you should use and explains when you should use them.

Becoming familiar with these tried and true camera shots will help you make decisions about your videos before you even take off your lens cap or switch to video mode on your cell phone. These shots are building blocks, and even though we're only trying to make online videos, the same basic rules apply. We want to use all the techniques and fundamentals to get our movies to look as good as they can, with as little hassle as possible.

Beyond that, understanding these basic shots will also inform your own video and film watching. The next time you're watching a movie, note how many times the filmmakers use just these basic shots, and how effective they are. What you may find is that you only notice the type of shot used if you concentrate on it, and that if it becomes apparent at any other time, it works against the film itself. Your techniques generally shouldn't draw attention to themselves. Like the best design, they should be invisible, and, unless intrinsically part of the story being told, shouldn't be noticed.

## The Static Shot

If in doubt, keep the camera still. Let the action take place outside the camera, not in it. This is called a *static* shot (see Figure 5-1). In a static shot, the camera does not move. Usually a good static shot is achieved with the use of a tripod. A tripod is not necessary, but it helps.

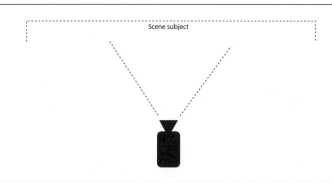

Scene subject

**FIGURE 5-1**   The static shot

If you've ever seen a Woody Allen film, then you've seen a static shot. With the camera in one position, the action takes place either right in front of it or in and out of the frame. This kind of shot can be used for several effects. For instance, comedy often takes place in the mind of the viewer, and not so much right in front of him. So combining a static shot with a sound effect, and have the action, say, a crash, or a person slipping on a banana peel off camera, in conjunction with a sound effect and a static shot works as *funny*. This is a good idea if you don't have a large budget, and don't want to spend too much on scenery and props.

In a drama, you can use the static shot for a simple monologue or a dramatic close-up.

## The Pan Shot

When the subject of a scene moves from right to left, you can do several things, but not all at once. If you want to keep the camera in the same spot, but follow the movement from one side to the other, you do a *pan* shot (see Figure 5-2). Pan is short for panorama. Swivel the camera from left to right, or right to left, keeping it at relatively the same height throughout the movement.

You can also pan up and pan down, but these shots often involve a crane or a very strong *grip* (the crewperson responsible for pushing the dolly, holding the cranes, or wheeling the chair).

Because panning moves the camera along a horizontal axis, it is often used as an establishing shot, when you want to show the landscape or environment where the film action will take place. When your landscape doesn't fit within the frame of your camera, or you want to give a shot some context, you can pan to the left or right. For instance, if your subject is standing alone on a rock, but that rock is on the edge of a cliff overlooking the Grand Canyon, you can either start from the subject and pan across to show the context of their precarious position or, to get a totally different message across, start your shot at the left or right extreme, taking in all the scenery, and slowly pan across until you come upon your subject on the rock at the edge of the cliff.

The two shots have very different effects. The pan from your subject to the vastness of the Grand Canyon reveals the context as dangerous, perhaps, or precarious. If that's what you want to say about your subject's situation, then this is a good shot to set up. The second example,

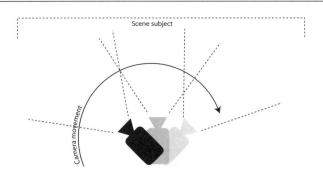

**FIGURE 5-2**    The pan shot

panning from the vast landscape and coming to rest on the subject, speaks not so much to the precarious position of the subject as to his position in the scheme of things. Is he just a small piece of something grand? Is he just a piece in a larger puzzle?

These are the kinds of considerations that just the starting and ending points of a simple pan shot can bring up. And all you did was set up a panning shot.

## The Tracking Shot

Sometimes you will want to follow a subject as they cross the frame from left to right or right to left. If you decide to do this, keeping your shot running parallel with your subject, it's called a *tracking* shot, or sometimes a *dolly* shot or *trucking* shot (see Figure 5-3). You *track* the subject from left to right or vice versa.

The tracking shot is related to the pan shot, only it moves along with the subject. In essence, you can pan with the subject always in view. This kind of shot can achieve many things for a video. You can use it as a discovery device. As you follow the subject, say a car driving across the screen, you're also putting the scene in context through the surroundings. The same goes for a person walking.

As you might expect, a dolly shot involves wheels of some sort. The idea behind the shot is a steady, smooth follow-along with the subject in frame. In the same vein, the dolly shot doesn't have to follow a subject at all. Instead, it can point and direct the viewer's eye, or act as a point of view (POV) shot. Try this: Stand in one corner of your living room. Close one eye and encircle the other with your index finger and thumb, as though you're looking through a telescope (like I'm doing in Figure 5-4). Now look to one side, either right or left depending on your room, and while keeping your head in that position, walk the length of the room. Make sure to keep your head at the same level as you walk. What you're seeing through your pretend telescope lens is what the dolly shot movement tries to effect.

You've seen this done in movies whenever there's a director looking for a shot. He'd put his two hands up, making a square in front of his eyes, framing someone, looking ridiculous. But there's actually a good reason why directors do this.

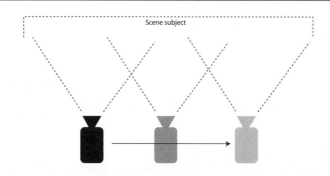

**FIGURE 5-3**    The tracking shot

**FIGURE 5-4**    You've seen guys do this in the movies, and you thought they looked silly then. Now you see why they did it. They still look silly, though.

Now do the same thing with your hand, but instead of walking across the room, focus on one object in the room, and walk toward it, slowly. You're now effecting a dolly zoom. Pull away, walking backward, keeping your focus on the object, and you're effecting a pull-away. We'll talk about that a little further on, when we discuss the ins and outs of the zoom.

You've seen the dolly shot in more movies than you can remember. But you probably didn't think about them because the shots made sense for the scenes they were depicting. A slow dolly shot from one character to another can intensify the sense of drama, or anticipation. Think of one of those spaghetti westerns you saw when you were a kid with the two antagonists facing off in a showdown. The slow dolly shot has been used more than once in scenes like these, starting at one character and moving over the ground to end at the other. Then a quick cut to a close up (static shot) of one of the character's eyes, and a quick cut to the other's face in a static shot. See how this all fits together?

**TIP**    *Here's an easy home-made way to make a dolly shot. Find either a chair that has good wheels on it, and place your camera, and probably your cameraman too, on the chair. Have a grip push them. Or borrow a shopping cart from your local supermarket, and use that as your dolly. Be sure to bring it back when you pick up the beers for the crew.*

## The Follow Shot

A variation on the tracking shot is the follow shot, or following shot (see Figure 5-5). This is similar to a tracking shot, but the subject's movement may vary back and forth, as well as side to side. The main idea behind the follow shot is to keep the moving figure onscreen at all times.

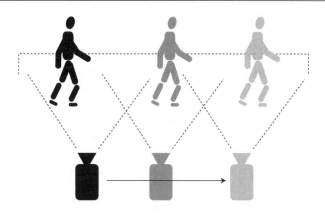

**FIGURE 5-5**    The follow shot

Although it may be tempting, try not to zoom when you're creating a follow shot. Keep the focal length consistent through the whole shot.

## The Zoom Shot

The zoom (see Figure 5-6), and its constituent zoom in and zoom out, is probably the most misused and overused shot of all when you put the camcorder in Mom's or Dad's hands. There

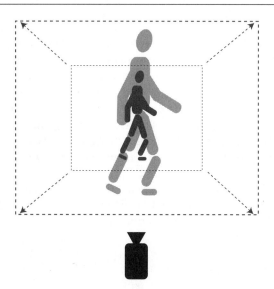

**FIGURE 5-6**    The often overused zoom shot

are few shots that can provoke land-based seasickness as easily as the misused zoom. When used correctly, a zoom can intensify emotion and drama. But when I say *correctly*, I mean to say *slowly*.

The misuse and overuse of the zoom is partly thanks to the fact that digital camcorder manufacturers and retailers all tout the zoom as one of their major selling points. And the reason they tout the zoom so much has a lot to do with the size of the lens on the camcorder and the fact that the lens can't be switched for another. To compensate for a single lens, that can't be removed, the manufacturers enhance the camera with a zoom function. And it's easy to use, too. Just flick your finger one way or the other on the wide/telephoto switch and wham! You're zooming.

But there is a problem with that. And that problem usually becomes apparent after you've done your video shooting, and you've sat down to watch it on your big flat-screen television set with surround sound. It's unwatchable. At least it's unwatchable unless you have taken some Dramamine. There are few things more difficult to watch than a quick zoom in an unsteady hand. And, coincidentally, that is what you find most parents and grandparents are most expert at doing.

There are appropriate uses for the zoom. The zoom is a great effect when used slowly. As an example, consider a scenario in which a character is giving a monologue and is speaking directly into the camera. This is sometimes referred to as the *fourth wall*, since we can see the two sides and the back (left wall, right wall, back wall) of the scene. The lens is the fourth wall. It's a dramatic convention that is very particular, and about as old as drama itself. The Greeks used it, Shakespeare used it, and you'll find it used in many contemporary films and stage plays.

Our scene starts with a long shot, meaning the subject of the shot is at a distance from the camera and thus appears to be small in the frame. As we begin the shot, our character is seated across the room, speaking. He looks directly at the camera. As he begins to speak, we slowly (very, very slowly) decrease the distance between the camera and the character. Let's say the distance we begin at is 20 feet away. The monologue is a two-minute piece. So we have to cover 20 feet in two minutes. That's slow. We end the scene with a close-up, just showing the character's face from his eyebrows to just above his chin. Dramatic, huh?

That's one way to use a zoom. It's almost imperceptible. Let's reverse that scene and see what kind of effect it has. So, we'll start with an extreme close-up and back away 20 feet over two minutes. It's interesting how, rather than increasing the drama and weight of what the character has to say, this zoom out seems to comment on the character. It diminishes his importance. It almost makes fun of him.

These basic shots are fundamental. You should not feel limited to only these shots. But in the next few chapters, you'll be drafting a story and creating a storyboard, and being able to define your shots, even at this basic level, will save you time and free you to make other decisions, and other camera angle choices.

## How to ...    Take Other Moving Shots

The following are a few other types of moving shots, beyond the basics, that you might consider using as well:

- ◼ **Tilt shot**   Tilt the camera up or down on a vertical axis, rather than on the horizontal axis used for a standard pan shot. There are many variations to the tilt shot. You can tilt pan, tilt up, tilt down, or use a so-called Dutch tilt, which is filming at an extreme diagonal, for a truly disorienting effect.

- ◼ **Head-on shot**   The action comes at the camera. It's a variation of a static shot, but the camera view acts as an active participant in the scene.

# Move on to Framing Shots

Framing shots describe the way you compose the shot, rather than the movement the camera makes while shooting. The terms defined in this section will help you to communicate and sort your shots both before and during your actual on-set shooting. If you are not working alone but actually have help, perhaps some unfortunate volunteer you roped into holding a microphone, light, or light reflector, then you'll need to communicate the premise of each shot to them so that they can better do your bidding. Sounds sort of megalomaniacal, doesn't it? That's what they call *directing*. And the person you convince to do that help is called your *grip*. At least, you can call them that, but not necessarily to their face. You might want to refer to them as your "Assistant Director." Why not? You're not paying them. It won't cost you anything to be nice.

## The Establishing Shot

The establishing shot is where you set the scene. It's a general term for the shot that visually gives us the context for the ensuing action of the scene. The establishing shot can be different from the master shot. The master shot contains your actors in the scene. The establishing shot can be a simple still, actually establishing the place for the scene, be it interior, exterior, in a restaurant, etc. Think of an establishing shot as a stage as the curtain rises, before the actors enter.

How we frame the establishing shot is important. Here are some choices:

- ◼ **High-angle shot**   Your subject is seen from above. The camera looks down on the action.

- ◼ **Low-angle shot**   A worm's-eye view, ground-up perspective.

- **Long shot**    The subject is filmed from a distance. There are relative variations on the long shot. You can take an extreme long shot, from a great distance, a medium long shot (also known as a mid-shot), or a wide shot, which is sometimes taken with a slightly distorted lens, bringing in more of the peripheral and background scenery than a flat, normal mid-shot.

- **Close shot**    Also called a close-up, your subject is shot from a short distance, filling the entire frame, without much if any background showing at all. Be sure that if you're shooting a close-up, the actor or subject doesn't have to make much if any movement. Every nuance is exaggerated because of the scale of the shot. As such, the close shot is often a static shot as well (described earlier in this chapter).

**TIP** *The close shot is a good place to start, but you'll want to either pull away using a dolly shot or reverse zoom, ending in a mid-shot, or even a long shot, depending on your intention for the scene.*

Once you have your establishing shot, you're ready to tell your story. This involves more shots…often taking the same scene with different types of shots. You would do this to give yourself more choices later on while editing.

## The Master Shot

If you are going to take multiple shots of the same scene, you start with what's known as a master shot. The master shot is a long, continuous take of the complete scene, usually starting with a mid-shot or long shot. Then you can go back and take various close and angled shots of different portions of the scene.

Let's say you have two people speaking in the scene. The mid-shot that takes both people in the frame is called a two-shot. (If there were three people in the frame, then it would be called a three-shot. This isn't exactly rocket science, or HTML, now is it?) So you can make your master shot a two-shot. Then your next shot would be an over-the-shoulder shot. This would be taken from behind one of your actors, showing part of the back of the actor's head, and the face of the other actor, as shown in Figure 5-7.

**NOTE** *This is that one point in production where you might want to bribe one of your friends to actually do a little more work than just hold up a reflector. Have someone take notes on positions and wardrobe. Use a digital still camera to make reference shots for continuity. Prop positions, cameras, and other things that you won't notice until you're in post-production can make a big difference in the believability of a shot—and a video as a whole.*

After taking an over-the-shoulder shot, you'd then take a reverse-angle shot of the other person. This shows their reactions to each other. So you take the whole conversation from one over-the-shoulder angle, and then take the conversation once again from the reverse. In editing, later, you can cut and mix and match.

**FIGURE 5-7**    The classic over-the-shoulder shot

TIP

*You may want to mix in a head-on shot of either or both of the actors, to further emphasize reactions and force.*

## Rules for Framing Shots

When framing shots, there are general rules one should follow.

### The 180 Degree Rule

The 180 degree rule states that when shooting a scene with two characters, or two objects, for that matter, these elements should always have the same left/right relationship to each other. So in your two-shot, when one character is on the right, the other character should be on the left. When you reverse shots, or do a close-up of each character, they should stay on their respective side of the frame and face the same way consistently.

### Eyeline Match

One very important aspect that I haven't discussed yet that concerns framing shots is known as eyeline match. If you find yourself cutting from one person to another, or from an actor to an object, you want to create the illusion that the actor in the original shot is actually looking at the actor or object in the subsequent shot. This is especially important with a head-on shot, where you are aware of the direction of the actor's eyes.

### Continuity

Most of the time, shooting isn't necessarily done in a normal timeline, but rather out of order, and with multiple takes, so it's important that you maintain consistency from one shot to the next.

If someone is wearing a hat in a two-shot, then make sure they keep that hat on in the over-the-shoulder cutaway. This is known as continuity. Continuity errors can cause a viewer to loose interest in a video or film.

To ensure that you have continuity from shot to shot, you can do either of two things (or both): have an assistant keep track of things, or check your shots between shots. If you do the latter, review your shots twice. First, review and keep an eye on details. Second, review for content and flow and the more artistic aspects of the shot.

### The Gate

When you finish shooting your scene, and you're ready to move on to the next scene, you'll want to check your lens to make sure there are no dirt particles or obstructions on it. You want to make sure your camera is working, and the aperture opens and functions. On a professional set, you'll hear someone yell, "check the gate." The *gate* is the aperture on the camera, and *checking the gate* is just making sure that everything is free of dust, clean, and functional. It generally refers to film cameras, not digital. On video shoots, you won't actually have to check the gate, if you can instantly see how clean the image is. But you may hear someone say it all the same, to signify that the scene is done.

# Know Your Audio and Lighting Options

Now that you understand the basic camera shots, you need to consider the mechanical and technical concerns that will affect your video in as intrinsic a way as whether you go for a three-shot establishing shot or use a dolly long shot. What about audio? How do you capture sound that is clear, crisp, and synchronized with your video? And what about lighting? You can have all your shots set up, ready to go, but without good, designed lighting, you won't get good results. So we'll cover how to set up your lighting in a basic way, to make sure that your video looks as good in the final result as it does in your head.

## Audio

In the context of a small video shoot, you have some fundamental choices to make about how you want to capture audio. You can use a boom microphone to an audio deck, a lavalier connected to either your camcorder or audio deck, the built-in microphone on your camera, an all-in-one digital recorder, a handheld wireless microphone, and finally a flash-drive based microphone. The following describes those choices:

■ **Boom microphone**    A boom microphone, one of those big microphones that look sort of like the hat worn by a guard at Buckingham Palace, on the end of a long pole, is one of the best ways to get good sound on your production. It's also the most expensive, and probably the most labor intensive. You need two people, at least, to operate the system. You will also want a synchronized audio deck, although you could plug it directly into your pro-level DV camera. The boom operator should have strong arms and good shoes, because they will be holding the boom and standing on their feet for a long time as you work.

- **Lavalier**   The alternative to the boom is the lavalier. A lavalier is a small clip-on microphone that can be hidden on an actor so that it can't be seen on camera. It is usually wireless, and sends the audio directly to the DV cam or audio deck. The beauty of a lavalier, other than its size, is its directional capabilities. When placed on a collar of a shirt, it picks up the actor's voice with clarity and isolation. It's also much less expensive than a boom microphone. Sometimes, you'll hear it referred to as a lav, or a lapel mike. Along with the lavalier microphone, you'll have a transmitter and a receiver to deal with. The transmitter usually looks like a pager (although it's larger) and clips on to a belt or a piece of clothing. Lavalier microphone systems can cost anywhere from $50 to $750 to buy, but you can always rent them for much less. For their versatility, they're among the best solutions you'll run across.

**NOTE**   *Lavaliers can also be used for great effect to pick up ambient sound. You can keep one lav for localized audio on vocals, and another simultaneously to record sounds of shoes walking, or crowds harrumphing.*

- **Built-in microphone**   The built-in microphone on your DV camera or camcorder is a cheap, easy way of getting muddy, wind-distorted audio packed with a lot of background noise. If you can't find a lavalier for rent or on sale, then you always have the plastic condenser microphone built into your recording device—this is not recommended, but when you have no alternative, you use what you've got.

- **All-in-one digital recorder**   A relatively cheap alternative to the built-in microphone is the all-in-one digital recorder. Some of these are about as big as a chewing gum package, and can act as cheap versions of a lavalier. You may have trouble converting the audio to your computer later, however, and find yourself outputting your audio via the earphone jack into the input plug on your PC.

- **Handheld wireless microphone**   These solid, hefty microphones are good for interview situations where you have a host or reporter controlling the audio input by directing the microphone to the speaker. A good-quality handheld wireless system will cost from $450 to $1500.

- **Flash-drive Microphone**   Finally, there is a new, although obvious, solution to the handheld audio input. The flash-drive Microphone looks like a traditional wireless handheld, but it's actually a lot more. Inside the shaft is a flash drive, similar to those keychain drives you carry with you all the time (you do carry one, don't you?). You turn the microphone on and record your audio into the mic, where it is stored on a memory chip. At the base of the microphone is a USB connector, so you can download your audio directly to the PC or Mac without any loss of quality. Unfortunately, at this writing, these new-ish microphones are on the expensive side, running from $1200 to $1500.

As you can see, when you're making a video, you're really making a video/audio. Even silent films have soundtracks. So it behooves you to make yourself aware of the basics involved with audio input. You needn't become an expert. As long as your audio is clear and understandable, you can use the video editing software tools discussed in Chapter 2, and later in this book, to help you put the whole package together, to make your video a complete and finished piece.

NOTE    *You can and probably will add the audio track during the editing process. So you could, in theory, film your video without sound, and then add the soundtrack later. Of course, it's a good idea to have both in place and then replace what you need to replace later. Chapters 9 and 10 discuss this further.*

## Lighting

Lighting is a touchy subject. Depending on the camera, the setting, the intention, and sometimes just the budget of your video, you can go all out and set up lights and strobes, diffusers, gels, and reflectors, or you can use natural light. If you're doing something more than amateur but less than feature film, the solution lies somewhere in the middle range. As a rule of thumb, it's best to keep it simple.

We'll discuss three types of lighting elements:

- **Key light**   The main light, the strong light. If you were to use just a key light, you'd create bright light on one half and a dark and stark shadow on the other half. Think of the key light as the sun on a bright day in spring. It's directional, and it's bright.

- **Fill light**   The light used to tone down, or balance, the key light. Not as bright as the key light, the fill light softens the shadows and reduces the contrast on your video elements or actors.

- **Back light**   A subtle way of balancing the balancing act in the foreground created by the key and fill lights. The back lighting is a very tricky thing to get right. If it's too bright, your actor will have a halo around her. If it's too low, you won't be able to see any of the details of the set behind.

Positioning the lights is about 70 percent of the problem. We'll use a very simple triangular diagram to set up our basic starting point, shown in Figure 5-8. Once you have your basic lights in place, you can fiddle with them while placing your actors on marks (or if you have a budget, your stand-ins) and adjust the lighting to work for your production intentions.

Lighting can take up more of your time than any other aspect of a shoot. If you've ever been on a professional movie set, you no doubt noticed that much of the time is spent in setup. That's why the actors have trailers. The trailers are convenient places to keep the actors out of everyone's way. You've heard the cliché command "lights, camera, action." It's more than just something to say when you're directing. Think of that phrase as a timeline for production. First, get your lights set. Then, set up your camera. Finally, call the actors in.

### Set Up Your Lights

Setting up lighting is tricky and takes practice, exploration, and experience. When you set up your lighting, you need to consider several things, among which are mood, effect, and continuity.

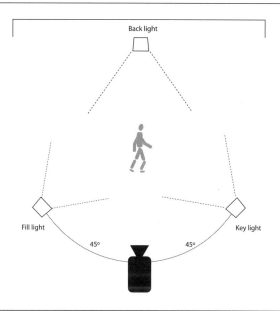

FIGURE 5-8    Basic lighting using key, fill, and back lights

To achieve mood, you can adjust the relative heights of your key and fill lights. Key light from above, say at a 45° angle, creates normal daylight types of shadows on a face. Lower that light to equal to head height, and your shadows become more dramatic and horizontal. Lit from below will give an eerie aspect. Monsters and mad scientists like to be lit from below. It's written in their contracts.

Once you've lit a scene and shot that scene for your master shot, you need to keep a record somewhere of your lighting setup for the sake of continuity. When you go back to do your subsequent two-shots and close-ups, you need to keep a consistent lighting ambience so that there is not a drastic difference from one shot to the next.

Set your key light, and then set your fill light. Start out by setting your key light at 45° from your main subject, and then position your fill light at the opposite yet equal 45° from the subject on the other side. With the two lights in place, adjust the distance from the subject, first with the key light, and then with the fill light. The key light is always first, then comes the fill light. When you have set your key and fill lights to an acceptable setting, it's time to work with the back light.

A back light can be reflected off a back wall to diffuse it and give the background some detail, but not blow it out or hide it in shadow.

## Choose Types of Lighting

A discussion of what type of lights to use could become a highly technical lecture, but you don't need to know too many technical details to choose your lights. Therefore, this section provides some basic guidelines for you to consider.

There are essentially four types of lighting for video:

- **Incandescent**    Incandescent bulbs are what we in the United States call light bulbs. They are the most common type of light bulb in our country, although not necessarily the best, or most environmentally friendly. But that's a discussion for a different book. Incandescent lights contain filaments kept in either a vacuum or a gas chamber with no oxygen. When the electricity is passed through the filament, the filament glows, or incandesces. While nowadays we have a small choice on the types of light these bulbs give off, usually they give video taken in them a yellowish tinge. Not the best thing.

- **Fluorescent**    Rather than having filaments that when charged glow, a fluorescent bulb is a so-called gas-charged light. Inside the glass enclosure is a mercury vapor in argon or neon gas. When electricity excites the mercury in such a gas environment, it causes a reaction that results in the gas glowing. Light. Fluorescent light gives video a greenish tinge. Also not the best thing.

- **Halogen**    Halogen lights are a special type of incandescent bulb with a tungsten filament. They get hot. They last longer than normal incandescents, and run blue rather than yellow or green.

- **HMI (hydrargyrum medium-arc iodide)**    HMI lighting kits are on the expensive side, starting around $2000. HMI lights are called continuous lights, because they stay on flicker-free and work well with digital video.

The cheapest lights to use are either incandescent or fluorescent. But they're not the best lighting for video. The particular tinge or color that they produce on video is always a factor to be dealt with. And here's how you deal with it.

In your camcorder, even the $200 kind, you have something called white balance control. Now, every camera is different, so the controls may also vary. White balance is a system that lets your camera know what color or shade is supposed to be white, and then adjusts the other colors it captures accordingly. In order to set the white balance, you generally hold the white balance button on your camera and focus your lens on a point in your scene or set that is "white." Once the white is set, your camera generally does all the rest. It automatically adjusts the entire spectrum to match that point you decided was the white point. Easy.

If you need further explanation, open the manual that came with your camera and see what it has to say. The manual may just show you how to adjust the white balance controls. You will more than likely want to set the balance and then forget it. Well, not forget exactly. You don't want to have to set it for each shot (although that's not a bad idea), but the white balance controls can be set to auto in most cases, and that should help.

# Learn Other Terms

The mechanical aspects of the shoot are pretty simple to learn. You've just been through a good set of basics. But there are other terms that you may want to understand in case you ever find yourself at Sundance or Cannes, and want to be able to talk to other filmmakers and film school graduates.

Many of these terms deal with the planning and ordering of your shots, which we'll go over in a subsequent chapter. For instance, when you have an idea of how to shoot the scene, you may want to block the shot. *Blocking the shot* simply means plotting out where the camera goes, where the actors or elements in the scene are, and, if there is movement, where they move to during the scene. This can become very involved, as you might imagine, using various shots. So in the planning on set, blocking is an essential step.

When planning the full scope of a project, you may want to have a scene at the beginning of the film that is referred to at the very end. These referring scenes, be it thematic or just at the same setting, are used as structural or framing devices that help tie the film together in the viewers' experience. Each of these scenes is referred to as a *bookend*. The reference should be obvious.

NOTE   *In case you're wondering, the short clip that comes before your actual video is called a* bumper. *It usually contains a logo or title.*

When you're planning out your video, you'll do so on paper first. You'll try to organize all your shots, angles, and ideas. The term used for this collection of shots, and all the various angles you have in your project, is *coverage*. It includes stage directions, notes, lighting setups, and anything else that you can put on paper that will help you establish an organized spreadsheet acuity for the project. You can also use this to help budget your video. If you're feeling like a snob, you can also refer to your arrangement of shots as *decoupage*. It's a French term that means more than just the arrangement of the shots. If you ever come across a French director, they will talk about their decoupage in a more thematic manner. If that director then talks about their *mise en scène*, they are using the French term for staging, or putting things in place within a scene.

Finally, when all is done, either for the day or for the shoot itself, it's called a *wrap*. After you wrap the shoot, the project isn't finished. In fact, it's really just beginning, because after you wrap your shoot, you have to go back into the computer and edit.

So let's add a bookend to this chapter. If you recall, the first paragraph of this chapter was filled with a lot of odd terminology and references. If we examine the scenario described in that paragraph once more, will we be able to make sense of it? Let's see.

Maybe the camera was shaking, or you missed some action, or you can't hear what the people are saying because you didn't use a *boom*, or even a *lavalier*. Maybe the light is too bright and you *backlit* your subjects, or your *key light* was not bright enough, or even too bright. Perhaps your audience has trouble following the action because there's no *continuity* to a shot, or you didn't follow the *180 degree rule*, your camera angle is wrong, your *bookends* don't box in the *sequence*, and your *coverage* is incomplete. Perhaps your *decoupage* is not ordered, and your *eyeline* doesn't match because you started with a *POV dolly shot* and cross-faded to a *Dutch tilt* instead of using a *head-on shot*. And all this could have been avoided if you had made a more complete *storyboard*, reviewed your *mise en scène*, used a *static shot* to start, *blocked* out some shots, and, before you called a *wrap*, made sure you checked the *gates*.

Does it make sense now? Of course it does.

And now that you know what all those terms mean, you can do one of two things. You can move on to the next chapter and learn about how to work out a story, and then plan that story using the technical know-how you've gained in this chapter. Or, you can put on an ascot tie, a dark blazer, and a monocle, crash some Hollywood party, and impress people with your filmmaking knowledge. The choice, of course, is entirely yours.

# Chapter 6

# Tell a Story

## How to . . .

- ■ Recognize the two kinds of stories
- ■ Apply the 30-60-30 rule to video storytelling

Storytelling holds everything together. I'm not just talking about the short videos that we are creating using the techniques introduced in this book. I mean everything that we call our human culture. Thousands upon thousands of years ago, a dirty, muddy, sweaty group of humans gathered around a fire and grunted to each other about their day. "Nearly got stomped on by a woolly mammoth today, dear. Boy, am I beat. How was your day?" "Oh, I had a good day, I discovered the wheel." That sort of thing.

Storytelling evolved into putting pigments on cave walls and stacking piles of stones on a hill. We put colors on our skin (and later shirts). We put beads in our hair. We made songs, and songs told us things about ourselves, and informed others about us. Stories in song, and stories on walls. We report our commonalities and our differences to each other and we leave records of our existence for others who come after us. We give instructions to each other of how to kill buffalo, how to sail a boat, how to lose weight, how to fix a computer, *how to make a video*.

Even a one-liner joke has a beginning, middle, and end. Videos should have the same, even at 20 seconds. This chapter explains how to structure your story, shows you how to estimate the length of your video based on your page count, and gives you an easy method of putting your ideas down on paper before capturing them on video.

# Understand the Two Kinds of Stories

Let's start by breaking down video stories into two types:

- ■ **The narrative, or three-part story**   This is what you normally expect, or think of, when you hear the word "story." There is a beginning, a middle, and an end. In other words, the story has three acts. Even a 30-second commercial that tells a story has three acts. Jokes have three acts. There's the setup, the exposition, and the punch line.

- ■ **The single-idea story**   This is as close to unedited video as it comes. Reportage. This type of story is more of an exploration, or a document. It reports more than it narrates. News footage is in itself a single idea. It captures an event. The lead in and exit that the footage is presented between may give it a context that makes it part of a bigger story. But the footage, like the videos on *America's Funniest Home Videos* on television, comprises single-idea stories. Many times, family videos, slideshows, and holiday collections of images are single-idea stories rather than narratives. Quick clips are single ideas. If you load a quick clip to YouTube, that's a single-idea story you're watching.

NOTE   *These descriptions are relegated to the U.S. style of story. There is a great difference between the U.S. story style and certain European story styles.*

The single idea story is similar to a point-and-shoot video. It doesn't need much more than an In and Out mark. So let's leave this alone, and focus on the three-part story instead.

Although we're not going to attempt anything on the scale of a long-form story, we are going to start our discussion there so that you understand the fundamental structure of a three-part story. We'll then use a condensed version of the same structure to tell a story in a two-minute video.

# Make a Three-Part Story

The long form in video storytelling is the feature-length movie. That's a 90- to 120-minute movie, which is not an easy project to pull off. Help is available, though. Whole schools have evolved concerning how feature-length movies are developed. There are authors, some of whom have never had a screenplay produced, who have made a living from breaking down the structure of screenplays and creating simple formulae that help others to write them. And if you ever move to Los Angeles, you'll meet more screenwriters than you ever thought existed. Every waiter, bartender, film student, car parking attendant, and even screenwriter is a screenwriter. They just haven't finished, sold, wrapped-up, conceived-of, produced, or written theirs. They're "still working on it." Remember to give them a good tip. Most commonly, they haven't actually thought about what goes into a story.

## Get Your Page Count Right

Feature screenplays work on page counts. The formula is that each page of a screenplay is equal to one minute of screen time. So if you have a 120-page screenplay, you have a two-hour movie. If you ever get the chance to have a producer look at one of your feature-length screenplays, the odds are that the first thing he will do is skip to the last page to find the page number. Or he might just ask you how long it is. To which you'll reply, not in terms of time, but in terms of pages. "It's 109 pages." "Perfect," he'll reply, and then he'll reach into his desk, draw out his checkbook, write you a check for $500,000, and off you'll go, laughing all the way to the bank. Moments later, of course, your alarm will go off, and you'll shower, get dressed, and head off to your dull, uninspiring drudgery of a job. In spite of that, you will have the knowledge that a screenplay has three acts, and they break down roughly into a 30-60-30 page formula. Within those parameters, there are things writers like to call *plot points*.

## Include Plot Points

Plot points are events or actions that occur to turn the progress of a story in a different, unexpected, or compelling direction. They work as marker buoys in a sailing race, points around which the story takes a different tack.

In the 30-60-30 format, the first major plot point comes at around page 28 or 29, just before the end of Act 1. The next plot points can occur two or three times in Act 2, but they are all minor twists until the end of the act, at which point you come upon the major plot point that sends us on to the resolution track of Act 3. So now you have an idea of how Hollywood movies get from A to B to C in two hours or less. The next time you watch a movie, keep an eye on your watch as well, and see how it works within the formula. You will probably find that most movies come within five minutes (pages) of the formula.

## Obstacles

Each plot point is an obstacle. You must have obstacles. This is very important. They move a plot forward. For example, let's say a man must get from point A to point B. But in between points A and B is an obstacle—something he must overcome. Let's say the whole story is that a man must cross his living room (we're keeping the scale of this very small, aren't we?). He must leave the couch on one side of the room to go to the other side of the room to get his book. But there is a problem. An obstacle is in his way. A large chair and ottoman block his path. Here is where the genre of the story comes into play as well.

For instance, let's call the story a comedy. So our protagonist decides he must get from the couch to get the book across the room, but he has to navigate the chair and ottoman to do so. Since this is comedy, the man can do a Dick Van Dyke–style pratfall over the chair, rolling and bouncing to his feet on the other side of the room, eventually ending up with the book in his hand. Intention, obstacle, and comedy.

Consider the same scenario as a drama. Our protagonist gets up from the couch, but just as he reaches the chair and endeavors to go around it, he pauses, sits on the ottoman, and looks back toward the couch he just left. He considers going forward to retrieve the book, but as he rises, he loses his balance. He has a fit of vertigo and collapses on the floor. Now the only thing he is focused on is reaching that book. That book is the answer to everything. Perhaps inside the pages he'll find the cure for his condition. He struggles to get up, and works his way across the room, falling to his knees again as he gets within arm's reach of his book. He reaches for the book, breathing heavily. Fade to black.

Finally, we can look at it as a foreign film. The man puts out his cigarette as he rises to cross the room. But as he reaches midway, he rests his arm on the chair, and considers how the light from outside lands on the chair's back. He glances toward the window, sits in the chair and smiles. Cut to the book, cover down so we can't even see the title. Fade to black.

Of course, the foreign film has nothing to do with the American sense of story. But it's filmed beautifully.

What you should see here is that even though we have two different types of story, the basic elements remain constant: point A, obstacle(s), point B.

So why am I explaining all this? As I mentioned earlier, I'm not trying to get you to make a two-hour film. You're not going to put a feature film online at YouTube—you can't, because there is a file size limit. Instead, we're going to adopt the 30-60-30 formula to condense three acts from 120 minutes into 2 minutes.

# Write a Two-Minute Video with the 30-60-30 Treatment

Let's condense the three-act form from 120 minutes into 2 minutes. To do this, we have to make some subtle adjustments to the formula. Two minutes equals 120 seconds, so we simply change the formula from minutes to seconds, to a 30 second/60 second/30 second format.

Let's now translate that into pages. Well, not exactly pages. Get yourself a box of index cards, preferably 3 × 5 inches. We'll substitute one face of one index card for ten pages of feature script (three index cards = 30 script pages). So that means we'll use three index cards for Act 1, six (if needed) for Act 2, and three for the final Act 3. In order to best explore this format, we should apply it to a short film.

So here is an exercise. Let's work out a 30-60-30 format treatment for a two-minute video. Try this as a starting point: What is your subject? We'll set a scene. A classroom. So, we fade in...

Act 1: A classroom setting—Written across the top of the blackboard are the words "Applied Logic." The teacher is writing on the blackboard, her back to the class. Our main protagonist, the problem student, is chewing gum...loudly. His attention is distracted by the basketball magazine he reads as he plays with a metal ruler. He holds the ruler with one hand flat on the desktop, and snaps the overhanging end with his other hand, making a boing sound.

The teacher of course becomes aware of the student's actions, stops what she is doing, and scolds the student.

Act 2: Detention—The student, now bereft of gum and ruler, sits bored and sad in detention. The teacher does paper work at her desk. Outside the window we can see other kids playing basketball, having fun. This only heightens our feeling of pathos (sympathy).

Act 3: Heroics—The teacher is walking to her car, carrying a bundle of books and papers. As she nears the curb, she drops her keys, and inevitably they fall down the storm drain, sitting just outside her reach. Desperation. But over her shoulder, we see our problem student, sullenly walking across the school yard, chewing his gum, slapping his ruler against his thigh. Cut to the student, using his gum on the end of the ruler to grab the teacher's keys from the storm drain grate. Smiles all around.

Fade to black.

A two-minute story in about 12 index cards.

**NOTE** *What we created is not a script or a screenplay but a treatment. A treatment is a simple document that is a precursor to a full-on script or screenplay. It outlines the story, with some directional attributes.*

Here's what our treatment accomplished in terms of the story: the main character, our problem student, would rather be playing basketball than paying attention in his Applied Logic class. Then we have conflict, as the teacher gives him detention. Inside that we have pathos and drama. Finally, we have the denouement of the story, and a small use of irony. The teacher's keys fall into the grate, but in a twist of the plot, our student applies simple logic, using the very elements that caused him his conflict in the first place, and he becomes the hero. All is well, and the story's own logic is satisfied.

**TIP** *The most important thing to remember in telling a story is to keep it simple. If you've ever heard a joke told by someone who can't tell jokes, you'll know that it's not the joke itself that is at fault. It's the telling of it. So keep the story simple.*

So we now have a story. Our next step is to use that story and plot it out as a shooting script. In order to do that, we'll first make a storyboard, which is a sort of cartoon or comic book version of our video. In the next chapter, we'll create a storyboard, and work out a shooting script.

# Chapter 7

# Storyboarding

## How to...

- Plan a story
- Create a storyboard
- Organize shots
- Use photo management software to create a storyboard
- Output a storyboard onto paper and online

Our short treatment from the previous chapter doesn't have all the formatting standards you'll find in a feature-length screenplay or a shooting script. For a short video such as ours, we don't need all the formatting standards. However, there are some conventions that would be useful to us. This is where we tie together the elements discussed in Chapters 5 and 6. Chapter 5, if you recall, discussed the various technical terms for camera shots, as well as film terminology used for cocktail parties. The cocktail party terminology can be saved for later, when you accept your award. But the camera shot terms are very useful when planning your video...even your short, two-minute epic.

With the treatment done, even to the extent of only having the basic sketch from Chapter 6, we can now start applying it using a combination of writing skills and camera direction. The idea is to make the shooting itinerary easier through pre-planning. And one of the best ways to do this is to create a storyboard.

If you've ever seen one of those "Making of..." documentaries that explain the movie-making process on some otherwise boring or blockbuster movie, you've probably seen the stage where they go over what looks to the civilian eye like a cartoon or comic-strip version of what the film eventually became. Those comic strips are actually storyboards. Storyboards can be as involved as having camera angles and great sketches, or as loosely put together as using stick figures and explanatory notes.

But since we have some great tools on our computers, we don't have to worry about how well we can draw. The point of a storyboard is to get your ideas out of your head and down in front of your eyes. And we have several possible solutions to achieve that end, as described in this chapter. Keep in mind as you read that one of the principal reasons we make a storyboard is to help us get a clear idea of what to shoot, and how to move our story along. That's its function. So whether you print it out and have a hard copy while on set, or just keep it on the computer and lug your laptop to the set, the act of creating the storyboard will inform your video for the better.

# Create a Storyboard Using Guerilla Methods

The guerilla method is the least expensive. Using this approach, we use what we can find, what we can get for free or very inexpensively, and what fortuitously washes up on our shores. So the first step using the guerilla method is to steal a pencil. Steal one from the bank, the golf course pro shop, or your kid. Remember, this is guerilla filmmaking. We take no prisoners. Now find a pad of paper on which to put that pencil to use.

This part of storyboarding is going to be the same in each of our approaches, so get used to it. Refer to the short treatment at the end of Chapter 6. We're going to pick out the key frames of each scene, and interpret them as camera shots. The idea is to make the storyboard a visual representation of our story, with as much economy as possible, and still keep the story's clarity. We're essentially translating the story form from word to image. The quality of the images isn't that important other than that they effectively communicate the action of the scene. So stick figures will work.

To start your storyboard, draw out four squares on a page. The easiest way to do this is to fold a piece of paper in half horizontally, and then turn the paper vertically and fold that in half, creating roughly equal quarters. Use the folds as guides for drawing your rectangles. (Remember this is guerilla, so we don't mention the obvious, which would be use a ruler, or even the drawing tools on your word processor.) Flip the page so that it is 11 × 8.5 inches, or what is commonly referred to as *landscape*. If you need a reference, take a look at Figure 7-1. You could also use index cards if you like.

**NOTE**   *We want to work in landscape because that more closely resembles the aspect ratio of a video, and a computer monitor.*

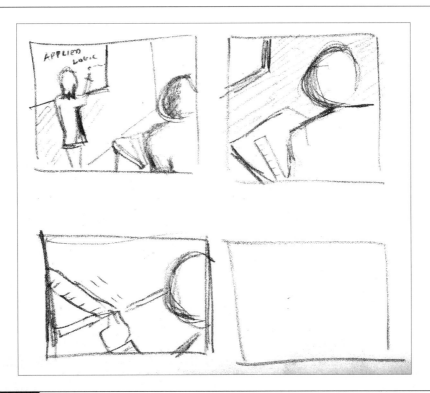

FIGURE 7-1     Basic layout

Ready with your pencil, it's time to review the simple story treatment established in the last chapter:

Act 1: A classroom setting—Written across the top of the blackboard are the words "Applied Logic." The teacher is writing on the blackboard, her back to the class. Our main protagonist, the problem student, is chewing gum…loudly. His attention is distracted by the basketball magazine he reads as he plays with a metal ruler. He holds the ruler with one hand flat on the desktop, and snaps the overhanging end with his other hand, making a "boing" sound.

The teacher of course becomes aware of the student's actions, stops what she is doing, and scolds the student.

So our first drawing should include the established setting, the classroom, with the all-important words on the blackboard clearly shown, as shown in Figure 7-2.

You may want to add the perspective over the shoulder, of the student. The drawing should be simple, just enough to get the basic point across. Simplicity is important. Feel free to write a caption. Remember, the storyboard is a tool, a way of planning things out. And even if it's written down, drawn out, and looks final, it's just a way of reminding you what you want the shot to look like. You don't have to stick to it. You're the director, and these are just notes.

Our next box will contain the next key action from the treatment. So you may want to draw a closeup of "the problem student chewing gum." And so on, filling up your boxes until you have the entire treatment illustrated.

**FIGURE 7-2**   Establishing shot

Sometimes this simple and very basic way of storyboarding is the best. It allows you to do certain things that the more sophisticated methods might overlook. The most important thing it does is force you to simplify. You already have enough to worry about with the setup and actually filming of the video. You don't need to waste your valuable time doing accurate illustrations of each shot.

Again, I can't emphasize enough that this is a simplification exercise. It will help you focus on what's essential in your story, and what isn't necessary at all. When shooting, this focus will help you to set up shots so that you know what to get from each shot. All of us have seen the depiction of the movie-making set where they shoot a number of takes until they get it right. As though what the director wants is a mystery, they shoot again and again until she says, "We got it, check the gates." What you didn't realize is that, before this moment, to *know* what she needed to *get*, the director developed her storyboards. And she probably had them on hand while shooting. Of course, she also had a budget, and so she worked with storyboard artists and assistants when she developed hers. Not so with us. We're on our own.

The bare structure and realization of our storyboard can work as a final product, and we can use it right now to begin shooting. Or we can use it as yet another starting point, a refining agent for our video.

# Create a Storyboard Using iPhoto or Picasa

A storyboard is just a visual story. But it's a visual story with a definite and specific function. A comic strip is not necessarily a storyboard, but if you employ that comic strip as a guide to making a video or film, then it becomes a storyboard. Our computers come with certain applications or programs that we can use to catalog, view, and order photos. These applications or programs work great when used for their intended purposes. But what if we were to use them for a different purpose? What if we were to use, say, iPhoto on the Mac, or Picasa (a free download from Google) on the PC, and instead of randomly dumping our photos into them, we set up albums that order our images to act as…storyboards? That's exactly what we're going to do.

## Make Your Storyboard Images

Before you can make a storyboard on the computer, you need to make the images. You can do this in any of several ways. Perhaps the best way, albeit the most time consuming and labor intensive, is to take photos of set shots, as you perceive the action of the video going when you actually do shoot it. You don't need to do this with real people, however. You can just use models, figurines, even Lego bricks. The point is to get a depiction of the key setup for each part of the video, and then put it on the computer in a digital medium.

You could also just scan the images and illustrations you used to make the pencil and paper version of your storyboard. When you have the images in digital format, transfer them to your computer (see Chapter 1).

If you are on a PC, skip the iPhoto section and go to the section on Picasa.

## Create a Storyboard Using iPhoto (Mac)

iPhoto is a great application on the Mac, as part of the iLife suite. It comes with every Mac, which means it's free. But it's also one of the most powerful image-management programs on any computer. So let's go through a simple method of creating a storyboard using iPhoto.

To start, we must, of course, have our script, or our treatment (see the previous section). Once again, we want to take only the key actions and key setup as the subject matter for our storyboard.

In the case of iPhoto, we can collect our images from stills, creating images, or taking photos or scans of illustrations and bring them into iPhoto. You could use models, toys, or anything that is recognizable and gets your message across. You could simply scan the hand-drawn images from the previous section's storyboard. If you don't have a scanner, you could use your digital camera as an ersatz scanner.

In iPhoto, import the images (File | Import to Library). If you're using a digital camera or a flash memory disk, iPhoto will let you give a name to the "roll" of images you're importing. This might be a good idea, since naming is a big part of the ordering process, which we discuss later in this chapter.

With your images in the main Library of iPhoto, you can now set up a separate album. But before you do that, let's set the viewing preferences for that Library:

1. Choose View | Film Roll. The selection should have a check mark now.

2. Choose View | Sort Photos | By Film Roll. See Figure 7-3.

Now that your photos can be viewed in digestible groups, it is easier to assess your images.

We've named our film roll, and we can see the images are all there, in no particular order, higgledy-piggledy. Let's say, for argument's sake, we already have a set of images that will work for our storyboard. And further, let's say that we want all of our imported images in the storyboard. Each image is essential to telling our story. What we need to do now is create an album of these images, so that we can order them and assess that order.

**FIGURE 7-3**    Sorting by film roll

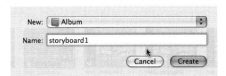

**FIGURE 7-4**    Storyboard1 is the new album for this example.

## Create an Album of Your Storyboard Images

In the left pane of iPhoto are the albums. Albums in iPhoto are simply collected images that speak to a particular event, or particular purpose. In the case of storyboard use, however, they are actually the bin from which we'll create the order and delivery of our storyboard. Let's make a new album:

1. Click the large + symbol in the lower-left corner of the left pane.

2. Name the new album. Use a name that is appropriate for the album's use. For this exercise, use **Storyboard1**, as in the example shown in Figure 7-4.

The newly created album won't have any images in it. By default, your new album will be located at the very bottom of the left pane. And when you created it, it was automatically selected. There are a few steps you'll want to take:

1. Deselect the album for now, and select the Library again. That should return you to the film roll from earlier.

2. In the main preview pane (also called the Gallery pane), click the name of the film roll to select all the images within it.

3. Click and hold on the film roll title head. Drag your cursor to the newly created album in the left pane. Your cursor should have a green plus sign next to it as you drag directly on top of the album's book-shaped icon, as shown in Figure 7-5.

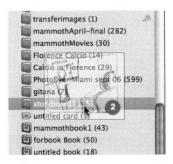

**FIGURE 7-5**    Fill the new album with selected images.

Select the new album from the left pane. Now we can get down to the real work. With our story images isolated in a neat group, we can order them, reorder them, and even edit them to a small extent.

## Order Your Storyboard Images

For the sake of order, let's first rename the images using a batch process:

1.  Select the new album (Storyboard1).

2.  Select all the images in Storyboard1. You can do this either by click-dragging across all the images in the Gallery pane or by just placing your cursor inside the Gallery and using the keyboard combination ⌘-A. You should see a light-blue border around each image, signifying its selection.

3.  Choose Photos | Batch Change.

4.  In the dialog box shown in Figure 7-6, choose Set Title to Text.

5.  Check the check box next to Append a Number to Each Photo.

6.  Type an appropriate title, like Storyboard. Click OK. The application will fill in the number.

You now have the images isolated from the general population, and you have assigned them numbers. With numbers assigned, if we reorder the images, we can immediately see our original order. Just a neat little trick to make our storyboard easier to maneuver. From here, we simply put the images into an order that makes sense.

NOTE    *Remember, one of the principal reasons to make a storyboard is to help you get a clear idea of what to shoot, and how to move your story along.*

Reorder your images by dragging and dropping them within the Gallery pane. When you have them in an order that makes sense for the video, it's time to put it into a format that you can take with you.

## Deliver Your Storyboard onto Hardcopy

You won't be able to print your images directly from iPhoto to a sheet of paper. But you can use a handy trick built into every Mac that can help you to print it. It's called the *screen grab*, which is a picture of your screen.

**FIGURE 7-6**    Setting up a batch process

There are several ways to create a screen grab. There's even an application that came with the Mac, called Grab, that will do it for you. But there is also an easier way to get a screen grab than opening yet another application. Using a keyboard combination, you can take a picture of your entire screen, or just an area that you designate. To capture the complete screen, use ⌘-SHIFT-3. To capture just a designated portion, use ⌘-SHIFT-4.

To take a picture of just the area on the screen that you want to print, do this:

1. Use the keyboard combination ⌘-SHIFT-4. Your cursor will now become a target, or plus sign.

2. Click-drag the cursor across the screen, outlining the area you want to include in the printout. When you release the mouse button, you'll hear a shutter-click sound.

3. Look on your desktop, and you'll see a new file there, generically labeled Picture 1.png. Double-click it, and it should open in Preview.

4. Print the file from Preview.

Now apply that methodology to the iPhoto Gallery pane that has your images in their correct order. See Figure 7-7.

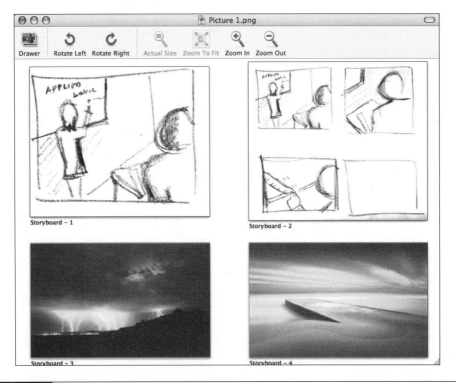

**FIGURE 7-7**    Printable version of your storyboard

iPhoto also gives us the option to print a contact sheet with image information. Choose File | Print, and in the ensuing dialog box, choose Contact Sheet from the Style drop-down menu. Be sure to check Show Titles.

You now have a printable version of your storyboard, and you can order and reorder your images as many times as makes sense, and then go through the screen grab process for each. That way, you can have variations to consider before shooting.

But we also want to test our story in another way. So next we'll create a mini movie of our storyboard, and see how the action flows from one image to the next.

## Export Your Storyboard into a Slideshow

Exporting our storyboard as a slideshow allows us to watch, rather than read, our storyboard. In some ways this makes sense, because as we experiment with the order of our images, we can also see them animated. If the story can be told through a simple slideshow, we can be reassured that the story will make sense in its final form as well.

Here's how we make a slideshow:

1.  With the Storyboard1 album selected, go to the tool icons at the bottom of the iPhoto window and choose Slideshow. You'll see the preview pane fill with your first image, and there will be myriad tool icons below it, as shown in Figure 7-8.

**FIGURE 7-8**    iPhoto slideshow tools

2.   Click Preview. The first two images will zoom and cross-fade into one another. You can change the transition settings, adjust the time each image is shown (Settings button), add music (Music button), and even adjust the color, crop, sharpness, and more for each image (Adjust button).

3.   Once you've finished playing around with all the settings, click the Play button. Your whole screen will be filled, and you can see if your storyboard is complete.

4.   Click inside the slideshow to stop it and return to the iPhoto window.

Your album is now transformed into a slideshow. If you look to the left pane, you'll see that there is now a Storyboard1 slideshow listed, with a number in parentheses designating the number of images contained therein.

Click the slideshow in the left pane to bring the edit window back up, and make adjustments. The upper pane of the slideshow preview window lets you reorder your selected images. So you can adjust the storyboard as much as you need.

The next step is to deliver the storyboard into a more moveable format. The simplest and most efficient format here is QuickTime.

### Export Your Storyboard into QuickTime

To export you storyboard into QuickTime, follow these steps:

1.   Select the slideshow from the left pane.

2.   Choose File | Export.

3.   The ensuing dialog box lets you name your file, choose a size for the output, and select a destination. To make it easy on yourself, use the name of the file for your video with _storyboard added to the end. Then select either Medium (320 × 240) or Large (640 × 480) and click Export.

You can now exit iPhoto and locate your exported storyboard on your computer. If you saved it in the default location, then it will be in your home account, under Movies. Otherwise, it will be wherever you decided to put it in the last dialog window.

You now have a working storyboard for your video. If it's good enough, it might even stand in for a video itself.

## Create a Storyboard Using Picasa

If you happen to be using a Windows PC, you may not have the advantage of a built-in photo gallery manager like that found in the Mac. But that shouldn't stop you. There is a free alternative on the Web called Picasa.

NOTE   *Picasa is available for both Mac OS and Windows. The controls are pretty much the same within the program whether you're working in Mac OS or Windows.*

Picasa is available as a free download from Google, at http://picasa.google.com. Click the Free Download link, and the download will start automatically. Or do a search on Google for Picasa. The results should lead you to Picasa.

Picasa is a very simple application that will help us organize our ideas to make a digital storyboard. Although we won't be able to print out the storyboard directly from Picasa in a simple page format, we can use it to create a slideshow from our key images. In that way, we can test the continuity of our story, which is one of the main functions of a storyboard.

But we *can* get output from this system. We'll just have to do it in an unconventional manner. But first, let's create our storyboard in Picasa. Picasa will import your images from your digital camera, scanner, or other media such as the flash micro disk that your camera uses to store its information. If you can get your images from your cell phone to your PC (see Chapter 1), then Picasa can import them.

## Import Image Files into Picasa

When you open Picasa, you'll find the Import button in the upper-left part of the window. You can also add files individually (File | Add File to Picasa) or whole folders to Picasa all at once (File | Add Folder to Picasa). So if you keep your images in your My Pictures folder, then locate them there. If you keep them on your Desktop, that's fine too. Just get them into Picasa.

Let's say we have a few images, for the sake of instruction. It doesn't matter if you have 5 or 12. We want to go over the basics for this process. Also, it's not just the images themselves but also how we order those images that makes the storyboard. With that in mind, we'll dump those images into the Picasa gallery. On the left side of the Picasa interface is the Library. This is made up of several categories, among them Albums, Folders, and Other Stuff. We'll concern ourselves first with Albums.

## Create an Album of Your Storyboard Images

By default, you may have some images already populating the Picasa Library, in which case you will see them in the gallery on the right. If you've imported your files already, then they too will be in the gallery on the right. However, they won't necessarily be a part of an album. They could be attached to a folder (the folder where they live on your hard drive) or Other Stuff, if they happen to be located anywhere else on your computer.

We want to keep a sense of order here, so we'll create a new album specifically for the storyboard images:

1. Choose File | New Album to open the Album Properties dialog box, shown in Figure 7-9.

2. Give the new album an appropriate name. For this exercise, use **Storyboard1**.

3. From the gallery where you have your existing images (on the right), select all the images that go into the album (to select multiple images, select the first one in the list, press SHIFT, and then click the last one in the list) and drag them over to the newly created Storyboard1 album.

**FIGURE 7-9**    Name the album

Your album should now show the number of images contained therein in parentheses after the album's name.

## Rename and Reorder Your Storyboard Images

To make the ordering process easier, we'll rename the images so that we can identify them and see how our ordering was originally and how we made it different:

1. Choose Picture | Batch Edit | Rename.

2. Type a fitting name (for this exercise, use **Storyboard**). Picasa gives all the images your designated name and appends them with a number.

Now that your images are numbered, you can reorder them to fit the story. As I said earlier, the reason we want to assign numbers *before* we do our final ordering is to give us an immediate visual clue at to where we started and how the images relate to each other.

While you have the Storyboard album in front of you on your screen, you can also type in a description of the collection, as shown in Figure 7-10. You can write annotations for your own information, or just put some text that helps you to see at a glance what you have in the album. If you were to create a second version of this storyboard, with another ordering system, you could use the Description area to give information about each version.

You can also edit a description by choosing Album | Edit Description or just by clicking the ghosted "Add a description" label in the storyboard itself.

**FIGURE 7-10**    Add a description.

Drag and drop the order of your images to fit your story, and make note of the new order. If the order ends up 1, 4, 3, 5, 2, write that down. That's a simple way of keeping track of the storyboard, a sort of mnemonic device, or memory trick. Finally, with all the images in the order you want, you export the gallery so that you can refer to it outside of Picasa. We'll use two methods. The first is a movie, and the second is a web gallery. Let's start with the movie.

## Export Your Storyboard into a Picasa Movie

There are certain intrinsic advantages to making a movie version of your storyboard. One is its portability. We can transfer the movie file from one PC to another. We can also upload that movie to the Web and use it as a reference point. Either way, creating the movie is an easy process:

1. In Picasa, select the images in the order you want them to run.

2. Choose Create | Movie to open the Create Movie dialog box, shown in Figure 7-11.

3. Picasa will create a movie and put it in your MyPictures folder. Double-click the newly created file to open and play it.

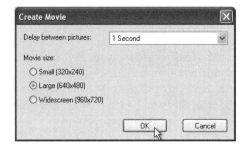

**FIGURE 7-11**    Create a movie.

One of the distinct advantages to setting up our storyboard as a movie is that we can test our movie to see if the story actually makes sense. When animated in this way, the storyboard is a quick version of the whole video. If it makes sense, then we've succeeded. Our story will work.

If you feel that the storyboard doesn't work well, or if you find that you need alternative sequences, just go back to the Picasa album and either add more photos or simply reorder them, and re-create the movie from there. You may want to create a new album for each storyboard version. That way, when you export your movies, they will have different names to reflect their different content.

## Create an HTML Gallery Page of Your Storyboard

The second delivery method from Picasa is the HTML gallery page. The advantage to this method is that, once created, we can look at the storyboard in our browser of choice and print the pages if need be.

Creating an HTML gallery page of our storyboard is a very simple process:

**1.** In the Storyboard album, select the images in the order you want them.

**2.** Choose Album | Export as HTML Page, as shown in Figure 7-12.

**3.** Select the size of the images for the page. Note the path for the folder in which your HTML gallery will live on your hard drive. You'll see that information near the bottom of the dialog box for Export as HTML page.

When you click Next, Picasa creates the gallery for you and automatically opens your default web browser to that page. Now that you have the images in the sequence you want, in a web browser, you can print this page as a reference point and storyboard.

**FIGURE 7-12**    Export the album as an HTML page.

You've now created a storyboard in two formats using a free application, Picasa. For most short video projects, this is about all you need to do before you go out and actually shoot your video. For those more intrepid, serious-minded, or budget-endowed, read the next section to learn about a professional-level dedicated storyboarding software solution.

# Evaluate Professional-Level Storyboarding Applications

Storyboarding is a serious thing. It's part designer, part illustrator, part editor, and part filmmaker. Storyboarding is a synthesis point for all of those skills, and it's an integral part of the process. You could probably make your living just being a storyboard expert.

Professional-level and so-called "pro-sumer" (as in professional consumer) storyboarding applications can cost from hundreds to thousands of dollars. The application you choose to use depends on your needs and your budget. But, let's be honest. If you're reading this book, you don't want to spend too much money on these sorts of things. This book is for those of us who are looking for practical solutions, who are economical and clever.

Any pro-level storyboarding application will have its own proclivities and interfaces. But the process is basically the same. You start with a script, screenplay, or treatment. You outline it in such a way as to develop key points and actions. That means you must break down your story into a series of shots and settings. From there, you sketch out those shots visually. The differences between what we did earlier in this chapter and what a professional storyboard software application does are the level of sophistication and the consideration of each shot. The final storyboard is not just a series of ordered drawings; it's a preliminary video composition.

For the purposes of demonstration, I'll introduce you to one pro-level storyboarding application that I'm particularly fond of: Storyboard Pro.

## Sample Storyboard Pro

Storyboard Pro, made by Toon Boom Animation (www.toonboomstudio.com), is a digital and flash-based animation application developer, so the producers of this software have a good sense of how to create, break down, and deliver stories for the Web. Storyboard Pro is a $900 professional storyboarding tool. That's not cheap. But it includes not only drawing tools, but text and soundtrack tools, as well as camera movements and numerous export formats. Within it, you can change camera angles, do very detailed drawings, make visual, textual, and audio annotations and descriptions, and output to any number of flat, printed, video, or animated formats. For cutting to the chase, as it were, you can also try out the lesser, but still viable, Toon Boom Storyboard (not Pro) at around $250.

NOTE    *The odds are, you won't use this level of tool for a two-minute video. But you should be aware of the existence of a program like this, in case your next venture into online video is more high end than just a cell phone.*

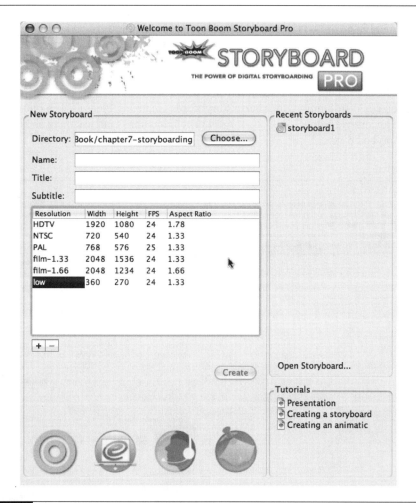

**FIGURE 7-13**    Creating a new storyboard in Storyboard Pro

Starting up in Storyboard Pro, as shown in Figure 7-13, you are immediately struck by the choices it offers for configurations.

After setting up a directory and a name for the storyboard, you select a specific resolution. These choices will change the aspect ratio of the drawing cells and, ultimately, the output. You can create your own resolutions and aspect ratios simply by clicking the plus sign below the settings.

The program itself is really a sophisticated drawing and animation application. The main interface, shown in Figure 7-14, is similar to most drawing applications, such as Adobe Illustrator and the like.

You'll find that with all the myriad tools, actions, and enhancements available to you in this application, or others of its professional level ilk, you are still creating a very basic storytelling device, just as you did earlier in this chapter. In fact, if you were ever to become a professional storyboarder, you could still import your basic storyboards created in Picasa's web output, or iPhoto's QuickTime movie output, or even scanned pencil drawings, and use them as basic templates for Storyboard Pro.

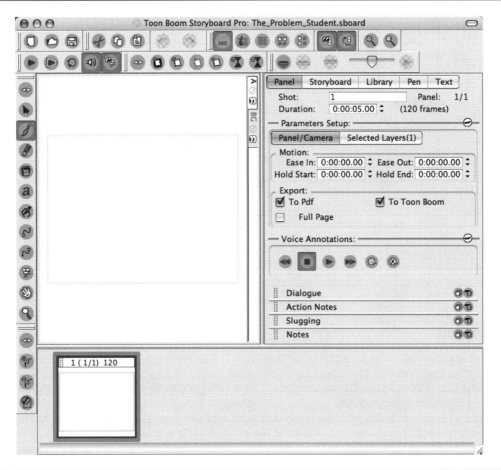

**FIGURE 7-14**    Basic drawing tools and more

The professional-level application affords you output and versatility—the very same things a pencil and paper give you, but with more repeatability and easier storage solutions. A program like Storyboard Pro has many other features as well, which, if you delve into them, can actually help you create a full-on animation without going outside to other applications.

Of course, the simplest—and for our needs, the most direct and useful—functions of a high-end application like Storyboard Pro are the layout, printout, and delivery options. In terms of layout, we have several views we can use. And even if you never buy this application (or something of its level), you can get an idea of the things you might want to include on a homemade version by looking at how it lays out the storyboard, as shown in Figure 7-15.

The inclusion of dialogue, production notes, captions, and drawings of camera angles is very important. Depending on how complex you want to make your production, these preplanned notes can save time and, as a direct extension, money.

If you plan out your shots using index cards or a folded, letter-sized sheet of paper, you can then apply them to a larger sheet, with production notes. But remember, production notes are just notes until you implement them into your shots. That means they aren't final, they aren't carved in stone, and they can be changed depending on circumstances, lighting, mood, or inspiration.

These are the things you must take into account as you go forward toward directing and shooting your video. So gather your notes, drawings, slideshows, and files. It's time to put some of these things together and make your video.

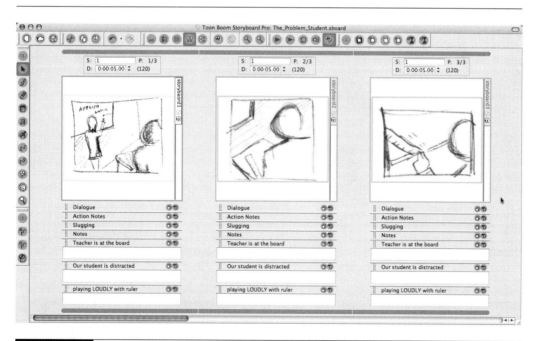

**FIGURE 7-15**   Layout options

# Chapter 8

## Be the Director

## How to . . .

- ■ Light your set
- ■ Adjust for white balance
- ■ Put your storyboard to use
- ■ Frame your shots
- ■ Time your shots

Although it's not necessary to sport jodhpurs, a riding crop, and a monocle when directing, it's always an option. They're not hard to procure, either, what with online shopping. And even though you may think I'm making a joke here, at the center of it, there is a reason behind my suggestion.

One of the keys to directing a video project, small or large, is knowing that it is your vision that carries the entity through. It may come down to your whim, or your practiced eye, to turn the camera one way or another, frame the shot this way or that. It is your intention that translates into the camera's eye. So why mention jodhpurs, riding crop, and monocle? Because those costume accoutrements signify something. On the set, or in movies that depict the set, they signify that the person wearing them is in charge. He's the bloke shouting *Lights! Camera! Action!* It's his point of view that's being recorded. It's his vision. It's your vision.

When you set up to shoot your video, it doesn't matter whether you're using a cell phone video camera or a high-end Sony HD DV camcorder as long as you're clear as to your intention for the shoot. All that planning I spoke of in Chapters 5 through 7—from story idea to treatment to script, from sketch to storyboard—leads to the moment you actually begin shooting your video.

But having said that, making a video is more than just putting together all the technical parts and following some rote idea of how a film is made. And there are no guarantees that anything we do on video is going to be a success. That's part of the crapshoot that any creative enterprise must deal with. Sometimes you don't know what you have until you finish it, let it sit, and then look at it. And other times you know it's just right...finished, great, done...the moment you do it.

So we set out the basic techniques to being a director so that you can use them as reference points. And so from there, you will be able to recognize, name, and repeat given skills or methods to improve on them to achieve better, more expected results.

# Be Prepared

Be prepared in your intention, your equipment, your manner, and your vision. If you feel it necessary to dress up in jodhpurs, by all means do it (but be prepared for the derision that might invite). Being prepared means have your material with you. Have your notes, your storyboard, your script, and your camera on hand. Know your set, know your crew. Know what points you want to cover.

## Use the Right Equipment

Aside from your camera and a backup camera (good for B-roll, or alternative, takes), get a tripod. I know that sounds like a mundane advisement, but you'd be surprised at how many times you might want a stable shot, and not have one for lack of a tripod. Shoulder cams are great, but they're not necessarily appropriate for every shot. Sometimes you just want a stable, clean shot, with no shake. So get a tripod.

## Set Your Lighting

Remember, in the final analysis, shooting video is just capturing reflected light. As you know, getting the right lighting can be one of the more tedious and time-consuming aspects of shooting a video. If you've ever had the opportunity to be present on a movie set, then you've no doubt witnessed the pace at which things move. Very slowly. Glacially slow. Slow. Most of that has to do with the lighting. On a movie set, the director wants a controlled environment, and everything points to the way the camera is going to capture the light and the actors. This is why actors get trailers—so that they can sleep or read or shower or play Yahtzee while the lighting director, electricians, best boys, and grips get the lighting right.

But we're not talking about a movie set. We're just doing a piddly little video shoot, so we have a few choices regarding lighting. The following sections describe the choice between controlled lighting and natural lighting, how to adjust white balance, and how to take advantage of a low-budget lighting trick for shooting night scenes.

### Use Controlled Lighting

Setting up controlled lighting is generally done by employing our basic three-light set (see Chapter 5): the key light, the fill light, and the back light. As Herr Direktor (the director), you'll want to oversee this. And if you happen to also be Herr Kameraman (the cameraperson), it's just as important that you have a say.

1. Put your subject in place. If that is an actor, or a stand-in, have them on set, on their marks.

2. Point your key light directly at your subject. This creates hard, contrasting shadows.

3. Point your fill light to balance and essentially neutralize those shadows.

4. Turn on your back light so that it does not create any silhouettes on your subjects (refer to Chapter 5).

5. Adjust each part of the lighting triangle to get the correct neutrality between all three.

### Use Existing Light

The other way to work with lighting is to use as much of the existing light that's there on location. If you're outside, bring reflectors (foam-core illustration boards work great as reflectors). Reflectors are not shiny. They are generally white and neutral. You can have colored reflectors, for effect, such as gold, silver, or even blue. But those should be used only for very particular situations.

When using a reflector, just experiment. Keep your eye on, say, an actor's cheek. Have a grip put the white foam-core board just out of frame, below and directed toward the actor, at an angle. Watch closely as the light values on the actor change. Sometimes they can change dramatically. This is good to know for close-ups, among other things. Again, the main thing is to experiment with the reflector.

## Adjust Your White Balance

Video camera images work best in full but not overly saturated light. In Chapter 5, I discussed the various types of lights you can use, so even if you don't bring your own lights, make yourself aware of what type of light is in the existing setup. If, for instance, you are shooting in an office that has fluorescent lighting, you need to know that so that you can adjust for the green color cast your video will have.

To counteract as much of the various color casts that you'll get with different lighting situations, you must adjust the white balance on your camera. (Even some cell phones have white balance controls.) Setting your white balance is really just saying to your digital camcorder, "This is what white is in this particular space." When the camera understands what white is, it has a reference point for all the other colors in the ambient spectrum, so that it can adjust accordingly.

You can be lazy and let your camera set your white balance with its own automatic settings. But that's a bad idea. Most of the time, you will get mediocre results from that. It's better to manually set your white balance. Here's how: Hold up the back of a white index card or a blank white piece of paper (or a white sneaker, white hat…something white) in front of your camera at the mark where your subject will be, and press the Set White Balance button on the camera. You're telling the camera, "Hey, this is the color white I mean." The camera will adjust accordingly.

If you're a particularly vindictive person with some issues concerning technology, you can also trick your camera. Try putting a gray piece of paper in front of the camera and tell the camera that it's white. Then film something and see how it changes the contrast and the colors of the resulting video footage. Your camera is dumb. It does what you tell it to do, and it sees only what you tell it to see.

## Use a Lighting Trick to Shoot Night Scenes

There are tricks for lighting scenes that could fill more than just one book, so I'm not going to go too far into them here. The best I can do in this limited space is give you a hint about how to leverage low-budget lighting to look good enough to make any deficiencies on the final footage look as if you meant to do it that way.

If you're shooting a night scene, you still need light. But bright light works against the idea of night, so use a technique that has worked well for low-budget filmmakers for many years: film during the day, but use a blue filter on your lights, giving your video the cooler look of evening. That may mean inserting a blue gel in front of your lights or just inserting blue cellophane in front of your lens.

Above all else, remember that lighting is the core element in the video's visuals. You can't tell a visual story in the dark. If you do, then it's not called video, it's call radio.

# Put Your Storyboard to Use

Chapter 7 was devoted to storyboarding. Now that you're on the set, use your storyboard to help organize the shoot. Remember, even the simplest of video projects should have a storyboard. It doesn't need to be an elaborate schema, as long as it gets your ideas down in a somewhat clear and organized fashion. You may want to refer to Chapter 7 one more time to make sure you have all of your ideas down on paper (or on QuickTime) before you show up on set with your riding crop.

Review your storyboard before shooting. Review it during the lighting setup. Review it as you are about to shoot. If you have a cameraperson other than yourself, or a director of photography, you will want to share each storyboard panel with those individuals before shooting. And then take one more look at the storyboard for yourself.

New ideas come at you when you least expect it. When you think you finally have everything you want ready in your head, take another pause. You may find that even though you've planned all of your shots in your head, and then on the storyboard, the reality of the location suggests that there is a better choice. Embrace change. The point of the storyboard is to provide a foundation for your ideas, not a set of chains for them.

# Keep a Few Things in Mind While Shooting

It's not enough to just point and shoot. You have to actually make some decisions about composition, and framing too. And while you are framing the shots, keep your eyes open for what we like to call happy accidents. Things never go exactly as planned. But mistakes aren't always bad things. But it all begins with how you set your shots up, and when you say, "Action!" Time your shots so that you have enough footage to edit, and make sure that you get the action where you want it in the shot.

## Frame Your Shots

All the setup and preparation points to the actual shoot. The most important thing to keep in mind while shooting is to keep it simple. Let the video action, not the camera, tell the story. Especially important for online video, where the screen is minute, the action is minimal, and the clarity is just out of your control, is simplicity of shots.

Use the rule of thirds. Segment your frame into vertices that break the frame into thirds horizontally and thirds vertically. In a two-shot, space the characters so that they are situated at the cross points of those vertices, as shown in Figure 8-1. This balances the shot and gives the video a simple yet compelling composition.

Center movement in the frame. When your subject is moving across a frame, or across the set, keep it in frame. The easiest target for that is the one that is centered in the frame. When the subject comes to rest, you can invoke the thirds.

**FIGURE 8-1**   The rule of thirds

Don't use only one shot. Take your scene from different angles. This will help later in editing, when you actually put the video together. A second camera, shooting simultaneously, is a great asset.

## Shoot Early

When shooting your video, shoot early. Whereas in script writing and storytelling the rule of thumb is "get in late, get out early," the rule of thumb for shooting is pretty much the converse of that.

Start shooting early, and let the cameras roll late. There are some reasons for this. Artistically, just letting the camera roll for a few seconds before and after the action of a prescribed scene sometimes helps to capture unexpected moments that might be useful in the final cut of a video. And functionally, it is vitally important to have a few seconds of footage before and after so that when you're editing, you have some room for transitions between scenes. You want a little mane and tail to hold onto when you're jogging through your edits, splicing things together.

## Shoot Extra Footage

If you have time, shoot extra footage. As I said earlier, the storyboard is a point of departure, not necessarily a destination. So while shooting, don't refrain from trying other angles, other shots, extended scenes, or even alternative scenes. Reaction shots, establishing shots, and so-called B-roll shots that take in scenery, crowds, or movement without any specific bearing on the scenes at hand are all vitally important.

TIP

*The more footage you have to begin your edits, the more choices you afford yourself during the editing process.*

Having choices, as you'll see in the following chapters, are at the core of the editing process. So finish your shoot, gather your footage, and prepare a comfortable chair. The real filmmaking takes place in the edits.

# Chapter 9

## Power Editing Basics: Using Adobe Premiere Pro

## How to...

- Create a sequence in Premiere Pro
- Photoshop your sequence
- Make a video using a layered Photoshop file
- Import your sequence into your video
- Export your video using Adobe Media Encoder

Sometimes simpler software applications just don't cut the mustard. Even though your project is a simple two-minute tale, using a higher-end video editing program such as Adobe Premiere Pro may actually be easier than wrestling with a program with limited capabilities such as Windows Movie Maker.

You do not have to become an expert, or exploit all the sophisticated tools available to you, when you're using Premiere Pro, although you always have that option. (Whether you have the *time* to learn it all is another question entirely.) The thing is, once you become even the least bit comfortable using the higher-end application, it becomes your go-to destination for even the simplest of tasks. The versatility of Premiere Pro's tools and output is an attractive feature. You may find yourself going back to Movie Maker and feeling as though your hands are tied, your ankles hobbled. Try working like that. Fuggetaboudit!

The fact is, the professional tools only look daunting until you start to use them. Then they open up and allow you to do magic. So let's do some prestidigitation.

# Get Familiar with Premiere Pro's Interface

Let's go over the basics of the workspace. While it is modular, the default layout for Premiere Pro and many other nonlinear digital editing applications is broken up into panes and panels, as shown in Figure 9-1.

NOTE     *Non-linear digital editing means you can access any frame in a video at anytime. It is non-destructive, which means that you are never editing the original but an edit of the original. So no matter what you do, you can always revert to the untouched original.*

There are essentially five panes to the layout. Within each pane are tabbed panels. As you work, you'll be able to move any panel into any pane. So, for example, if you want to have the Effects panel, which by default is located in the lower-left pane, in the upper-left pane, you can just drag the Effects panel and place it there. The same, of course, goes for any of the panels. But there are also some you just won't want to move, for obvious space reasons. The Timeline panel, for instance, should remain where it is, in the bottom, central location.

The top, central location, by default, is the Source panel, as well as other more control-oriented panels. Let's call it the Control pane. This is where you'll find yourself doing a lot of the hands-on editing. But more of that in a minute.

To the right of the Control pane is the Preview pane. When you're previewing your film sequence, this is where you'll do that.

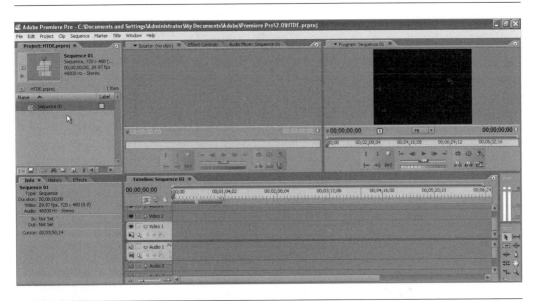

**FIGURE 9-1**   Premiere Pro's default layout

Below these panes are several and varied jog and edit controls, mainly to work with the Timeline.

# Make a Sequence

A *sequence*, in editing terms, is an ordered collection of clips, transitions, effects, and soundtrack in a particular timeline. You can have numerous sequences in your project, and when you're ready to output, you can join them together, on a timeline, or you can output each individually. In this section, we're going to cover the basics of creating a sequence in Premiere Pro. Let's begin by starting a new project, and then cover the basic elements of turning that project into a sequence.

## Start a New Project

When you first open Premiere Pro, you get to choose either an existing or a new project. If you're about to start a new project, as we are here, the choice should be obvious. Select New Project, and you're taken to the New Project window with the Load Preset tab displayed. Since we're working with online video, you can select a 16 × 9 aspect ratio. By default, it is a standard 4:3 ratio, as shown in Figure 9-2.

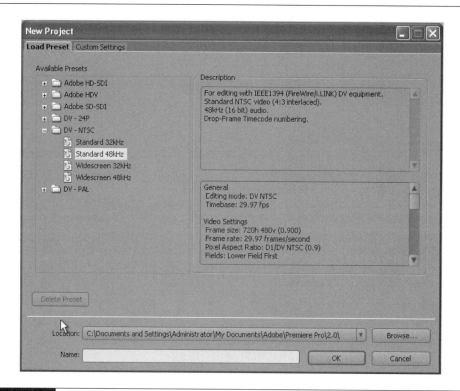

**FIGURE 9-2**   Presets: Each choice has a corresponding description to help you make the right decision.

NOTE

*The Load Preset tab offers myriad choices that affect the shape and output of your videos. The presets on this tab cover most types of video you'll find yourself working with.*

There are two main ways to get existing clips into a project. The first is to choose File | Import (CTRL-I), navigate to your media files, and then import the clips into the project. The other, more intuitive way is to simply double-click in the Project panel. The same navigation dialog box opens, letting you locate your files.

NOTE

*Any setting you make, either customized or preset, as well as any workspace configuration, can be saved as your own custom preset. The sidebar "Create and Save a Custom Workspace," later in the chapter, explains the basics.*

If your footage is still on DV tape on a camera, you can do a direct capture as well. Both audio and video files live together in the Project panel (see Figure 9-3).

**FIGURE 9-3**    Video and audio files are listed together in the Project panel.

## Prepare Clips for the Timeline

Now that we have imported our clips into our project, let's prepare our clips for the Timeline:

1. Double-click one clip in the Project panel. The clip opens in the Source panel.

2. Set your In and Out marks for the clip.

3. Scroll through the clip until you find your In mark. Press I or click the In marker in the bottom part of the Source panel.

4. To make your Out marker, press O or click the Out marker in the Source panel. For a closer look at the In and Out marker buttons, see Figure 9-4.

Repeat this process for several clips. Note that if you have more than one clip in your Project panel, you can SHIFT-click to select multiple clips, and then drag all of your selected clips into the Source panel. When you want to edit a particular clip, click the drop-down arrow in the Source panel and select the clip from the drop-down menu.

**FIGURE 9-4**    The cursor is hovering on the Out marker. The In marker is to the left.

## Put the Clips into the Timeline

After you've set your In and Out markers for a clip, drag the clip directly to the Video 1 track in the Timeline. The default mode for putting clips into the Timeline is Overlay. That means that if there were a clip already present, by dragging directly over that clip, you would be dropping your new clip on top of that existing one.

Dragging directly from the Source panel to the Timeline is fine for the first clip. But if you have an existing clip in the Timeline that you don't want to overlay with your new clip, then you need to use Insert mode, which involves pressing the CTRL key while you drag the new clip from the Source panel to the Timeline. This inserts the new clip next to the existing clip, keeping them both on the same track, both in sequence.

Figure 9-5 shows a clip being added in Inserted mode (CTRL-drag) rather than Overlay mode. Use this method to drag several clips from the Source panel into the Timeline.

## Order Clips Within the Timeline

After you have a bunch of clips in your timeline, you may find that they aren't in the correct order. Using a similar drag-and-drop technique, with the Insert and Overlay modes, you can easily reorder your clips.

Suppose, for instance, that you have three clips in your timeline but they're out of order: your second clip should be third, and the third should be first. The solution is simple:

1. In the Timeline, click and hold the top portion of the third clip, where you see the clip's name.

2. Drag the clip upward from the Video 1 track into the Video 2 track. Do not release the clip yet.

3. Drag the clip to the very beginning of the Timeline and position it back in Video 1, just before the first clip. If you were to release now, you'd overwrite the existing clip. Remember, the default setting is Overlay mode.

4. Instead of releasing the clip, first press the CTRL key. You will note that the insertion icon appears. Now release the clip. The clips will move to the right, making room for your inserted clip.

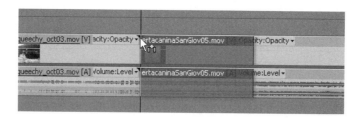

**FIGURE 9-5**     Inserting a clip without overlaying the existing clip

| FIGURE 9-6 | Insert clip controls

If you don't feel comfortable using the drag-and-drop method, there are also controls in the Source panel that let you do the exact same thing. What you must remember is to place the playhead in the Timeline in the correct position, and then select one of the insert buttons (found to the right of the playhead controls in the Source panel, as shown in Figure 9-6). You can insert or overlay from these controls.

## Extract Clips from the Timeline

If we're working in the Timeline and we have a few clips out of our preferred order, we can extract clips and replace them in correct positions. Suppose we have a clip in the middle of our sequence and we want to move it to another position. Let's say, for simplicity's sake, that we want to take the clip and move it to the very beginning of our sequence.

If we just grab the clip and drag it up and out of the Timeline, that's what's known as a *lift*. It certainly takes the clip out of that track, but it leaves a gap where it once resided, as shown in the example in Figure 9-7, where queechy_oct03.mov is being lifted, leaving a gap in the Timeline.

We don't want to have a gap like that in our timeline, so we are going to do something slightly different. When we begin our lift, we hold the CTRL key, and the space is automatically closed by the clip to the right of our extracted clip, as shown in Figure 9-8. That's called an *extraction*.

Keep holding down the CTRL key after you extract the clip and then insert the clip at the beginning of the sequence. All the clips shift to the right in the Timeline to make room for the inserted clip, and we have a gapless sequence.

| FIGURE 9-7 | Lifting a clip from the Timeline (which leaves a gap)

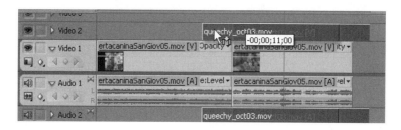

**FIGURE 9-8**    Extracting a clip from the Timeline (which fills the gap)

## Adjust Your In and Out Marks

After you've repositioned your clips, if you find that your In and Out points in a clip aren't exactly where they should be to best tell your story, you can adjust them on-the-fly.

Using the CTRL key, you can extend or curtail the In and Out points while still in the Timeline. This is called a *ripple* edit. Hold down the CTRL key, position your cursor over the edge or end of a particular clip, and drag it either to the right or left, depending on whether you want to extend or cut into the length of the clip. The adjacent clips shift over without leaving a gap. Figure 9-9 shows an example of a ripple edit in progress.

NOTE    *Having extra footage on either end of the clip, referred to as a mane and tail in the previous chapter, gives you more versatility in ripple edits. Ripple edits are real-time edits done by dragging along the clip, usually holding the CTRL key at the same time. They allow us to shorten or lengthen our clips in the Timeline without having to revert back to the Source panel.*

If you forget to hold the CTRL key while performing a ripple edit, the Timeline reacts as if you were extracting a clip. In other words, you'll create a gap on the Timeline. You may do so intentionally, of course, but be aware that if you do it by accident, you can easily rectify the mistake simply by undoing the action, by pressing CTRL-Z.

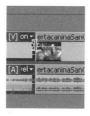

**FIGURE 9-9**    Ripple editing In and Out points

By repositioning and then editing your clips, you can get a real-time sense of how to make your video as powerful and clear as possible. If you still have your storyboard from the shoot, you may want to refer to it as well during the editing process. Even if your final footage doesn't cohere exactly to the storyboard, it may still act as a jumping off or reference point for your video's continuity.

## Add and Adjust Transitions

Once you've figured out the basic edits for your timeline, you'll want to think about transitions between your clips. The trick to transitions is to keep them simple. Sure, you can always go the cheesy route, with page flips, 3-D cubes rotating, and star-shaped irises or wipes. But that stuff is distracting. And if it doesn't add anything to your video, then it's extra baggage. It's visual baggage. Transitions should be simple.

Adobe Premiere Pro comes loaded with transitions. If you look in the Effects panel, under Video Transitions, you'll see several folders containing various types of transitions, as shown in Figure 9-10. In your editing work, you'll more than likely want to explore all of these transitions, but after you've played around with them, you'll likely settle on one or two as stalwart go-to transitions for the overwhelming majority of times you need them.

NOTE    *The most used and useful (read simple) transition is Cross Dissolve, which overlaps and fades from one clip to the next. If the clip is at the beginning of the sequence, without any other clips before it, then Cross Dissolve acts as a fade-in transition. If you place it at the end of a sequence, it acts as a fade-out transition.*

**FIGURE 9-10**    Premier Pro provides a host of video transitions.

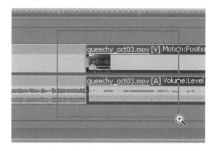

Magnifying the work area

## Apply a Transition

To apply a transition to either a single clip or a pair of clips, you first should increase the magnification on the area of the Timeline where you plan to apply the transition. This will make the whole process much easier. Increasing the magnification is easy. In the bottom-right corner of the workspace, there is a Tools panel containing a number of editing tools. Click the magnifying glass icon to open the Zoom tool. Now, just as with any other graphics application, to use the Zoom tool, you click the Timeline in the spot that you wish to concentrate on (magnify) and then drag out to select an area, as shown in the example in Figure 9-11.

Now that you have a clear and up-close view of the clips, you can more easily apply a transition. The default transition for Premiere Pro is—you guessed it—Cross Dissolve. The easiest way to apply this transition is to place the playhead at the point where you want the transition to occur, and press CTRL-D. If you place the playhead at the beginning of the sequence, then you'll get the fade-in effect I spoke of earlier.

Once you've applied a transition, you can check it in the Program panel in the upper right of the default workspace. Press the SPACEBAR, or click the Play button in the Program panel controls.

## Drag and Drop Transitions

Dragging and dropping transitions is almost as easy as applying transitions in the method described above. Again, you'll find all the transitions in the Effects panel. The Cross Dissolve transition is located, obviously, in the Dissolve folder. You can use any transition you like, frankly. I just chose Cross Dissolve because it is the most basic, least-apparent transition in the collection.

Select the transition you want, and drag it directly onto the Timeline at the point where you want it to occur. The cursor lets you know when it's possible to successfully drop the transition in place (cursor will change its form). When you do drop a transition in this manner, however, the duration of the transition might not be long enough for your needs. This is where it's important to have a magnified view of the Timeline. Up close, you will be able to ripple edit the transition longer or shorter according to your needs (see Figure 9-12).

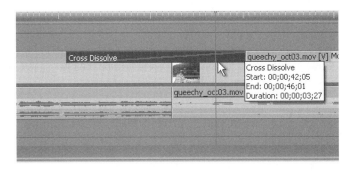

**FIGURE 9-12**   Ripple editing a transition. Here we are applying a cross dissolve.

## Adjust Transitions with the Effect Controls Panel

If you want to adjust your transitions further, double-click the transition icon in the Timeline. This opens the Effect Controls panel just above the Timeline panel. The Effect Controls panel gives you a variety of frame-by-frame details and control, with an A/B configuration so that you can see the clips in direct reference to one another. Figure 9-13 shows a basic view of the Effect Controls panel.

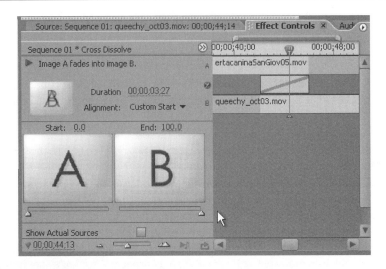

**FIGURE 9-13**   A/B clips and transition control

In the panel, you can change the overall duration of the transition by inputting numbers into the Duration readout, or you can drag the ripple edit controls and adjust it that way.

If you are working on one transition in the Effect Controls panel, you can easily change over to control another transition simply by selecting the other transition in the Timeline. The Effect Controls panel remains open, but the transition you control will be the one selected below in the Timeline.

## Apply Audio Transitions

We've thus far added transitions to the video, but we can just as easily add transitions for audio as well. Applying audio transitions works in very much the same way as applying video transitions. Rather than dragging a video Dissolve transition onto a clip, for example, you can instead go to the Effects panel (*not* the Effect Controls panel, but the panel on the left) and open the Audio Transitions folder.

Drag an audio Crossfade to the Timeline. Just as with the Cross Dissolve video transition, if you apply the crossfade audio transition to the first frame, it will fade in, and if you apply it to the end of a sequence, it will fade out, fading the audio to nil.

In the Timeline, you can press the CTRL key and ripple edit your audio track in the same way you ripple edit your video clips.

A big difference here from applying a default transition as we do with standard video clips, is instead of CTRL-D, we press CTRL-SHIFT-D to automatically drop in a crossfade audio transition.

NOTE    *CTRL-SHIFT-D automatically adds the default crossfade audio transition to your audio track where you put the playhead.*

Premiere Pro treats digital transitions of all types in the same way, but the transitions affect only their like kind: audio transitions affect only audio, and video transitions affect only video.

# Add Effects

This section explains how to add effects to your timeline by presenting the specific example of applying color correction. The process is pretty much the same for the application of any effect, so once you understand the first principles of the process, you should have no trouble applying any other effects.

## Correct Color

Recall that in Chapter 8 I discussed white balance control while shooting your video, and how to ensure that your original footage has the correct color tones and cast. I discussed basic lighting, and how to compensate for ambient light by using the so-called white balance controls on your capture device—essentially letting your camera know what it should regard as white, so that it has a point of reference to profile all other colors, lights, shadows, and such. Even in the best conditions, however, color on video won't be completely consistent. From one shot to the next, the light may change, with the colors gaining a particular hue or cast. We'll take it as axiomatic that clips need color adjustment. But fortunately, color correction in Premiere Pro is as easy as applying transitions.

In the Effects panel, you'll find the Video Effects folder. There are many effects from which to choose, but we are going to concentrate on color correction:

1. Drill down to the Color Correction folder and find Fast Color Corrector.

2. Drag the Fast Color Corrector effect over any of your video clips in the Timeline.

3. Look at the Effect Controls panel (above the Timeline panel, not the panel to the left), and you'll see a triangle next to the Fast Color Corrector folder. Click the triangle.

4. A color wheel and various other color-specific adjustments will appear. At this point, you may want to reassess your basic working layout. See the "How to Create and Save a Custom Workspace" sidebar for instructions.

5. In the Effect Controls panel, click the eyedropper icon next to the White Balance sample.

6. Drag the eyedropper over the preview image on the right, and find a point in it that should signify absolute white. Click at that point. Note two things here: the shift in colors in your preview, and the White Balance sample box in the Effect Controls panel.

7. To make sure you can make the best adjustments, check the Show Split View check box in the Effect Controls panel.

8. Now look at your preview. It will have the new color adjustment on the left side or, if you chose a horizontal split, on the top, and the original color scheme on the alternate side.

One last step after white balance is to make sure that the Black point in the clip is what you want it to be as well. Scroll down in the Effect Controls panel to the Auto Black Level and click. Or, you can follow the same procedure we ran through with the White Balance eyedropper, only this time use the Black Level eyedropper.

## Apply Adjustments Consistently

You can apply these adjustments to each clip on your sequence. If you want to be consistent in each clip, there are two easy ways to go about this:

■ Click the Fast Color Corrector tab in the Effect Controls panel and press CTRL-C. This copies those settings to the clipboard. Find the next clip in the Timeline, select it with your cursor, and press CTRL-V, or paste the correction directly to the clip.

> TIP    *If you're following along here, you'll note the uniformity in processes. If you can copy and paste the color effect, then you can copy and paste any video effect.*

■ Make a preset. Right-click the Fast Color Corrector tab in the Effect Controls panel and choose Save Preset, as shown in Figure 9-14. Give the preset a name and save it.

# How to ... Create and Save a Custom Workspace

You can have as many workspace presets as you like in Premiere Pro. Sometimes it's a good idea to have specific workspaces for specific tasks. For example, instead of working in the standard and somewhat cramped default workspace, you can set up a workspace specifically for the color correction adjustment:

1. Place your cursor on the Effect Controls panel tab and drag the panel to the far left. It should reposition and lock into place over the original Project panel.

2. Make any adjustments you like to make sure that the Program panel is large enough for you to see clearly and yet still have easy access to the Effect Controls panel on the left.

3. When you're satisfied with your setup, choose Window | Workspace | Save Workspace.

4. Name your new layout something like Color Correction and click Save.

You've now made your very own preset, which you will be able to access via the Window | Workspace menu path at any time in the future.

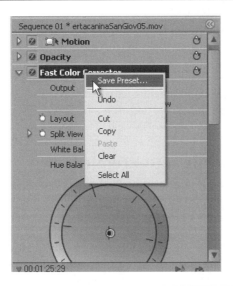

**FIGURE 9-14**    Saving adjustments as a preset

You will now be able to apply your color adjustments as a universal preset, by locating the preset in the Presets folder of the Effects panel (*not* the Effect Controls panel). You can now use this preset as a simple drag-and-drop effect to ensure color continuity between all your shots.

# Photoshop Your Sequence

One of the great features of Adobe products nowadays is their increased integration with one another. We're dealing primarily with Premiere Pro in this chapter, but I would be remiss if I didn't mention its integration with Photoshop. So, even after you've shot and collected all of your footage and put it into sequence in Premiere Pro, you might go back to your storyboard and realize that you could punch things up with a few stills and maybe some simple animation. Hence, Photoshop.

Premiere Pro can take layered Photoshop documents, import them into clip sequences, and animate each layer. What that really means is you can make nice title plates and introduce basic panning text or colors or images—whatever you have on separate layers in Photoshop—and make them a part of your video.

This is sophistication on the cheap. Before we do anything, let's reset our workspace to the default, which you will find under Window | Workspace | Editing. Now our workspace should have the Project panel on the left, the Source panel in the top center, and the Program panel on the right.

## Start with a Photoshop File

Let's start with a layered Photoshop document, or image as it were. Perhaps a still from the shoot. On the background layer, you have your basic image. One layer above that, you could have text, on another layer you could have a title, and on yet another layer you could have a gradient. The image that you use is up to you, but make sure that the Photoshop file is the same size and aspect ratio as your video. So if you're going for 640 × 480 pixels, make sure the image is that size.

Create the image and save it in its native Photoshop format, with layers intact. With that ready, we can look at how to bring that file into Premiere Pro and make it work as a separate animated sequence.

## Import a Photoshop File into Premiere Pro

This section assumes that you have already created a layered Photoshop file. Depending on how you're set up to work in Premiere Pro affects how you go about importing the file.

If you're working with Premiere Pro as part of the complete Adobe Creative Suite 2 or 3, you'll probably want to use the Adobe Bridge application. Adobe Bridge is a sort of digital holding tank and resource reservoir for all types of image and motion files. You can use it to sort images, movies, and other assets (like PDFs), order them, get info, and finally import them into and share them throughout the Creative Suite of applications. It has extensive search tools as well, so if you can't remember where you left your files, a quick search and drill down of your system through Bridge's search functions will most probably find the asset.

If you're running Premiere Pro as a stand-alone application, you can locate your assets the old-fashioned way. That is, from within Premiere Pro, select File | Import and then navigate to your file.

Whichever method you use, the result is the same: you'll find your Photoshop file and select it for import. When you do choose the Import File, the Import Layered File dialog box appears, shown in Figure 9-15. In the Import As drop-down list box, you need to choose in what format you would like to import the file.

Since we're importing a layered file, one that we plan to animate, choose Sequence.

NOTE    *Select Footage for single-layer files, stills, or untouched video.*

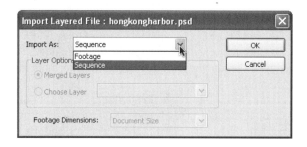

**FIGURE 9-15**    Choose the Sequence import option.

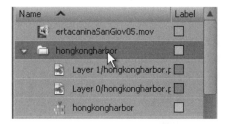

**FIGURE 9-16**    Imported sequence in Premiere Pro

After the layered Photoshop file is imported into Premiere Pro, you'll find it in your Project panel, not as a single file but as a folder. Inside the folder you will find every layer as a separate file (see Figure 9-16), and one extra Sequence file.

Double-click the Sequence file. A new sequence opens in the Timeline, with each of the constituent layers as separate simultaneous tracks. Switch your Source panel to the back by selecting the Effect Controls panel. In the Timeline, you should see all layers as clips. You should see your file in the Program panel on the right, with the effects that govern that clip displayed in the Effect Controls panel.

## Work with Motion and Opacity

Now we can pay attention to two resident effects that we ignored in the previous section. You may have noticed the Motion and Opacity controls in the Effect Controls panel. Now we get to use them.

Take a glance at Figure 9-17. The top track has the text overlay and the bottom track has our base image.

1.  Select the text track (refer to the example in Figure 9-17).

2.  In the Effect Controls panel, select and open the Motion effect. When you select the Motion effect, note the transform anchor points that surround the layer, visible in the Program panel on the right.

3.  In the Timeline, move the playhead all the way to the left.

4.  In the Program panel, drag your text off the visible area all the way to the left.

**FIGURE 9-17**    Our imported sequence in the Timeline

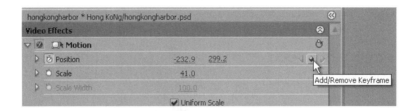

FIGURE 9-18    Toggle keyframes

5.  In the Position control, toggle the small icon to the left of the word Position. This assigns a keyframe to the layer. When you toggle the small Position button on, you also see a keyframe icon on the right, as shown in Figure 9-18.

6.  In the Timeline, move the playhead to midway through the clip.

7.  Make sure to select the Motion effect in the Effect Controls panel, and then do one of three things:

    ▪  In the Program panel, drag the text to the preferred position in the frame.

    ▪  Position your cursor over the numeric controls in the Effect Controls panel and scrub the text to the original position.

    ▪  Click the Reset button in the upper-right corner of the Motion control.

Now you see a tracking line that shows you the movement the text will make during its animation, or movement over time, as shown in Figure 9-19.

That's it. Click Play and watch how the text animates into frame. This is the basic process for creating animation. You can adjust things further with scale and opacity as well. You can make each layer animate independently of the others. Again, the controls are simple. The choices are yours.

FIGURE 9-19    The animation path

# Import the Sequence into Your Video

With the animation finished, you'll want to bring it into your existing video. We'll use it as a title clip, in this instance. The animated sequence can now be treated as a complete clip in itself.

We already know how to add clips to a timeline sequence from earlier in the chapter. We can select the sequence from the Project panel and CTRL-drop it on the sequence, or we can CTRL-drag it from our Source panel and drop it on the sequence.

To open our animated sequence within our main sequence, do the following:

1.  Open the main video sequence for the project.

2.  In the Project panel, CTRL-click the animated sequence. It opens in the Source panel, but still *within* the main sequence.

3.  Now you can CTRL-drop the animated sequence on the main sequence timeline. Refer to Figure 9-20 to see how you're still in the main sequence but dropping the animated sequence in.

**FIGURE 9-20**   CTRL-drop the animated sequence into your main sequence.

This is a nice way to add dramatic and simple titles and effects. But Premiere Pro also has a dedicated titling engine, as described in the "How to Add Titles with the Titler" sidebar.

## How to ...   Add Titles with the Titler

Before you access the Titler, position your playhead in the Timeline in the position you want your titles to begin. The Titler is sort of hidden. You can access it via the Project panel, in the series of small icons situated at the bottom of the panel. Find and click the New Item icon (it looks like a page turning). In the New Item drop down, select Title. The Titler opens, showing the frame where you positioned the playhead. Click inside the frame to position your text tool. The interface for the Titler is pretty simple.

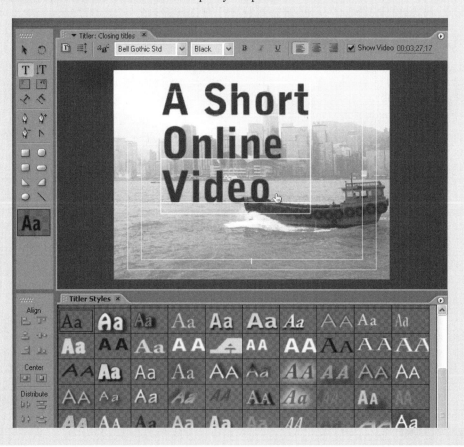

Choose from the array of Titler Styles and then type your title. You can change the style by selecting the text and clicking a new style. When you're finished, close the Titler window. Premiere Pro treats your title as a part of the project, and you'll find it in the Project panel. You can apply it to the sequence by dragging and dropping it into the sequence, and you can apply movement and opacity to it in much the same way as you would apply them to any clip element.

You can also create animated titles using a preset. Often, you'll want to have what's known as a *crawl*, where the credits roll from the top to the bottom of the frame. The easiest way to do this is to choose Title | New Title | Default Crawl.

The Titler will open, but this time it will be animated for you. Again, once you're finished with the specific information in the Titler, you'll be able to drop your titles directly onto the Timeline in the appropriate spot.

# Export Your Video with Adobe Media Encoder

This section assumes that you've finished assembling your sequence and are ready to wrap up your video and put it into the correct format for online viewing. That means you've put your clips in order, given the clips appropriate transitions, added effects, added a soundtrack using the same method as you would adding clips and effects, and written and applied your credits and titles. Fade in, fade out, everything is in place. It's time to put your baby into the world at large.

This is the easiest thing you'll do all day. Select File | Export | Adobe Media Encoder. The Adobe Media Encoder lets you get a sample of what the video quality of your output will be in

## Codec Means Compression/ Decompression

Here's a really dumb and inaccurate way of analogizing what a codec does. Think of your digital video file as a balloon filled with air. You don't want to transport the balloon filled up, so you want to deflate it, put it in your pocket, and then reinflate it when you get to the party where you are the clown act. Essentially, codecs determine the way a digital video file is squeezed and then reinflated. There are many ways to do it, some *lossy*, meaning they give up some information, and some not so lossy, or *lossless*. Choosing a codec can be like trying to have a dinner conversation with a software engineer. You end up nodding your head a lot, and trying to change the subject to one you both can understand. If he says you should try this instead of that, you just take him at his word. Choosing a codec is very much like that, only a lot less painful and uncomfortable. Most codec's are explained in brief in the software or, at the very least, labeled as better for achieving some things than others.

**FIGURE 9-21** Output and Source tabs in Adobe Media Encoder

a real sense. The Encoder presents two main tabs, one for your Source and the other for Output (see Figure 9-21). The codec settings are to the right of the preview.

At this point, you choose the file format and the various settings for your video. As with virtually all of the settings in Premiere Pro, you can also customize them and create your own presets. But for now, it's a good idea to look at what Adobe has available. Figure 9-22 shows what to expect.

**NOTE** *If you experiment, you may find that MPEG is a good way to go. It keeps the clarity of the source, and gives you many size variations.*

When you're happy with your settings, click OK and save the file to your Desktop. The default name of the file will be the name of the sequence. Of course, you should name your file whatever you decide to name your video.

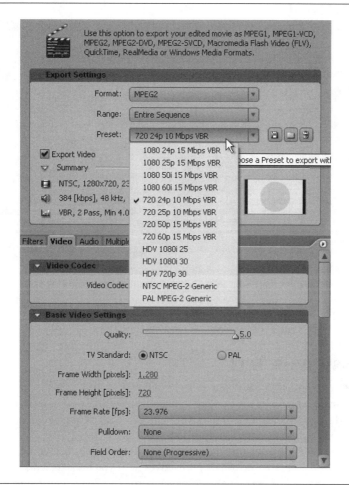

**FIGURE 9-22**    Presets for export

## Opt for Simple Export

Another quick and easy way to export your finished video sequence into a usable format is found under File | Export | Movie (or CTRL-M). Choosing this route, you are immediately greeted with a dialog box for saving the file. Choose settings before you do anything else. In the ensuing Settings dialog box, shown in Figure 9-23, you can select from among many presets for format, size, compression, and more.

When you finally find the settings that work best (QuickTime, for most online video uploads), click OK and save your file to your Desktop. Refer to Chapter 3 for the various choices for upload.

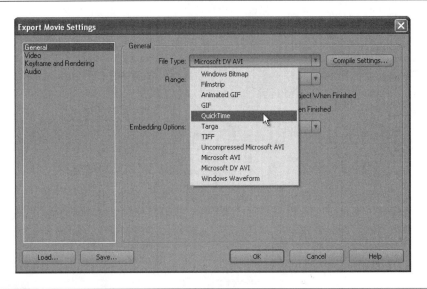

**FIGURE 9-23**    The easy way out. As we know, QuickTime is a great format from which most of the other online formats can be specified.

# Are We Professionals Yet?

In this chapter, we went through a basic *how to use Premiere Pro to edit* path. I didn't tell you what choices to make on which clips, how long to make your video, or whether you should do a hard cut or not. I didn't go into the high end of After Effects, with chroma key compositing and CGI effects. That is all beyond the scope of this book.

What I did do was give you a leg up on a very powerful tool that, once you start working with it, will open itself to you in ways you can't discover until you do start working. But, hopefully, I also gave you enough knowledge to be dangerous. If you become familiar and comfortable with the way this program works, the way it sees assets and editing, and the intrinsically nondestructive method it lets you use to explore and experiment, there's no going back. There's no going back to handcuffing your skills and your vision by using something like Movie Maker. There's no going back to saying, "I'll just take a poor-quality video and leave it at that." The only direction to go is forward. The only path to take is improvement. And the only venue to make it happen, of course, is online.

The difference between the amateur and the professional is not so much what gear they have available, but rather what vision and skill they apply to using whatever gear is on hand. As you explore your own vision, and work with editing applications like the one discussed in this chapter, you'll begin to hone your skills and create better video. It's not in the gear. It's in your choices.

# Chapter 10

## Power Editing Basics: Using Final Cut Express HD

## How to ...

- Find your way around the interface
- Load clips into Final Cut
- Preview and trim
- Apply clips to a sequence
- Edit in the timeline
- Apply transitions and effects
- Work in LiveType
- Add and edit audio
- Finalize production

Sometimes simpler software applications just aren't sufficient to enable you to achieve the results you want in your video. Even though your project is a simple two-minute tale, using a higher-end video editing program such as Apple's Final Cut, whether Final Cut Express HD or Final Cut Pro, may actually be easier than wrestling with a program with limited capabilities such as iMovie (HD or '08).

Because Final Cut Express HD offers everything you need for online video, and everything you need to learn the basics of power editing, we're not going to examine Final Cut Pro. If you decide to go the extra mile and dive into Final Cut Pro, you'll find that the basic tools and interface, as well as the workflow, are pretty much the same between Express and Pro.

This chapter teaches you a basic work process in Final Cut Express HD so that you can edit and deploy your video with professional tools and a professional look. After you become even the least bit comfortable using this higher-end program, it might very well become your go-to destination for even the simplest of tasks. The versatility of Final Cut Express HD's tools and output is an attractive feature. If you're familiar with iMovie HD, then you should adapt to this level of editing pretty quickly. Even if you've never bothered with the lower end and are diving in right here and now, you shouldn't have too much trouble. The fact is, the professional tools only look daunting until you start to use them. With a specific goal in mind, you'll find that using these tools will become almost second nature.

# Get Familiar with Final Cut Express HD's Interface

Unlike iMovie, which has one large preview window and a clip well and control panel, Final Cut Express HD has a professional-level interface, shown in Figure 10-1, with a Viewer window and a Canvas window. To the left of these two windows is the tabbed Browser window, which holds all the video and audio assets you bring into the project.

Below these windows is the all-important Timeline. The Timeline is itself broken up vertically into the Video tracks portion in the upper half and the Audio tracks portion in the lower half.

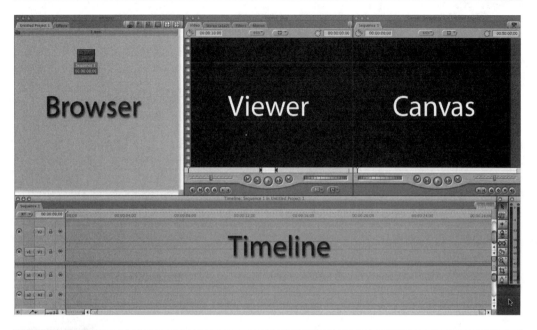

Browser    Viewer    Canvas

Timeline

**FIGURE 10-1**    The basic Final Cut Express HD workspace

The Browser and Viewer windows are where you do most of the organization of your video. Essentially, think of the workflow for Final Cut Express HD as a clockwise path, starting with the Browser, which is where you store your raw footage:

1. Access your footage in the Browser.

2. Drag the footage you want to view and edit to the center Viewer window. Find and assign your In and Out points.

3. Add your footage to your sequence by dragging it to the Canvas on the right. Preview your footage in the Canvas, which automatically puts it in the Timeline.

4. Edit your sequence in the Timeline.

We'll go through this process in more depth in the following sections.

# Load Clips into the Browser

Upon opening, Final Cut Express HD always asks you for a direct connection to your preferred capture device. In other words, if you took your video footage with a camcorder to a mini-DV tape, you will want to plug that camera into your Mac via FireWire before you open Final Cut Express HD. This direct connection downloads your information with time codes intact from the shoot.

## Did you know?

# You May Need to Stripe Your Tape

Time codes are pretty important when you're dealing with higher-end video editing. Sometimes it's a good idea to do what's known as *striping* your tape. Every tape comes with a sort of built-in time code, starting from when you begin taping. If you're using a tape that's been used before, your time code may be set already, and it may not jibe with the time code of the project in the particular software you will be using. When you stripe a tape, you erase that time code and set it at a universal zero. But you have to do this before you use the tape, not after. In order to stripe a tape, you need to keep a lens cap on your camera, shut off any audio input, and let the tape record darkness and silence for the length of the tape. What you are really doing here is establishing a time code for the tape. Everything put on the tape from then on will be according to the tape's time code.

There are other ways to replace DV time code, if you don't have a stripped tape. You can connect a tape with data on it to another tape recorder, and connect the two recorders, and dub the original tape onto a zeroed-out tape. But once again, you should try to start out with striped tape before you do any shooting. It may not be essential in a short video, but it makes life easier all around.

If you already have your footage on your hard drive, because it came from alternate sources, then all you have to do is import the files into the Final Cut Express HD project. Choose File | Import and navigate through your system to find the footage. You can select either single files or folders. Importing files in this manner brings them directly to the bins (folders) panel of the Browser window.

If you haven't named your project before you import files, Final Cut Express HD asks you to do so. You must have a name for the project to enable Final Cut Express HD to successfully import your files. As soon as you do, your files will reside in a bin in the Browser, which will have a tab emblazoned with the name you just assigned for the project.

In the upper-right corner of the Browser is a button bar that you can use, instead of key commands or shortcuts, to launch your most commonly used actions. You can customize the buttons, or just leave the defaults. To customize the button bar, choose Tools | Button List. In the Button List, shown in Figure 10-2, you'll find a myriad of choices for each category of use within Final Cut Express HD.

You probably won't want to customize the button bar until you've spent some time working in Final Cut Express HD. But you should be aware of this option when you get to the point that your wrist is sore from repetitively changing some formatting option in the Timeline or opening files. Make the action a button and speed up your workflow. You simply select from the Button List the action you want to assign to a button and drag it to the button bar.

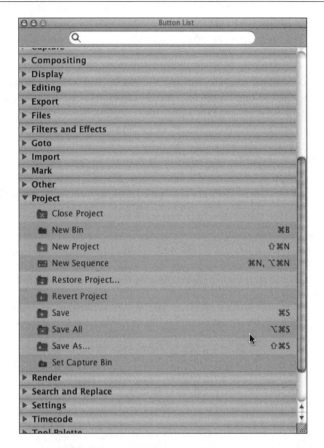

**FIGURE 10-2**    Choosing the button function

# Preview and Trim Clips in the Viewer

The Viewer is where you'll spend a lot of your time. This is where you preview the raw footage and apply your In and Out markers. The Viewer has four default tabs: the Video tab, which is the default position, the Audio tab, which is set to Stereo by default, the Filters tab, and the Motion tab. We're going to work with the Video tab here, and we'll use the Audio tab later in the chapter.

If you double-click a video file in the Browser, it opens in the Video tab of the Viewer. Once it is in the Viewer, you can watch the footage from any point by dragging the play arrow and clicking the Play button, or you can use the shuttle control (on the left) to scrub through the footage. For more precise control, the jog tool on the bottom right lets you go frame by frame.

*You can press the SPACEBAR on the keyboard to initiate the video play. Alternatively, you can use the L key to start the clip, the K key to stop the clip, and the J key to move the clip in reverse. If you press a key repeatedly, you can change the speed of the playback up to eight times normal speed.*

Note the two time codes in the upper bar of the Video tab. The one on the right shows you where you are in the footage; the one on the left, the duration code, shows you the total length of the clip (or, as you define your In and Out points, the duration of your selection). In between those readouts is the video scale on the left (set by default to Fit in Window) and a guide drop-down button on the right. You will want to use the drop-down button later when you're applying titles or overlays. For now, you can leave it in its default state, Image. When you click the drop-down button, you also see options for Image + Wireframe, Show Overlays, and Show Title Safe, as shown in Figure 10-3. Keep Show Overlays activated and, if you don't find it distracting, activate Show Title Safe too.

NOTE    *The time code is represented by pairs of numbers separated by colons, or at the end a semicolon. Reading from right to left, these pairs are frames, then seconds, then minutes, and then hours, or hh:mm:ss;ff. So a time code of, say, 00:43:12;04 can be read as 43 minutes, 12 seconds, and frame 4.*

**FIGURE 10-3**    Activating Title Safe from the drop-down menu

Title Safe gives you guides that help you to ensure that your titles don't run offscreen. If you keep within the parameters of the guides, you can be sure that no matter the screen, the titles will read. We'll need this later when we apply titles and credits.

## Place In and Out Points

So, you've dragged your clip from the Browser bin, or just double-clicked it. It's in the Viewer. Play the clip (using the SPACEBAR is easy). Once you've watched the clip, decide where you want to have your In and Out points—in other words, determine which part you actually want in your video sequence.

The In and Out marker buttons are on the bottom portion of the Video tab, just under the shuttle control. You can designate your In and Out points by dragging the playhead to the precise point you want to place the In or Out point and then clicking either the In or the Out button. You can also use the I and O keys, respectively.

You can use one long clip as many times as you like in different instances, for different In and Out points. Once a clip is designated with In and Out points and then put into a sequence, you can adjust those specific In and Out points at any time, without disturbing other clips from the same footage. For instance, if you have one long take in one long clip, and you need parts of that same clip but they're not contiguous, or back to back, you can mark your clips with In and Out, put them in the Timeline (using a method I'll show you in a moment), and then mark others and put them in the sequence. On the Timeline, they work as separate clips, even though they're from the same source clip.

To summarize, here is how to mark your In and Out points:

1.  Scrub to a point near your intended In mark. When you are near it, within a few frames, use the jog tool to get to the precise frame you want.

2.  With your playhead at the precise frame, take note of the time code on the upper right of the Video panel and write it down.

3.  Press the I key (or click the In marker button). You'll see the marker in the playhead move to the In point.

4.  Play your video clip to the end point of the clip.

5.  Find the precise frame where it ends the clip you need.

6.  Press the O key (or click the Out marker button).

Note in the progress bar that your clip is now framed on either side by markers. Figure 10-4 gives you an idea of what that looks like.

**FIGURE 10-4**    A clip area with In and Out points

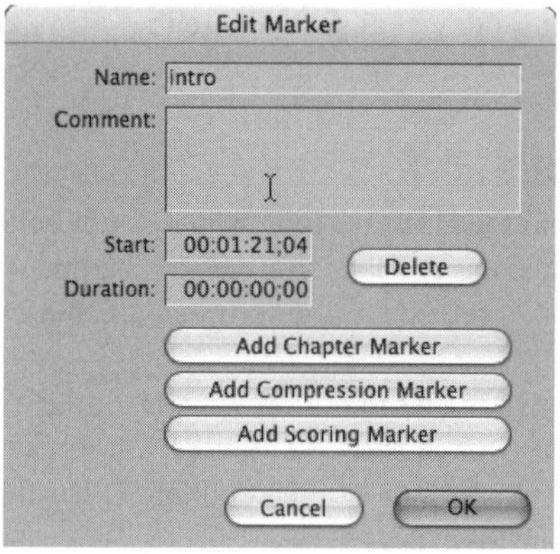

**FIGURE 10-5**    Marker choices

## Place Markers

Now that you've designated your In and Out points, there is one additional bit of housekeeping you may want to do: put a marker on each point. That way, if you accidentally drag your playhead off to the left and hit the I key again, you can always retrieve your originally intended marks.

There are other, more important reasons for making a marker, as well. When you have a marker, you can use it as a reference point for scoring a soundtrack, for adding a Chapter Marker (if you want to put your video on a DVD), and for simple organization later on.

Placing markers is as easy as placing In and Out points:

1. Position your playhead on the In point and press M on your keyboard.

2. Press M again. An Edit Marker dialog box opens so that you can name your marker and give it other designations, as shown in Figure 10-5.

You now have a clip with In and Out points and some markers. It's time to put this clip to work. We want to put it on the Timeline and make it part of our video sequence.

# Apply Clips to the Sequence in the Canvas

You could just drag your clips directly to the Timeline, but if you were to do that, you'd be cheating yourself out of some control and some editing options. So instead of acting wildly without reasonor rule, shouting ya-hoowhile and waving your mouse-free hand in the air, choose the more sophisticated, demure, and professional method. Drag your selected clip from the Video panel to the right and drop it in the Canvas.

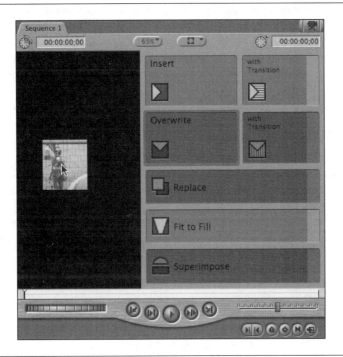

FIGURE 10-6    Applying your clip to the Timeline via the Canvas

Let's take a quick look at the Canvas, shown in Figure 10-6. At first glance it seems to mirror the Video panel of the Viewer from the previous section. For instance, the jog control, which was on the right side of the Video panel, is on the left side in the Canvas. Likewise, the shuttle control mirrors that of the Video panel, residing here on the right.

The time code readouts at the top of the Canvas, however, are in the same configuration as those found in the Video panel. On the left is the duration readout, which tells the complete length of time for the entire sequence, not just for the one clip. And the time code on the right reads out the playhead position in the entire sequence—again, not just within the selected clip.

The Canvas is a representation of your entire video sequence. Its controls refer to the Timeline, not to the clips. Whenever you click Play while working in the Timeline, you see your video sequence in the Canvas.

So why, then, do we not drag our clips directly into the Timeline? Follow along here and you'll see why. Select your clip in the Video panel and *slowly* drag it across to the Canvas. As your mouse drag enters the Canvas window's space, a group of command areas automatically appears, as shown in Figure 10-6.

Each of the colored areas represents a method of applying your clip to the Timeline. This is sort of a built-in shortcut.

By default, if you were to drag your clip to the Timeline directly, you'd do so as an insert. But when you drag your clip to the sequence via the Canvas, you have more choices. You can choose Overlay, for instance, or Fit to Fill, or Replace, or Super Impose. (Super Impose becomes important later, when we make our titles and credits.) But more than that, note that you can also automatically insert or overlay your clip *with transitions*. (Transitions are discussed later in the chapter in the "Apply Transitions and Effects" section.)

# Edit Your Sequence in the Timeline

The Timeline represents the sequence of our video clips. It's where we do the majority of our editing. You have no doubt noted that I use the term *sequence* a lot here. In a video project, we can use as many sequences as we like and string them together before we output the video. But since we're really dealing with short video for online delivery, we'll probably be working with at most three or four sequences. In fact, most of the time, we'll just have one sequence. You can have up to 99 tracks of video and audio in a sequence. For our simple work here, we're using one video track and two audio (stereo) tracks (since we are just using the simple audio included on the clips).

When you create a new sequence, you'll see it as a tab on your Timeline. But we don't even have any clips on our Timeline yet, so let's put a few clips into our Timeline and get this sequence going:

NOTE    *A sequence, as you might remember from Chapter 9, is an ordered collection of clips, transitions, effects and soundtrack set in a timeline, and eventually ending up as your output video.*

1.  Load three or four clips into the Browser.

2.  Drag and drop those clips into the Viewer and create In and Out points in each clip.

3.  Drag each clip to the Canvas and drop them over the Insert area (refer to Figure 10-6). As you do this, each clip drops into the Timeline as well. The next clip will drop in directly after the previous clip. Notice that the playhead in the Timeline moves to the Out point of the clip that is dropped, as it is dropped, each time.

You can scrub the playhead (move quickly through your footage) in the Timeline anywhere you like, if you feel that the next clip you're loading into the sequence should go at a particular spot. It's also easy to move the playhead around the Timeline using the UP and DOWN arrows on the keyboard. Press the DOWN arrow to move forward to the end of the clip, or on to the end of the next clip. The UP arrow moves you back toward the beginning of the sequence. Pressing the SPACEBAR toggles the sequence to play or pause.

Did you know?

# Timeline Settings You Should Know

Playback is a very important aspect of the Timeline. In the upper-left corner of the Timeline, just below the tab name, you'll see the RT button. Clicking this button opens a drop-down menu of the RealTime playback settings. This setting is important for the quality of your playbacks, especially when working with effects. Most of the time, you should keep the setting at Unlimited RT, which, if your processor supports it, gives you greater latitude and on-the-spot dynamic playback, where Final Cut Express HD automatically adjusts the quality.

In the upper-right corner of the Timeline are two innocuous buttons. Place your cursor over them and the explanatory pop-up text of Linked Selection (left button) and Snapping (right button) appears. By default, these buttons are depressed. The Linked Selection button lets you work with a clip either with or without its linked audio. So, for instance, if you would like to overrun one clip's audio into the next clip's video, you can deselect the button and then ripple edit or curtail your video back. This button allows you to work with the audio or video portion of the clip on its own. The Snapping button, when depressed, enables the playhead to move along the Timeline from point to point with a magnetic movement, meaning that it snaps from one clip end to the next instead of moving along frame by frame.

TIP

*Depending on the speed of your processor, and the RAM you have installed, Final Cut Express HD might or might not do what's known as RealTime Rendering. When you drag the playhead in the Timeline, if you find that you get a warning signal and, instead of showing your video, the Canvas says Not Rendered, then your processor isn't employing RealTime Rendering. But you can get around that. Choose Sequence from the menu, and select the appropriate Render command. It may take a few minutes, but you'll soon have your sequence rendered and ready to go.*

Once you have your clips in the Timeline, you can start using the tools found in the editing palette on the right side of the Timeline. The editing palette, shown in Figure 10-7, can float anywhere on your workspace; it doesn't have to remain on the right. For most of your needs, you will just use the Selection tool, and maybe later the Roll Edit and Ripple Edit tools. Let's go over the tools quickly, in order starting from the top:

- ■ **Selection tool**   The first tool is the selection tool, which is the one you'll probably use the most.

- ■ **Edit Selection tools**   This is a group of tools that you can use to bring your specific clips into the Video panel, not the Canvas. You can just as easily use the basic Selection tool for any of these functions.

**FIGURE 10-7**    The editing palette

- **Select Track Forward tool**    This tool enables you to easily select clips from one point forward. Placing this tool on a point in the sequence and dragging it to the right selects that portion of the sequence.

- **Roll Edit and Ripple Edit tools**    The fourth tool icon includes both the Roll Edit and Ripple Edit tools. The Roll Edit tool affects two clips that share an edit point or abut each other. Using a roll edit means you can simultaneously adjust the Out point of the earlier clip and the In point of the following clip, without changing the overall length of the sequence. You're rolling the cut edit one way or the other. When you use the Roll Edit tool, the preview in the Canvas shows you both clips at once, so you can fine-tune your adjustments. The Ripple Edit tool, on the other hand, adjusts the length of the clip you are editing, and hence the overall length of the sequence. It's best to play with these tools to get a good understanding of the finer points they afford you.

- **Slip Edit and Slide Edit tools**    These tools, located on the fifth tool icon, simply enable you to make fine adjustments to a roll edit.

- **Razor Blade tool**    This tool enables you to cut a clip into two clips. The single razor works only on one track, but the double-razor works on all tracks.

- **Zoom tool**    Lets you adjust the scale of your Timeline.

- **Cropping tool**    Enables you to make adjustments to clips while working with motion effects and overlays.

- **Pen**    Enables you to make keyframes from motion effects.

Now that you have a basic idea of the tools available, let's move on to what we'll probably spend most of our time doing: making transitions and effects.

## Apply Transitions and Effects

Transitions are very important, as discussed throughout this book. The trick to transitions is to keep them simple. Sure, you can always go the cheesy route, with page flips, 3-D cubes rotating, and star-shaped irises or wipes, but that stuff is distracting. And if it doesn't add anything to your video, it's extra baggage. It's visual baggage. Keep transitions simple.

As I mentioned earlier, you can apply transitions automatically with your clips as you overlay or insert them into your sequence through the Edit Overlay, which are the choices that are presented to you (refer to Figure 10-6) as you drag the clip to the Canvas. We'll apply transitions to our sequence in a bit.

Alternatively, you can add your clips to the sequence, as described earlier, and then add transitions and effects. Let's take a look at the transitions and effects that we have available to us.

In the Browser, click the Effects tab, which is where the Video and Audio Transitions and Effects are located, as shown in Figure 10-8. Drill down through the various choices in the Video Transitions bin. The most commonly used transitions are found in the Dissolve, Iris, and Wipe folders. Again, remember to keep the transitions simple, not distracting. Make them fit the content. Choose appropriately. The best transitions are the ones you don't notice.

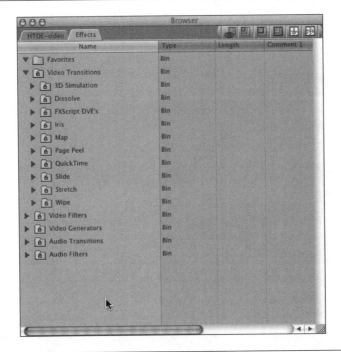

**FIGURE 10-8**    The Effects panel holds all the transitions and effects.

Applying an effect or transition to your sequence is easy:

1. In the Timeline, place the playhead at an edit point between two clips.

2. From the Effects panel in the Browser, select the Cross Dissolve transition.

3. Drag the Cross Dissolve transition directly to the Timeline and place it over the edit point so that its icon overlaps both clips.

4. To adjust the duration of the transition, double-click its icon. The transition appears in the Viewer, as shown in the example in Figure 10-9.

5. Place your cursor on one end point or another of the transition and drag it to make it longer or shorter. Check the Canvas on the right to see how it looks. (The buttons just above the transition can help you to find the center point or end points of the transition.)

**NOTE** *Removing transitions is just as easy as applying them. If you want to remove a transition, use the Selection tool to select the transition in the Timeline and then press the DELETE key.*

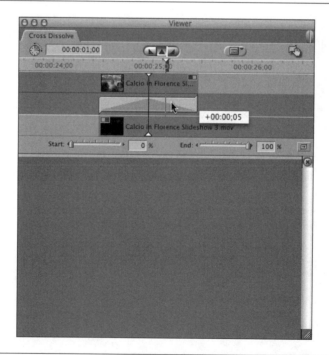

**FIGURE 10-9**　Adjust your transitions in the Viewer.

This same drag-and-drop and adjustment method works for video effects and filters. Select the clip in the Timeline and drag and drop the filter on your clip, and there it is.

You can also apply filters to part of a clip rather than to the whole thing. To do this, you need to use the Range Selection tool from the editing palette (one of the Edit Selection tools). Select the Range Selection tool and drag across a range, or area, of your clip in the Timeline. Now select Effect from the Effects tab of the Browser and either drag it directly on top of your selection, or choose Effects | Video Filters and select your filter from the choices there.

# Add Titles

Titling in Final Cut Express HD can be accomplished either within the application itself or by using an external, but bundled, application called LiveType (in this case, LiveType 2). First, let's look at the external method.

## Add Titles with LiveType 2

LiveType 2 is essentially a type animation program. It comes with a large set of preset styles, each of which can be customized by size, face, color, and movement. It also has preset 3-D forms for type. With any of these, or any combination, you can find an interesting and probably overly enthusiastic title sequence to put into your video.

LiveType 2 is pretty straightforward. It will look familiar to most Mac users who have taken a stab at iMovie. It has four windows:

- **Canvas** The main window, which takes up the most real estate on the screen. This is both the preview window and the workspace for your titles.

- **Inspector** Allows you to control font size, color, style, effects, and timing.

- **Media Browser** Contains LiveFonts, which are the preconfigured animations already mentioned. The Media Browser also gives you access to your fonts, textures, objects, and effects.

- **Timeline** When you draw up a title using the three windows above the Timeline, your title sequence is applied to the Timeline.

Before you begin adding your title, take a look at the LiveFonts tab in the Media Browser, which will give you a good idea of the presets. There are quite a few LiveFonts settings to look at, so take your time and check them out. If you don't mind, I'll just take a nap while you go about your business. Wake me when you've decided on one.

Zzzzzzz.

Ready? Great. So you've decided on something I agree with. We'll use a simple preset called "Gust." Good choice. Now let's work with it:

1. In the Inspector, type your title. For this example, I'll use the title of this book, HTDE [line break] with [line break] Online Video.

2. Move over to the LiveFonts tab in the Media Browser and select Gust.

**FIGURE 10-10**    LiveFont Defaults. Note that the text can be changed to suit your project.

**3.** Back in the Inspector, click Use LiveFonts Defaults.

**4.** In the Canvas, click Play. You should see your title displayed in the LiveFont you have selected, as shown in the example in Figure 10-10.

Note in the Timeline that you have a lot of time before and after your title effect animates. But you can adjust that. On the upper part of the track, where you find the time code, are the In and Out handles. These handles are on either side of the LiveFonts active area and can be pulled left or right to suit your timing. LiveType will export only the area you designate.

Below that area on the track is the velocity of the animation. That's not to be confused with the frame rate, which is something altogether different. Slide the edge of the lower portion of the track and see how it condenses the animation, speeding up the whole effect. The duration of the animation remains the same as what you designate with the In and Out points. The Timeline provides information about the duration and frame rate to the left, as shown in Figure 10-11.

The preceding adjustments are all well and good, but when we look at our Canvas, we see that the text is sitting too far down on the screen. To move it to a good spot, balanced in the screen, click and drag up the blue line at the center, as shown in Figure 10-12.

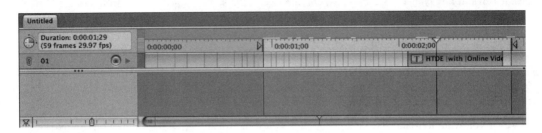

**FIGURE 10-11**    Duration and frame rate information

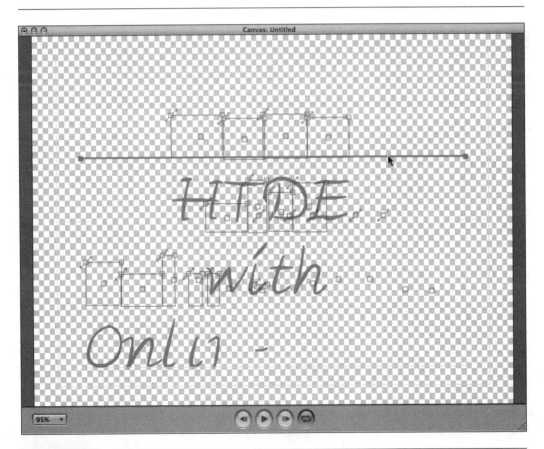

**FIGURE 10-12**    Positioning the text onscreen

**Format Titles in LiveType 2**    We can also change any of the settings of the type, from color to font to size. Here's how:

1. In the Inspector, select the Text.

2. Click the Attributes tab.

3. Using the various sliders and color wheel adjustments, make your changes to the type. You can watch your adjustments in real time in the Canvas to the left.

4. If you want to make style changes, click the Style tab and click the Enable button. Now you can add glow, drop shadow, and other stylistic effects.

5. Skip over to the Media Browser and click the Fonts tab.

6. Change your font. Again, it's live in the Canvas, so you can experiment with real-time read out.

Before we go back to Final Cut Express HD, we should look at one more set of title effects. Click to the Effects tab in the Media Browser. Scroll through the various and sundry text effects here. When you find one you like, select it and click Apply. Then click Play. Your effect will show immediately in the Canvas.

NOTE    *Effects take up extra layers in the Timeline, which means they can be removed or adjusted at any time. Remember, things in the Timeline are fluid, and by using the sliders and In and Out points, you can change their settings and make them your own.*

**Save Your Title in LiveType 2**    After you've had enough, and you're done fooling around with all the possibilities, or even before that, it's time to save your title so that you can import it into Final Cut Express HD. Save the file with an appropriate name and put it in the folder where you're keeping your Final Cut Express HD project.

Then select File | Render Movie. Here's where it is important that you pay attention. At the bottom of the Save dialog box are two check boxes, as shown in Figure 10-13:

■ **Render Background**    If you have a background (from the Textures tab in the Media Browser pane) and want it as a part of the title, then check this box.

■ **Render Only Between In/Out Points**    This option is more important. Check this box. It will cut down on processing time, by only rendering what you want rendered (what's in between your In/Out Points, of course).

Upon saving the title by clicking the Save button, you get to preview your title as a mini movie. Run it and make sure it does what you want it to do.

**Import Your Title into Final Cut Express HD**    So let's now import our title into Final Cut Express HD:

1. In the Browser in Final Cut Express HD, click the View as List button to change the file view.

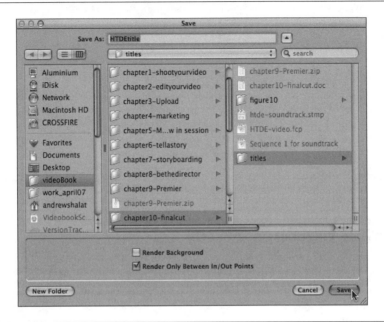

**FIGURE 10-13**    Saving and rendering a title

**2.** While still in the Browser, place your cursor over an empty area and press the CTRL key. Choose New Bin. Name the new bin **Titles**.

**3.** Import the LiveType file you created earlier. When it is in the Browser, drag it into the Titles bin.

**4.** Press the HOME key on the keyboard to set the playhead at zero.

**5.** Drag the title clip to the Canvas and choose Insert from the edit overlay. The new title clip will drop into the Timeline at the beginning.

**6.** Run the sequence and see how it works in your video. If you're not satisfied with it, select it in the Timeline and simultaneously press the CTRL key. Choose Open in Editor, as shown in Figure 10-14. The editor, in this case LiveType 2, will open, enabling you to make any changes to the file. When you save the file, it will automatically be updated in Final Cut Express HD. Therefore, you can continue to experiment with textures, backgrounds, and different settings in LiveType without worrying about destroying anything you've created thus far.

You can treat the title with any transitions you want, such as Cross Dissolve, and it will blend into your video sequence nicely.

Choose Open in Editor to make edits to your title.

## Add Titles Within Final Cut Express HD

We've created our titles in LiveType 2 and integrated them into the live sequence in Final Cut Express HD. But when it comes to credits, you don't need to be so elaborate. You can use Final Cut Express HD's built-in tools for titling and credits, meaning you won't have to open any other applications.

The trick with using titles within Final Cut Express HD is that we superimpose them rather than give them their own clips. We'll do these titles as final credits, but as you go through the drop-down menus, take note of the other choices. Here's the process:

1. Select the clip over which you'd like to place the credits.

2. If the clip is too long, you may want to use the Razor Blade tool to slice it and make the final clip just long enough to have your credits roll over them.

3. Place the playhead in the Timeline at the In point of the final clip.

4. In the Viewer, locate the small button in the lower right that looks like a piece of film with a letter A in frame. Hold down that button and select Text | Scrolling Text (see Figure 10-15).

5. Click the Controls tab in the Viewer.

6. In the Text area, type your credits. Choose a center alignment for the text. A little trick here is to put an asterisk after your title and then type the name. So, for instance, if you want to say Producer*Andrew Shalat, that asterisk will ensure the spacing on the output. Press RETURN and continue typing all the credits you need.

7. When you have all your credits typed in, make whatever stylistic alterations you want. Then click the Video tab.

8. Drag the text clip to the Canvas and select Superimpose (see Figure 10-16).

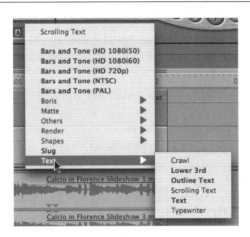

FIGURE 10-15   Scrolling Text for credits

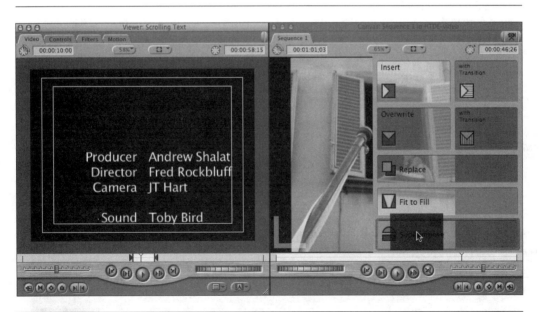

FIGURE 10-16   Superimpose the scrolling credits.

The Timeline now has your credits on the V2 track, just above the final clip. Final Cut Express HD automatically times the superimposed text clip to match the clip in the sequence above which it sits. That's why we shortened the final clip earlier.

Now review your video. The final touch before exporting the video for the Web is working with sound.

# Add Audio

There are two distinct ways of working with audio in Final Cut Express HD. The first is within Final Cut Express HD itself, and the second is to work outside of it with the bundled software application called Soundtrack.

## Add Audio Within Final Cut Express HD

From within Final Cut Express HD, audio is pretty straightforward. The audio tracks work much the same as the video tracks. If a video clip was captured with audio included, the audio will appear on the corresponding audio tracks located just below the video tracks in the Timeline, as shown in Figure 10-17.

The most important thing you must be aware of here are the audio meters. Few things can ruin a good video more than bad or distorted audio. In the following chapter, I'll give you a set of basic guidelines for audio adjustments before you output your final video.

Next to the editing palette, on the right side of the Timeline, are the audio meters. Keeping an eye on these meters is always a good idea. Make sure that your levels never light the little red bulbs at the very top. If you see one of the red lights light up, then your output sound will be distorted. And you don't want that.

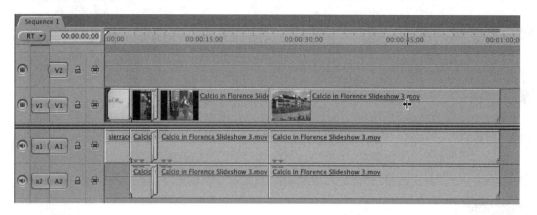

**FIGURE 10-17**    Audio tracks

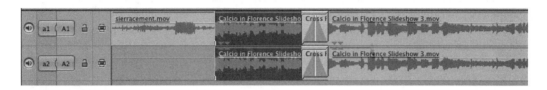

**FIGURE 10-18**   Wave form

Audio tracks can be worked on visually. (You *can* shut audio off by using the small audio button on the left side of the audio tracks.) Sometimes it's best to work with audio tracks in what's known as wave form (see Figure 10-18). Wave form shows the volume of the audio graphically. The loud parts look bulbous, while the quiet parts are thin. To see your audio in wave form, press OPTION-⌘-W.

> **NOTE**   *With some practice, you'll be able to see at a glance whether a wave form is a human talking, a piece of music, a sound effect, or ambient noise. The trick is to be able to recognize that in speech, there are lots of peaks and valleys, and equal flat parts. The peaks, or thick parts, are syllables, and the flats are the spaces between words. Music is continuous, with few thin flat parts. Valleys are opposite of peaks.*

Editing your audio is something to be taken seriously. It's not the easiest thing in the world, and until you're comfortable with it, you might want to stick with adjusting the levels. But if you are forced to make edits, remember to make your cuts at the thin points of the wave form, and not at the thick ones. As you improve, you'll be better at overlaying thick parts and using audio transitions to smooth things out.

> **NOTE**   *See Chapter 12 for some more technical guidelines on audio.*

Final Cut Express HD lets you directly import any audio format compatible with QuickTime. Most likely you'll be dealing with MP3 or AAC files. If you are intent on editing the imported audio, however, you'll only be able to do so with uncompressed file formats such as AIFF and WAVE.

Double-click your audio clip and you can attempt your edits in the Viewer. Using the Pen tool, you can assign keyframes, or points at which you can make changes in the levels of specific parts of your audio clip. You can also adjust the level wholesale, using the levels tools in the stereo panel.

## Add Audio with Soundtrack

The subject of working with audio could fill a book all on its own, so my goal here is limited to giving you a basic introduction to some of the audio tools at your disposal. Although the audio tools within Final Cut Express HD are pretty basic, they might be all you need. If, however, you find that those simple tools are hampering your creativity, you can opt to edit and create audio for your video using the bundled application Soundtrack.

Before you open Soundtrack, you should choose a video sample from Final Cut Express HD that is made just for this occasion. You can export a simple version of your video sequence to use in Soundtrack as a scoring guide to help you set up sound effects, and narration, or musical score. In order to do this, you must export a version of your video:

1.  Select File | Export | For Soundtrack.

2.  In the Save dialog box, shown in Figure 10-19, name your export in the Save As field.

3.  In the Include drop-down list, choose Video Only.

4.  If you haven't made specific audio markers in Final Cut Express HD, choose All Markers in the Markers drop-down list.

5.  Click Save to save the file.

The next step is to bring that video-only file into Soundtrack.

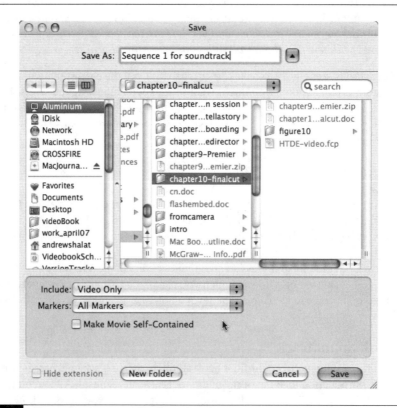

**FIGURE 10-19**  Preparing to export for Soundtrack

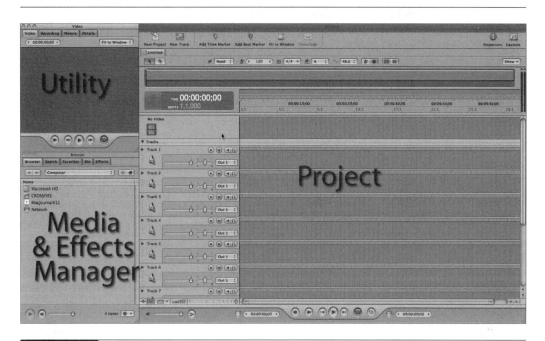

**FIGURE 10-20**    Soundtrack interface

**Bring Your Video-Only Sequence into Soundtrack**    Soundtrack is a simple interface with three main windows, as shown in Figure 10-20: a Project window, a Media and Effects Manager window, and a Utility window. If you've ever had any experience with the web site GarageBand, then you may find Soundtrack to be somewhat familiar. And after working in Final Cut Express HD for a while, you should have an idea of how tracks work. For instance, you should pretty much understand by now the drag-and-drop and slide-around method of putting objects or clips on tracks. You should have a good idea of what time codes are (although the time codes for audio are not exactly the same as for video), and you get a good idea of movement over time, which is what a timeline represents.

It's pretty much the same thing here, only we're talking about *sound* over time rather than *movement* over time. Adding one track over another doesn't cancel the lower track out. Each track has its own levels and controls, and at the bottom is a master mixer.

Soundtrack has its own editing tools, which are located in the main Project window, just under the project tab, and you can work on more than one project simultaneously. But we're not interested so much in the composing-from-scratch aspects of Soundtrack as we are in its integration with our existing video sequence back in Final Cut Express HD.

Let's put our video-only sequence into Soundtrack:

1. Open Soundtrack.

2. Go out to your Finder on the Mac and locate your video file.

3. Drag the video from the Finder directly into Soundtrack. Place the video file into the upper-left, Utility window. By default, the Video tab should be on top.

4. Your video appears in the Video tab of the Utility window, as shown in Figure 10-21. Note the playback controls. You also see that the entire video sequence now occupies the video track on top of the Project window tracks.

We can think of Soundtrack now as a sort of locked-down Final Cut Express HD, where we can't change any of the video but we *can* edit the audio to our heart's content. We have our video on top, so we can continuously refer to it for markers and synchronization.

What we want to do here is get in and get out, put some sound effects in certain places, maybe use an Apple Loop to create a background theme, and get this back to Final Cut Express HD, where we can finish off our video and export it for online delivery.

**Add Sound Effects in Soundtrack**   So we already have our video in place. Next we want to use one track for just sound effects. We find the sound effects by clicking the Search tab in the Media and Effects Manager window. Scroll through the various types of sound effects in the Keywords column,

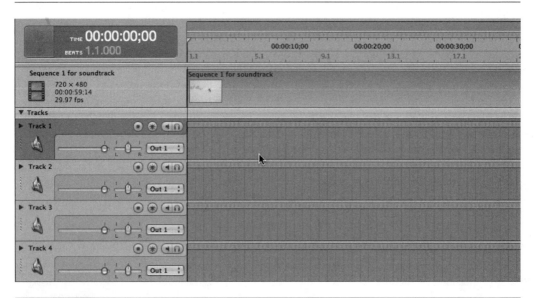

**FIGURE 10-21**   Video track in place on top

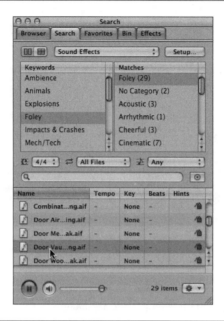

FIGURE 10-22   Choosing sound effects in Soundtrack

as shown in Figure 10-22. There are all types of effects for ambience, applause, explosions, sci-fi… pretty much whatever movie sounds you'll want to use. Choose one at random. For instance, in Figure 10-22, I've selected a door vault opening.

Before I go ahead and put sound effect on my timeline, I may want to gather more sound effects and put them somewhere where I can access them as I go through the video. So I select the sound effect, right-click or CONTROL-click it, and choose Add to Bin from the context menu.

Add to the bin as many sound effects as you think you'll need. When you've found a good number of sound effects you're likely to use, click the Bin tab. All the sound effects you sent to the bin should be available here.

Now, with the bin open, you can go through the various sound effects you have on hand, and simply drag them to the top track just under the video track in the Timeline, as shown in Figure 10-23. The spot where you place them correlates directly to the point in the video above. You can check it by scrubbing the playhead and watching the video preview, while your sound effects play at their appropriate points.

You can also manipulate the duration of sound effects by dragging their edges, ripple editing them, and shifting their positions on the Timeline.

**Create a Soundtrack in Soundtrack**    The idea of making a musical soundtrack to go along with your video might be more intimidating than the thought of adding sound effects, but actually the procedure is just as easy. Any experience in GarageBand will actually help you quite a bit here.

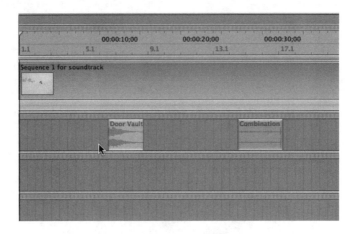

**FIGURE 10-23**    Sound effects in place on the Timeline

Back in the Search tab of the Media and Effects Manager window, select Instruments rather than Sound Effects. You can then further delimit your choices to looping or nonlooping. The loops are excellent samples of instrumentation and beats. The process is the same as what we did with sound effects.

1. Find the instruments, beats, and melodies all in loop form and put them in your bin.

2. When they reside in the bin, you can apply different beats or music (I make no claim to being a musician here) on the various tracks that correspond to the video. I recommend you work with loops, especially with short video for online delivery. Using a loop is easy.

3. Drag and drop a loop of a bass beat on the next track under your sound effects.

4. Place your cursor over the right edge of the loop and drag to the right. You'll see it continue, but in packets, or loops, until you stop dragging. Having a loop lets you apply a beat, which is really a complete piece of music, and repeat it seamlessly for as long as you need (see Figure 10-24). Now, we're dealing with the simplest of all tasks in Soundtrack, but still we want it to be effective.

Each track, you should note, has its own level controls, mute, Record button, and output settings. The bass beat we applied will add subtext to our video, a simple soundtrack if you will. We can adjust its output levels, and make it fade in or out.

If you click the triangle in the bass track, more controls are revealed. If you recall earlier, I talked briefly about the Pen tool in Final Cut Express HD. In Soundtrack, we don't need the Pen tool to make a keyframe. We just click the newly revealed volume line, and it gives us a point.

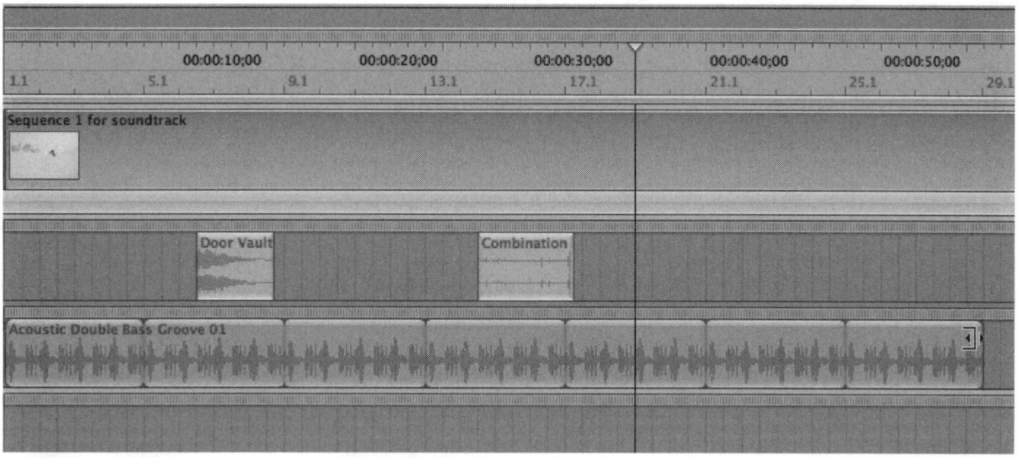

**FIGURE 10-24**   A continuous loop

That point acts as a sort of thumbtack. You can pull the line before it down so that it leads up to it, or you can move the point itself to a different level.

The upshot of all this is that creating a basic score is easy.

**Save Your Mix File for Final Cut Express HD**   But how do we get the mix file into Final Cut Express HD? Just as we did in LiveType 2, we can export this mix, or just the track we like, in an appropriate format for Final Cut Express HD. Choose File | Export | Export Mix.

Now we have some choices to make. The default setting for output has two important features: bit depth and sample rate. The default bit depth in Soundtrack is 16 bit, and the sample rate is 48 kHz. You don't have to know exactly what these mean, although I'll give you a brief explanation in Chapter 12. Just know that 48 kHz is the standard sample rate for most broadcast video. And while 16 bit is also a standard, we could get away with 8 bit for online use. However, since we'll take what we can get, we'll leave the audio export settings at the default. Name your mix, and click Export. This will create a soundtrack file that is now ready for import into Final Cut Express HD.

**Import Your Mix File into Final Cut Express HD**   In Final Cut Express HD, select File | Import | Import File. Navigate to your mix file from Soundtrack. It will come into the Browser. You can now place the mix file directly into its own audio track, aligning it with the far-left starting point of the video.

Run your video and make sure it works. Sounds good? Looks good? Good. It's time to finish this baby off.

# Export Your Video for Use Online

Save your Final Cut Express HD file:

1. Select File | Export | Using QuickTime Conversion.
2. In the Save dialog box, name the file.
3. In the QuickTime format drop-down menu, choose MPEG4.
4. Click Save to save the file.

You've now completed your video using Final Cut Express HD. There is no need to do anything more here except open your YouTube account and upload your video. You know the drill.

# Chapter 11

# This Just In—iMovie '08

## How to . . .

- Capture and collect video in iMovie '08
- Create a project sequence
- Trim clips
- Create transitions
- Add audio
- Crop video
- Fix color
- Add titles
- Share directly to YouTube

You'd think we'd be done now. You have everything you need to get your video online, from cell phone, video camcorder, digital camera, or just your webcam. You know how to use the software, and you understand the concepts of frames, timelines, and time codes. But then along comes this new version of iMovie, iMovie '08, part of Apple's iLife '08 application suite. And what do you think? Apple changed everything.

> **NOTE**   *What's in a name? iMovie '08 can also be referred to as iMovie 7, according to the version number of the program. I know it's confusing, but if you hear someone referring to iMovie 7, you'll know that they mean iMovie '08, or vice versa.*

Really. Everything is different. No Timeline, no Clips well, no time code. No destructive editing. iMovie '08 presents a whole new way of creating and finishing your video and uploading it directly from within the application to YouTube. And, despite the removal of some features found in iMovie HD, the new workflow is easier and more efficient than anything else out there.

# Take a New Approach to Video Editing with iMovie '08

iMovie '08 may throw iMovie veterans for a loop. iMovie '08 is a radical departure from its namesake. In fact, in many respects, it takes a different approach to video editing from all the other video editing software applications discussed in this book. It pretty much leaves behind the timecode-based editing and replaces it with what it calls Event-based editing. Instead of relying on frame numbers and timecode numbers, iMovie '08 collects your clips as Events in your life, not clinically enumerated clips. It also introduces nondestructive editing to iMovie, joining higher-end applications like Apple Final Cut and Adobe Premiere Pro in being able to revert to original footage after editing, without the worry of having lost something forever.

> **NOTE**   *Nondestructive editing lets you keep the original content untouched. Instead of editing the original, you edit a copy of the original. In other words, you don't lose anything. You can always revert to the original.*

Don't be discouraged by the new interface. iMovie '08 is intended specifically for making quick work of editing video and sharing it online. The loss of Timecode references and other more traditional tools is not to hobble your editing experience, but rather to economize it. Once you familiarize yourself with the basics of the application, you will find that your editing process is a lot faster than before. Of course, those who are still stuck in the old-school timecode timeline methods may scoff at you. Not to worry. Your prodigious speed in production and delivery will silence them quickly enough.

**NOTE**    *Don't panic! If you're quite content with iMovie HD, you can still use it even if you install the new iLife '08. The installation keeps your older version of iMovie, placing it in a folder called iMovie-Previous Version. So if you find the newer way of doing things in iMovie '08 too limiting, or just too foreign, you can always curl up in your comfort zone and work your magic with iMovie HD. Apple also offers iMovie HD for free when you purchase the new iLife '08.*

# Get to Know the New Interface in iMovie '08

The new main iMovie window is broken up into several panes. These various panes can change according to your project, your preference, or the tools you happen to be using. To make things simple, I'll just go over the default layout. Any adjustments we make during production will be explained at that time. By default, you have five basic panes contained in one main window, as shown in Figure 11-1. Reading from the upper left and moving clockwise, these are the Project Library, the iMovie Project pane, the Preview (or Viewer) pane, the Source Video pane, and the Event Library.

As you will note, the new interface is somewhat more fluid than its predecessor. iMovie '08 collects all of your video from every source into a centralized library, which in turn allows you to create and organize these clips and footage as parts of Events. Events are the new ordering system that Apple is using across the iLife '08 application suite. iPhoto, in particular, now uses the Event designation to sort images. So what are your Events? One Event could be your trip to Europe. Another Event could be your ski vacation, a third could be your sailing excursion, and so on. When do you ever work?

You're always on vacation! Well, the price you pay for all that free time is that now you have to sit down and edit your videos *taken during that free time.*

So even if the various clips you want for a particular project are from disparate times and reside in different places on your hard drive, you can group them together as a single Event. In so doing, you can then access all the related clips from an Event with a single click.

**NOTE**    *iMovie '08 works with Events and projects. An Event is a collection of clips that you relate to one another as a group, no matter where the files reside or when the footage was taken. An iMovie project is an umbrella for the video you want to create. The project contains all the Events you want to add to the video as well as the music and effects. You can share Events between projects, but you cannot share projects between Events.*

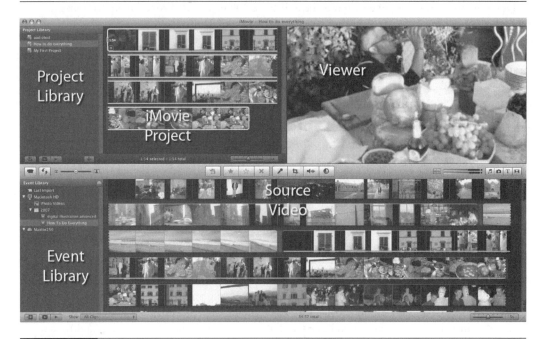

FIGURE 11-1    The new iMovie '08 interface organizes video project production into five basic panes.

The best way to understand how this new interface works is to work with it. So let's explore it in a production setting. We'll start by importing video.

## Import Video Footage

iMovie can import digital video footage you have either resident on your hard drive or on a video recording device, such as your cell phone, digital camera, or digital video recorder (see Chapter 1).

Let's start by importing video from an external video recording device:

1. Open iMovie. When you open iMovie for the first time, or when you start a new project, you see the iMovie window, but the panes are blank, as shown in Figure 11-2. The Project Library lists any of your current projects and enables you to create new projects.

2. Connect your video recording device to your Mac using the appropriate cable. For instance, if you are using a DVD, HD drive, or flash memory recorder, use a USB cable. If you have a FireWire camcorder, use a FireWire cable.

3. Within iMovie, click File and choose the appropriate Import menu item (see Figure 11-3) that fits your situation. You can even capture video directly from your iSight into iMovie (see Figure 11-4). Or you can attach your camcorder, hard disk, or any media and copy files either directly to iMovie or via your resident Macintosh HD to iMovie.

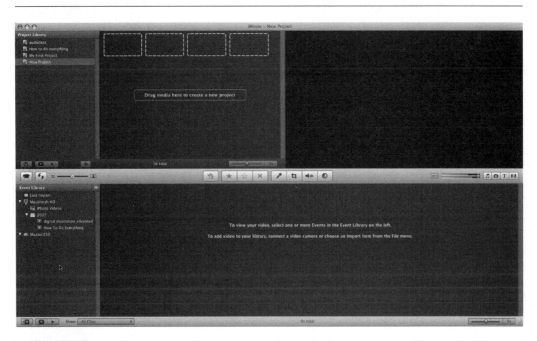

FIGURE 11-2 When you start a new project, the iMovie Project pane shows placeholders for your clips.

FIGURE 11-3   iMovie gives you several menu choices for importing your video.

**FIGURE 11-4**    Through iMovie, you can capture video directly from your iSight using a simple Record/Stop button and a large time display.

**4.** When you import your footage, be it a movie file from your disk, captured video from your iSight, or video footage from a camcorder, you are presented with several choices as to how to organize it, shown in Figure 11-5, including whether to add the file to an existing Event or create a new Event from it. When you have made your selections, click the Import button.

**5.** Repeat steps 1–4 as necessary to add more footage to your existing Event, or to create a new Event.

After you import your video file either as part of an existing Event or as a new Event, it is included in the Event Library (by default, the lower-left pane of the iMovie window), which contains all of your Events (which are in turn collections of related clips available for video projects). If you select a particular Event listed in the Event Library, the clips contained therein appear as a series of thumbnails in the Source Video pane to the right of the Event Library, as shown in Figure 11-6. You begin editing in iMovie '08 after you gather all your clips into Events.

NOTE    *Events are the new ordering system that Apple is using across the iLife '08 application suite. iPhoto, in particular, is now using the Event designation to sort images. So what are your Events? One could be your trip to Europe. The next event could be your Ski vacation. A third is your Sailing excursion. When do you ever work? You're always on vacation!*

FIGURE 11-5  Importing a movie file into an existing Event

FIGURE 11-6  The Source Video pane shows thumbnails of the video clips contained in selected Events.

# Create and Edit a Project in iMovie '08

We've imported all of our video footage, set up various Events as we did so, and now we want to put those Events to use. In the Event Library, select the Events you plan to use in your video. The Source Video pane is populated with thumbnails of your Event clips. As this section explains, you'll select clips, or portions of clips, from the Source Video pane and drag them up into the iMovie Project pane. Much of your trimming and initial editing is done in the selection process in the Source Video pane.

## Create a New Project

Before we begin our edits in iMovie '08, we need to create a new project. Choose File | New Project or press ⌘-N. Creating a new project sets up the Project pane with placeholder icons, as shown in Figure 11-7. The Project pane takes the place of the Timeline from previous iMovie versions. This is where you do the actual sequence.

## Edit Clips in the Source Video Pane

The first stage of the editing process is to make adjustments to the clips in the Source Video pane:

1. Select an Event in the Event Library. All the clips included in the selected Event appear in the Source Video pane.

2. Find and click the particular clip you want to include in your video. A yellow border appears around your selection, as shown in Figure 11-8. The left edge of the clip shows the duration, in seconds, of your selection.

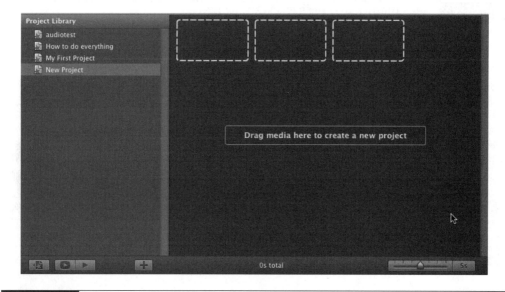

**FIGURE 11-7**    This is where you make your video sequence.

**FIGURE 11-8**  Don't worry if the yellow border doesn't have all the parts of your clip. You can adjust that.

3.  Place your cursor over either the left or right edge of the yellow border and slide it left or right to capture more or less of your video clip. Notice how the duration readout changes with the sliding motion.

4.  As you adjust the length of your clip, watch the Preview pane above to coordinate the exact frame you want to either make your in marker (left handle of the yellow border) or out marker (right handle). You are trimming the duration and in and out marks of your clip right here.

## Move Clips from the Source Video Pane to the Project Pane

After you have edited the points and duration of your clip in the Source Video pane, you are ready to move it to the Project pane, as follows:

1.  Place your cursor inside the yellow border. It becomes a hand icon, as shown in Figure 11-9.

2.  Click and drag the clip from the Source Video pane into the Project pane and drop it directly on one of the placeholder icons, as shown in Figure 11-10.

3.  Repeat this process until you have a basic sequence of video in the Project pane.

4.  After you've placed your clips into the Project pane, you can preview them by placing your cursor over a clip and dragging or by pressing the SPACEBAR. The clip runs in the Preview pane.

**FIGURE 11-9**  When you place your cursor within the yellow border, you can drag the clip to the Project pane.

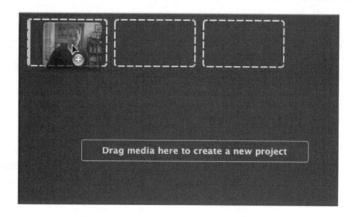

Drag media here to create a new project

**FIGURE 11-10**    Drag your clip directly onto the Project pane.

**NOTE**    *You can see which parts of which Event clips are live in the Project pane by looking at which clip thumbnail in the Source Video pane is underlined in orange.*

## Trim Clips in the Project Pane

As the previous "Edit Clips in the Source Video Pane" section explained, when you select a clip in the Source Video pane and move the yellow border left or right over the clip, you are in effect trimming your clip. The Preview pane gives you a heads-up, real-time display of the footage as you proceed.

Clipping and editing doesn't end in the Source Video pane, of course, but carries on throughout the video production process. There's always something to tweak here or there in the actual sequence. And you can just as easily trim your clips in the Project pane as you can in the Source Video pane, as described next:

1.    In the Project pane, select the clip you intend to trim.

2.    Just as you did earlier in the Source Video pane, drag the left or right handles of the yellow border to the in and out points you prefer.

3.    Choose Edit | Trim to Selection (or press ⌘-B). The unwanted frames from your clip are removed.

Here's another way to trim the duration of your clip, with some more precision:

1.    Select your clip in the Project pane. Notice the small icon with a clock in the lower-left corner of the first frame of the clip's thumbnail, as shown in Figure 11-11.

**FIGURE 11-11**    Clicking the clock icon opens the Trimmer window. The other small icon to the left is for fine adjustments to the start point of the clip.

**2.** Click the clock icon (officially called the *Clip Duration button*). A new window opens, called the Trimmer.

**3.** From within this window, select your in and out points for the video clip. Preview your changes by clicking the Play button in the Trimmer. When you're satisfied with your edit, click Done.

**TIP**    *For those of you who think in a more analytical manner, you can always find a duration timer at the bottom of the window.*

As far as clip trimming, that's pretty much it. You'll notice that this methodology is much more organic, more visually oriented than the numeric Timecode method from previous versions of iMovie. It makes for quick editing in a visceral manner.

## Add Transitions

Adding transitions between clips is a very simple process:

**1.** Choose Window | Transitions, or click the Transitions button in the iMovie toolbar (the Transitions button is found furthest to the right, just below the Preview pane).

**2.** With the Transitions window open, you can preview and try out all the available transition styles. Place your cursor over a transition thumbnail and watch.

**3.** Click and drag your preferred transition into the Project pane and drop it between the clips you want it to affect.

**4.** To preview the transition in your project, double-click anywhere in the clip preceding the transition, or just drag your cursor across the transition as quickly or slowly as you like and watch in the Preview pane as you do.

To delete a transition, select the transition icon and press the DELETE key. Since this is nondestructive editing, your original footage is never changed. Just the piece you are working on is changed.

To close the Transitions window, just click the Transitions button again.

*If you are importing some of your older projects from, say, iMovie HD into this version, you will most likely lose those carefully thought-out transitions and effects that made your previous project sing. You'll have to find and apply their equivalent transitions in iMovie '08, or make other decisions.*

## Add Audio/Music

One of the biggest complaints about iMovie '08 is that it limits your audio control. Separating audio from video, as you did in earlier versions of iMovie, is not possible at the time of this writing in iMovie '08. But you do have great control over clip volume. There are two basic ways of adjusting sound levels in the video clips. You can reduce the maximum volume or you can adjust clip volumes individually to fit within a volume level range, what the application calls a "normalized" clip volume.

You adjust the volume in the Audio Adjustments dialog box, as follows:

1.  Select a clip and click the Audio Adjustments button. The Audio Adjustments button will appear after you select the clip, and let your cursor hover in the clip area. See Figure 11-12.

2.  Make the appropriate adjustments to the audio. Either raise or lower the volume or select a normalized clip volume. Clicking the Normalize Clip Volume button sets the volume range so that volume within the project won't go beyond a certain level range.

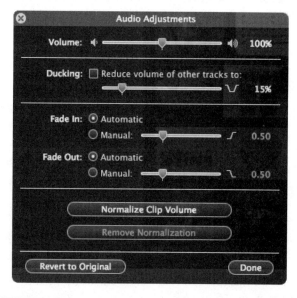

FIGURE 11-12    You can reduce the maximum volume of the clip, or set a "normalized" volume range.

**FIGURE 11-13**   You can test out any sound file by double-clicking it.

Adding background music to your project shows how iMovie integrates with iTunes. You have the choice of using pretty much any of your iTunes music tracks or adding one of the included, preset sound effects and jingles that iMovie provides.

1. Click the Music and Sound Effects button in the iMovie toolbar, or choose Window | Music and Sound Effects.

2. The Music and Sound Effects pane slides out from the bottom right. In this pane, shown in Figure 11-13, you can select from iMovie '08 Sound Effects, iLife Sound Effects, any GarageBand soundtracks you may have, or from your entire iTunes library.

3. Select a music file and drag it to the Project pane's background. Be very careful not to drag the music directly on any one clip. The background area that contains your clips will turn green (see Figure 11-14). This indicates that the clips within that green background have the music you put there as a background soundtrack.

4. If you want to adjust the in and out points of the music, click the green background to select it.

5. Choose Edit | Trim Music (or press ⌘-R) to open the Trim Music window, shown in Figure 11-15.

   The waveform represents the music or sound. If you look closely, you'll note that part of the waveform is pink and the rest is black. The pink waveform represents where the music is accompanied by video. The black shows you where the music extends beyond the video.

6. Move the left and right selection handles to adjust where the music begins or ends.

**FIGURE 11-14**    The green background shows you that your background music underscores the video clips.

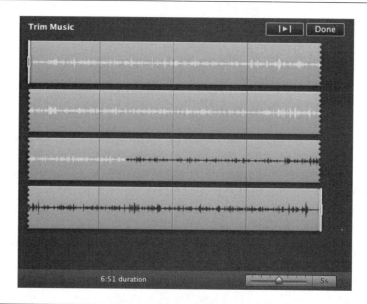

**FIGURE 11-15**    The Trim Music window lets you adjust your in and out points for the background sound or music.

## Add Sound Effects

To add a sound effect to the video, open the iMovie '08 or iLife Sound Effects list in the Music and Sound Effects pane and follow these steps:

1. Click and drag your preferred sound effect to the Project pane and drop it at the point in the project where you want it.

2. A green icon appears below the clip to show where the sound effect resides. You can make it shorter by dragging the end toward the left.

## Add Voice-Over or Narration

You can add voice-over or narration to your project as follows:

1. Click the Voiceover button (the button that looks like a microphone) on the iMovie toolbar.

2. Select the microphone you will record from.

3. Drag the Input Volume slider to the right or left to adjust your levels.

4. Use the Noise Reduction slider to eliminate ambient noise.

5. Select Voice Enhancement to smooth your voice sound.

6. When you're ready to record, click the point in a clip where you want the narration to begin. You'll get a countdown from three to one.

7. Begin speaking with the prompt. To stop recording, press the SPACEBAR or click anywhere in the iMovie window.

Shorten the voice-over by dragging the end of the voice-over to the left. You can move the placement of the voice-over by dragging it to a different point in the Project pane.

## Crop Video

One of the more advanced features of iMovie '08 is that it enables you to crop, resize, and rotate your video clips. The following steps show you how to crop video images:

1. Click the Crop button and then select a video clip.

2. In the Preview pane (or Viewer), click Crop. A green bounding box shows you the borders of your image, as shown in Figure 11-16. Reposition the size of this green border to fit your vision of how the image should be cropped.

3. After cropping, you may not want a black border where the cut parts of your image once were, so click the Fit button to make the image fit the full frame.

4. When you're happy with your work, click Done.

NOTE    *The maximum crop is 50 percent of the original size.*

**FIGURE 11-16**     You can crop your video to focus on what's really important.

## Enhance and Color Correct Your Video

If you're familiar with the adjustment controls in iPhoto, then this procedure will be quite familiar to you:

**1.** Click the Adjust Video button (or press v). The Video Adjustments dialog box opens, as shown in Figure 11-17.

**2.** Select a clip to adjust. It appears in the Viewer (Preview) pane.

**3.** In the Video Adjustments dialog box, you can brighten, darken, adjust contrast and saturation, and even set the white point for your clip.

**TIP**    *Remember that all of these adjustments are nondestructive, so if you aren't happy with what you've done, you can simply undo the changes (choose Edit | Undo). To restore media to its original state, select the clip you want to restore, reopen the adjustment tool that you used to make the changes that you want to undo, and restore the settings to their original state (by clicking the Revert to Original button).*

## Add Titles

The titling controls in iMovie '08 produce surprisingly sophisticated results, but are extremely easy to use. You can overlay text at any point in your video project. And iMovie has an ample set of prefab title styles built in. To add titles, follow these steps:

**1.** Choose Window | Titles, or click the Titles button.

**2.** In the Titles pane, shown in Figure 11-18, select the title style you prefer.

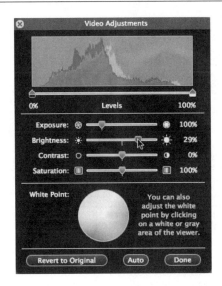

**FIGURE 11-17**    Adjustments are easy to make and are immediately apparent.

**FIGURE 11-18**    Preset titles are numerous in iMovie '08.

**FIGURE 11-19**    Note the Title icon on the clip in the Project pane, and the actual applicable template in the Preview pane.

3. Click and drag the title thumbnail to the point in the Project pane where you want it and release (see Figure 11-19).

4. Click the Show Fonts button in the Preview pane to adjust fonts and colors.

5. To adjust the title's duration, in the Project pane, hover your cursor over the Title icon until the cursor becomes a vertical line, as shown in Figure 11-20, and then drag at either end of the title icon.

# Share Your Video on YouTube

When you're finally happy with the project, it's time to publish it to YouTube. Save your project.

1. Select your project from the Project Library.

2. Choose Share | Publish to YouTube (Yeah! It's built right in.)

3. Choose your account from the Account pop-up menu. If you don't have a YouTube account (see Chapter 3), set one up by clicking Add. You'll be directed to the YouTube web site, where you can set it all up.

**FIGURE 11-20**    The cursor changes to a vertical line, letting you adjust the duration of the title.

4.  Type a name for your movie in the Title field. Give it a short description.

5.  Type in your tags and keywords.

6.  Select a size. Medium is usually best.

7.  Choose whether you want this video to be publicly viewable or private. Click Next and then click Publish. iMovie automatically uploads your video.

8.  Click Visit to see the video live online.

Well, that's it. Probably the simplest, most efficient way of creating and publishing video you'll find for now. Mind you, we haven't covered all aspects of iMovie '08, but I hope this chapter has given you enough information to be dangerous. Explore this application, experiment, and be bold. The world is changing, and we're riding on the crest of the wave. Good luck, and do good work seekers. See you on the Internet.

# Chapter 12

## Online Video: That's a Wrap

## How to . . .

- Stay on top of things
- Be resourceful

Even as I write this, the online video terrain is changing. Corporations are conducting meetings, trying to figure out how to make some pennies out of this phenomenon, servers and domains are changing hands, advertisers are looking for space on the margins, and new forms of software applications are being developed.

And through it all, some basic things remain. The impulse that makes us want to create video, to tell a story, to make fun of someone else's story, to express our view of the world, continues unabated. It's an intrinsic fiber in the human anatomy. Whether it's on a cave wall, a scrap of paper, a napkin, or the Internet, we need to tell a story.

This book, I hope, has given you some of the tools to express yourself through online video. Although I haven't been explicit on the finer details of every piece of video software, I've given you the principles and the approach to working with pretty much any piece of video software.

# Remember the Rules

I do need to address some specifics and technicalities, which I'll do here. This section offers some basic rules to remember when you are creating your video and getting ready to put it online.

There are really two different types of video: video intended for broadcast media, and video intended for computers. You can use the same source material, again and again, but when you decide to deploy that work, you need to be aware of some technical issues that you just aren't going to get around unless you know what settings you need to employ:

- *Set up your capture device, if possible, as progressive.* Video output should be set as progressive, not interlaced. Interlaced is for television sets, and it builds the image on the screen differently from the way a computer screen builds it. An NTSC television image builds from the top down, every odd line first, and then every even line. This method is known as interlaced, and it doesn't work for a computer monitor. Computers, and hence the online world, use a different method, called progressive. This image builds each line, in a row, top to bottom. The image is sharper and contains fewer artifacts on the edges. For online output, if asked, choose progressive.

- *Check the white balance on your shots.* Digital cameras are prone to color casts depending on the ambient light. You can adjust for most of this (see Chapters 5 and 8). Digital video also has a slightly higher tolerance for whites. These are spoken of in the industry in percentages. Where a broadcast white can tolerate 100 percent or less, a digital white can be up to 109 percent white, which is very bright. Where it may look great on a digital screen, on a television, it will flare and have trailers. Not good form. So keep your whites under 100 percent.

- *Keep your framing simple.* Keep subjects toward the center, or follow the rule of thirds (see Chapter 8) for more complex compositions. Simplicity is often underrated. Believe me, the simpler your shots, the more your audience appreciates what your video has to say.

- *Be aware of title-safe parameters in your shot.* In Chapter 10, I discussed the title-safe guides in Final Cut Express HD. Keep them in mind when you're framing your shots. If you have action in your shot, try to keep it within the title-safe area at least, but within the action-safe area for sure. The action-safe area is 5 percent from all edges. The title-safe area is 10 percent from all edges. Since you want to keep things as viewable as possible, it's a good idea to keep these areas in mind, even though on a computer, these are not necessarily important settings. Simple, clear, and viewable.

- *Be aware that audio settings are tricky.* It's a whole different world from video, really. But there are two main things to remember about recording and saving audio: sample rate and bit depth. I won't go too far into the technical reasoning behind these settings, but I will give you the basic parameters for success in your work:

  - **Sample rate**   Often given as a ratio of cycles per second, such as 32K, 44.1K, or 48K. The standard sample rate for digital audio is 48K. Choose 48K if you can.

  - **Bit depth**   Essentially determines the range from softest to loudest. If 0 is loudest, then softest can be something like –124 dB. Each bit depth, usually represented as 8 bit, 16 bit, and 24 bit, represents a range. 8 bit, which is usually the minimum for online audio, has a range of 0 to –96 dB. 16 bit, a video standard, is 0 to –124 dB. 24 bit, which is what is used in theatrical releases, is 0 to –143 dB. For your uses, stick with 16-bit audio and you're already beyond what you'll need. If you are pinched for space and download time, you can bump it down to 8 bit.

- *Keep an eye on your levels when you are recording audio during a shoot.* In mixing audio, here are some basic guidelines. Dialogue should be from –6 dB to –12 dB. Sound effects can range from –12 dB to –18 dB. Music should float around –18 dB. Don't go beyond that if you want to avoid any distortion.

# Visit Web Resources

As we know all too well, the list of resources on the Web is fluid. Sites come, some stay, some go. More sites appear. So, at the risk of dating this book, I'll list several sites you might want to visit as resources or as sharing outlets.

## Resources

Below are some resources that might help you out in your online video sojourn. While the field is continually changing, there are always some stalwart sites that I continually find to be of use. So I've collected several of them here for your own use as well. Browse them, explore them, and get the most from them. Don't be scared to contact the support teams behind the sites either. They often will help in pointed situations.

- **www.adobe.com**   The source for all things Adobe
- **www.apple.com**   The source for all things Apple
- **www.apple.com/itunes**   An online gateway to iTunes
- **www.dvcreators.net**   Training and resources for digital video creators
- **www.lynda.com**   A commercial site for digital software education
- **www.vodstock.com**   A how-to site for video blogs and vodcasting
- **www.bbc.co.uk/films/oneminutemovies/howto**   A short tutorial on how to make a one-minute movie

## Sharing

The following are just a few of the sites you'll find for sharing. Every day more pop up on the Web. One of the easiest ways to find a sharing site other than word of mouth is a simple Google search for "video sharing."

- YouTube.com
- MySpace.com
- Yahoo video (http://video.yahoo.com)
- Photobucket.com
- Grouper.com
- Soapbox.msn.com
- Dailymotion.com
- Ning.com
- iFilm.com (Spike)
- Metacafe.com

# More Software Options

In this book, I've covered only a few particular software video editing packages. MovieMaker, iMovie, Premiere Pro, and Final Cut Express HD are not the only applications available to you, by any stretch. But I chose these few for several reasons. The first and most important reason is usability. All four of those applications are easy to start using, and make getting your work done easy. Although you may get other recommendations to use Avid Free DV (discontinued!) or even the full-blown Final Cut Pro, I didn't use those applications in this book because, in my opinion,

Final Cut Pro is too powerful and the interface of Avid Free DV was too Byzantine. Final Cut Pro gives you more than you need for online video, and Avid Free DV is now a moot point since they've discontinued the product.

But that doesn't mean you shouldn't check out those or any other editing applications. You should. Avid Free DV is, after all, free. It's just a download from the Avid web site, along with the obligatory surrender of personal web information. And it does come bundled with a video tutorial. If that makes sense to you, then by all means, go ahead and try it out.

If you find that Final Cut Express HD is not sufficient to meet your needs, the instruction that I gave you in Chapter 10 should at least give you enough knowledge to get a jump start on the big boy, Final Cut Pro. (By the time you need Final Cut Pro, you won't need to talk to me anymore anyway. Knowledge is funny that way. It's a step ladder.)

Hopefully after reading this book, you are now a videographer, a movie maker. If you have only the bare minimum of equipment and software, this book has given you at the very least a methodology to follow to create and refine your story in video format ready for the Web.

I don't have to wax poetic about it. The availability of capture devices and easy-to-use software editing solutions gives us all more power as members of a world community than ever before in the history of…well, history. So there I go waxing. Enough blather. You have what you need. If you need more, you know where to find it. Now charge your batteries, grab your reflectors, and get a crew. It's time to make videos. I'll be looking for your work online. Believe me, I *will* be looking.

So for now, that's a wrap. See you online.

# Index